**Connecting with the Enemy**

# Connecting with the Enemy

A Century of Palestinian-Israeli
Joint Nonviolence

SHEILA H. KATZ

University of Texas Press ⌇ *Austin*

Requests for permission to reproduce material from this work should be sent to:
Permissions
University of Texas Press
P.O. Box 7819
Austin, TX 78713-7819
http://utpress.utexas.edu/index.php/rp-form

⊗ The paper used in this book meets the minimum requirements of
ANSI/NISO Z39.48-1992 (R1997) (Permanence of Paper).

University of California Press granted permission to reprint excerpt from Halit
Yeshurun, "Exile Is So Strong Within Me, I May Bring It to the Land: A Landmark
1996 Interview with Mahmoud Darwish," in *Journal of Palestine Studies* 42, no. 1
(2012) with permission conveyed through Copyright Clearance Center, Inc.

Martin Buber quote reprinted with the permission of Scribner, a Division of
Simon & Schuster, Inc., from *I and Thou* by Martin Buber, translated by Walter
Kaufman. Copyright © 1958 by Charles Scribner's Sons. Copyright renewed
© 1986 by Raphael Buber and Simon & Schuster, Inc. Translation copyright © 1970
by Charles Scribner's Sons. All rights reserved.

Additional thanks to Bloomsbury for use of that same quote © Martin Buber,
*I and Thou*, Bloomsbury Academic, an imprint of Bloomsbury Publishing Plc.

**Library of Congress Cataloging-in-Publication Data**

Names: Katz, Sheila H., author.
Title: Connecting with the enemy : a century of Palestinian-Israeli joint
nonviolence / Sheila H. Katz.
Description: First edition. Austin : University of Texas Press, 2016. Includes
bibliographical references and index.
Identifiers: LCCN 2016003036 (print) LCCN 2016004743 (ebook)
    ISBN 9781477310274 (cloth : alk. paper)
    ISBN 9781477310625 (pbk. : alk. paper)
    ISBN 9781477310281 (library e-book)
    ISBN 9781477310298 (non-library e-book)
Subjects: LCSH: Arab-Israeli conflict—History. Jewish-Arab relations.
Reconciliation—Social aspects—Israel. Reconciliation—Social aspects—Palestine.
Classification: LCC DS119.7 .K328 2016 (print) LCC DS119.7 (ebook)
DDC 956.04—dc23
LC record available at http://lccn.loc.gov/2016003036

doi: 10.7560/310274

*For Ari, Aliza, and Noah*

*It is impossible for me to evade the place that the Israeli has occupied in my identity . . . Israelis changed the Palestinians and vice versa. The Israelis are not the same people that came, and the Palestinians are not the same people that once were. In the one, there is the other. . . . The other is a responsibility and a test. Together we are doing something new in history. . . . Will a third way emerge from these two?*
MAHMOUD DARWISH


*All real living is meeting.*
MARTIN BUBER

# Contents

# List of Maps

# Notes on Transliteration and Translation

In order to balance accessibility for the general reader with clarity for the specialist, I've mixed the use of scholarly convention with popular transliterations. So on one hand, you will see *fallahin* instead of *fellahin*, but on the other hand, *fedayeen* instead of *fida'iyyin*. I have omitted most diacritical marks for Arabic and Hebrew terms and names, and I have not designated *ayin* or *hamza* except in the middle of a word, where it clarifies pronunciation, as in Bi'ina and *ma'abarot*. But clarity of pronunciation defers to spellings chosen by the founders of joint nonviolent initiatives, such as Wahat al-Salam, rather than as-Salaam. Proper names with widespread recognition in English render Faysal Husayni as Faisal Husseini and Musa al-Alami as Musa Alami. Place names use Anglicized spellings— for example, Beersheba instead of Hebrew Be'er Shev'a or Arabic Bi'r as-Sib', and Shefaram instead of Arabic Shefa'Amr or Hebrew Shefar'am. Sometimes the same proper name has different renderings in English. So, for example, Umm al-Fahm is an Arab town in Israel, but its residents Romanize the gallery they founded as Umm el-Fahem Gallery. Different individuals also choose different spellings for the same name, so you will see, for example, Muhammad and Mohammed; they may also choose different structural formats, such as Abu-Nimer and AbuZiyyad.

# Preface

Four decades ago I went to Israel with a backpack and a question: Is it possible for Arabs and Jews to work together in mutual respect? The Vietnam War had just ended, but the Arab-Israeli wars continued. I was one of those Americans reared on the Civil Rights movement, arrested for protesting Vietnam, and empowered by second-wave feminism. At that moment in history, age-old injustices like racism and imperialism seemed tractable.

Israel turned out to be an epiphany for a young woman who had lived her entire life as a minority and was suddenly experiencing the safety and spaciousness of belonging to the majority. My personal religious holidays were suddenly national holidays. I shed some of my internalized stereotypes of Jews as I witnessed the diversity of my people: blond-haired or black-skinned, truck driver or president. I listened to tales of courage and survival, of exile and holocaust that brought this rainbow people home to their ancestral lands.

Yet the dark side of dominance tempered this relief and pride. I listened to Palestinians' heart-wrenching stories of exile and destroyed villages, of second-class citizenship in Israel, crushed dreams for independence, and daily dangers under Israeli military occupation. Palestinians' unprecedented hospitality and welcome into their communities moved me. My admiration for the Palestinian people was born in the same soil as my love for Israel. I couldn't accept that one people's political and cultural renaissance was another's devastation, that each people saw the other as the obstacle to freedom. The near-absolute segregation between Jews and Arabs seemed a terrible loss to both of them. A daily disregard for the human dignity of the other contradicted the deep compassion expressed in each people's heritage and way of life.

In an effort to make sense of it all, I talked to Israelis and Palestinians and read everything I could on the subject. Forty years ago, the only writings available told two totally different stories. It was outrageous to read Zionist accounts of history that either omitted Arabs or included them only as obstacles or murderers. It was painful to read Arab accounts of Jews as monsters and imperialists, and of Zionism, the Jewish national dream of political freedom, as racist. This initiation bred in me a suspicion of facile dichotomies between villains and heroes, victors and vanquished, as well as skepticism about the incessant cycles of blame that sanctified victimization. It taught me that the ways we tell our stories have life-and-death consequences.

My stereotypes of Arabs and Jews were not the only ones to be challenged. Through my newly opened feminist eyes, I looked for other women to continue the radical explorations of the realities of being female and ended up founding the first feminist group in Jerusalem. The myth of gun-toting, liberated farmer/soldier Israeli women dissolved into a more nuanced reality of inequalities in a militarized society. The myth of oppressed Arab women gave way to a more complex understanding of their different kinds of power that are invisible to Westerners. The exhilaration of starting this group gave me a paradoxical sense of both the dynamic democracy of Israeli society, with its deeply rooted Jewish imperative for social change, and the entrenched ignorance that undergirded Israeli institutionalized inequalities for women, Palestinian Arabs, and the half of the Jewish population of Israel who were from Middle Eastern and North African countries.

I later returned to Jerusalem to apply what I had learned in an undergrad sociology course with Professor Maury Stein on intergroup work on inequality. Co-counseling theory and practice allowed people from both sides of a power imbalance, oppressor and oppressed, to work on racism, sexism, classism, and anti-Semitism. People who had been targets of injustice communicated to members of the dominant group that perpetuated injustice. I led classes and workshops for Palestinians and Israelis who for the first time directly witnessed the other's suffering and dignity. They whispered, cried, and shouted details of their lives that exposed the one-way nature of oppression, as well as the insidious internalization of oppression that causes people in the same group to turn against each other. Israelis heard Palestinians' personal tales of upheaval and exile, which shattered the myth that stories of these hardships were merely propaganda aimed at Israel's destruction. Israelis began to understand their part in Palestinian suffering. Arabs listened to the struggles of Jews who were minorities under Arab regimes, in European societies, and in the Holocaust, and began to understand their part in Jewish suffering.

Israelis and Palestinians awakened to the daily consequences of orientalist racism that institutionalized anti-Arab attitudes in Israeli society. They began to see the hidden two-part nature of anti-Semitism that first allowed some Jews to attain visible power as agents of an oppressor and, second, isolated them and blamed them for other peoples' suffering. Oppressed people who expressed their rage at Jews were diverted and defeated, while the real power causing oppression remained intact. Together we untangled intertwined, multiple, one-way oppressions to learn who was responsible for standing up against what in order to end harm and become allies.

Co-counseling was one of a handful of initiatives in the 1970s that created opportunities for encounters that challenged the status quo. New possibilities for alliances arose with Partnership, Oasis of Peace, Interns for Peace, and some elements of Peace Now. No one had much funding, but each group built bridges across a bloody chasm. This handful of taboo-breaking initiatives multiplied after the first war with Lebanon in 1982, the first intifada in 1988–1992, and the Oslo Accords in the 1990s, as hundreds of Palestinian-Israeli joint nonviolent initiatives attracted thousands of participants.

Meanwhile, I returned to the United States in the 1980s to study more formally what I'd learned on the street, when Harvard generously funded my study for a doctorate in Middle East history. When it came time to choose a dissertation topic, the Arab-Jewish work was hardly history and was still a mostly hidden, fragile presence. In fact, Israel had just passed a law making it illegal for Israelis to meet certain Palestinians. So instead, I investigated how the changing construction of gender roles helped form early Palestinian and Jewish nationalism and the conflict between them. I completed my doctoral thesis within moments of the 1993 handshake of Yasser Arafat and Yitzhak Rabin on the White House lawn that launched the Oslo Accords. By the time I finally published the results of my research in my book *Women and Gender in Early Jewish and Palestinian Nationalism*,[1] Oslo had collapsed into an orgy of blood in the second intifada.

I wondered why the work I'd experienced with Arabs and Jews in the 1970s, and watched blossom in the '80s and '90s, seemed so alive and vital while most people ignored or dismissed it. Why was there such a persistent gap between the dramatic changes experienced in our lived encounters with the so-called enemy and the marginalization of this work by pundits and even participants? Why were these alternatives to violence not even known by most people living there or elsewhere? The epitome of this syndrome occurred on the White House lawn in September 1993 when President Bill Clinton said that the historical handshake of Arafat and Rabin was an example of "the leaders leading the people." He dismissed the thousands of Palestinians and Israelis who had taken enormous risks for decades to nurture constituencies that demanded change, in a striking case of the people leading their leaders.

As the second intifada raged, I began to search for answers to these questions. I started with a narrow focus on why the groups I had founded in the 1970s with Palestinians and Israelis had been so successful and had attracted so many people who were willing to risk fears of facing each other for the first time, and to shatter presumptions about themselves, each other, and their histories. It was soon clear that this initiative was one of many Arab-Jewish nonviolent initiatives that dated back to the beginning of the conflict itself and stretched forward into the present.

There was no comprehensive account of the history of joint nonviolent initiatives. Most of the related literature focused on neither joint work nor history. Pieces of the puzzle were nestled in accounts of Palestinian and Israeli anthropology, social psychology, politics, activism, ethics, theology, and conflict resolution. Fragments existed in articles, flyers, and leaflets from my own informal archive collected over decades. There were clues in manifestos, treatises, and polemical pleas. The abundant books on the official "peace process" made passing references to grassroots joint interactions, as did writings by scholars and activists on peace and protest movements, advocacy, human rights, and social change, but these were mostly focused on separate Palestinian and Israeli societies.

Accounts that did concentrate on joint work employed a variety of disciplinary lenses that were valuable though not historical, or if they were historical, they focused on one particular time period. Social scientists and psychologists produced detailed analyses and critiques of the work. Monographs about single initiatives offered particulars about specific groups. Memoirs of individual Palestinians and Israelis revealed partnerships. There was an edited compendium detailing the work of over forty joint initiatives by over forty writers, and a directory of hundreds of initiatives up to 1992. My sources extended from the late 19th century through 2010.

I worried that publicizing some initiatives would "out" a person or organization and expose them to the condemnation rampant in both societies, so I resolved to include only those that were already visible in print, digital, or other media. Fortunately, their public presence expanded exponentially during the first decade of the new millennium, with an explosion of websites created by the groups themselves, as well as online lists of links and articles. By 2012, an internet search turned up well over a thousand groups. The quality and quantity of information varied greatly, but it was not difficult to distinguish between organizations that were actually engaged in what they claimed as their purpose and those that hoped to attract funds to implement dreams.

An abiding challenge for the research was an imbalance of sources that reflects the imbalance of power between the two peoples. Jewish sources predominated, in part because the Israeli state is organized and supports writings about itself. Palestinian sources get "lost, destroyed, and incorporated" into Israeli archives.[2] Before the creation of the State of Israel in 1948, Arabs had fewer reasons to record the joint work. They were a dominant, established culture with their own political aims, and they experienced the Jews as a minority serving Arab society in useful ways. Like any minority, Jews had to learn more about the dominant society in order to survive. Arabs were less concerned about getting along with this growing minority and more concerned with opposing Zionists' political goals, which threatened their own expectations for sovereignty. Most Zionists did not care about joint work either, except to validate their vision of liberating Arabs along with Jews. Yet some Jews and Arabs recognized the necessity of reaching for their neighbors as allies in a mutual quest for refuge in ancestral lands.

Scholar and activist Mohammed Abu-Nimer pointed out some of the historiographical pitfalls related to the dominance of Jewish sources:

> During the first phase of historical development of the coexistence field, all of the documentation was written by Israeli Jews affiliated with the major political parties or Histadrut. They wrote reports to illustrate the Arab minority acceptance of a Jewish state and to describe a manufactured reality of peaceful Arab-Jewish relations. Only during the second and third phases of the field's development were more serious . . . reports produced.[3]

Shany Payes further contends that the "limited and unequal nature of the encounter between Jews and Palestinians" shaped joint activism and, I would add, access to its evidence.[4] At certain points in history, Arabs faced higher risks for participating in joint encounters and were less likely to record them. So, for example, I discovered the existence of a Palestinian-Israeli theater performance at the Ramallah Summer Festival from an

Israeli website, but I could find no mention of it on the Ramallah Festival website. Palestinians' antinormalization concerns made participants fear being seen as collaborators with the enemy while the occupation continued.

I have included resources intended to shepherd the reader through the enormous volume of information and to give spatial and temporal guideposts to hundreds of initiatives over a hundred years. Historical and current maps locate almost all places mentioned in the text. Maps 1–4 locate places in chapters of the same number, including some towns and villages that no longer exist. Map 5 locates places in chapters 5–10 and shows Arab and Jewish towns that are not often found together in a single map. A chronology of Palestinian and Israeli history provides a timeline and definitions of events. A list of the initiatives divided by categories (arts activism, dialogue, political activism, women, youth, and so on) references chapter numbers to locate initiatives both in time and by field of endeavor. That list alone provides a powerful snapshot of the tremendous efforts of thousands of people to touch both painful and joyful aspects of their lives during protracted conflict, war, and occupation, with the very enemy who inflicted them. Together that suffering suddenly ceased to be a source of revenge and turned into a chance to live, if for only a few moments, the reality of their profound interconnection.

# Acknowledgments

The writings and support from Palestinian, Israeli, Arab, Jewish, and other scholars, activists, and friends made this volume possible. The magnitude of their input and my debt to them will become evident as you read, but I would like to especially thank those whose work was foundational to this project: Mohammed Abu-Nimer, Ziad AbuZayyad, Sami Adwan, Dikla Alush, Hanan Ashrawi, Uri Avnery, Mubarak Awad, Mordecai Bar-On, Gershon Baskin, Carol Birkland, Bishara Bisharat, Lisa Blum, Julia Chaitin, Naomi Chazan, Peter Demant, Bishara Doumani, Ayala Emmett, Michelle I. Gawerc, Varda Ginosar, Daphna Golan, Rabah Halabi, Sara Kallai, Reuven Kaminer, Edy Kaufman, Maxine Kaufman-Lacusta, Herbert Kelman, Rashid Khalidi, Baruch Kimmerling, Judy Kuriansky, Zachary Lockman, Joel Migdal, Nadia Nasser-Najjab, Sari and Lucy Nusseibeh, Roger Owen, Benny Morris, Shany Payes, Wendy Pearlman, Suha Sabbagh, Walid Salem, Raja Shehadeh, Hanna Siniora, Nava Sonnenschein, Gila Swirsky, and Rebecca Torstrick.

I am particularly grateful to Gordon Fellman and Stephen Zunes for their close readings of the manuscript and valuable comments. Maisa Khaishbon, a Palestinian Brandeis University student from Nazareth, contributed to this work as my research assistant in its early phases during my sabbatical year as a scholar-in-residence at the Women's Studies Research Center. My appreciation goes to University of California Press, Bloomsbury, and Scribner, a Division of Simon and Schuster, for permission to use quotes by Mahmoud Darwish and Martin Buber.

Berklee College of Music offered generous funding, with time off from teaching for research, travel, and writing. My students, who hailed from every continent and many conflicts in their own lands, widened my perspective and challenged me to articulate the unique nature of this particular history. Harvard's Widener librarians helped me access more resources than one could process in a lifetime. Staff and faculty at Harvard's Center for Middle East Studies provided encouragement.

Cecelia Cancellaro gave careful reading and intelligent support to the manuscript. Jim Burr, my editor at University of Texas Press, provided encouragement for guiding the project to completion. Sally Blazar read with fine sensitivity to nuance, joy, and sorrow in the text. I thank my family for their love and for their own work for transformation, in their own individual ways, that strengthens and sustains me. Unwavering support from Eduardo Stern anchored my work.

And finally, my appreciation goes to all those on the front lines of Palestinian-Israeli joint nonviolence who refuse to accept the unacceptable and who reach for the enemy to forge a just peace. Each initiative detailed in the book constitutes a unique piece of a vast mosaic of a century of joint nonviolent work. My intention is to present the initiatives and their participants as they desire to be seen. I regret having to omit so many worthy initiatives due to space limitations that required me to privilege breadth over depth in order to give contour to a wide sweep of history.

The opinions, ideologies, and approaches of these many groups do not always align with my own points of view, nor will they all align with yours. My intention was to cast a wide net, beyond the limits of my own perspective, and I hope that you, the reader, will do the same. May the telling of this hidden history challenge our presumptions about these two peoples and make us better allies to them both. I hope that the errors, limits, omissions, and shortcomings in this volume will goad others to hone and expand research into the ways that Palestinians and Israelis have dared to risk connecting with the enemy.

**Connecting with the Enemy**

# Introduction: Subversive Encounters

*This land, this Palestine, this Israel, does not belong to either Jews or Palestinians. Rather we are compatriots who belong to the land and to each other. If we cannot live together, we surely will be buried here together. We must choose life.*[1]

ELIAS CHACOUR, PALESTINIAN MELKITE PRIEST, *WE BELONG TO THE LAND*

*We must begin the process of creating a new partnership, an internal alliance that will alter the array of narrow interest groups that controls us. An alliance of those who comprehend the fatal risk of continuing to circle the grindstone; those who understand that our borderlines no longer separate Jews from Arabs, but people who long to live in peace from those who feed, ideologically and emotionally, on continued violence.*[2]

DAVID GROSSMAN, ISRAELI WRITER, "AN ISRAEL WITHOUT ILLUSIONS"

Three Hamas militants captured and killed a nineteen-year-old Israeli soldier, son of an Orthodox Jewish family. When the father discovered his son's clandestine peace activism, he refused the customary official consolation that promised revenge and instead sought out Israeli and Palestinian families whose children were killed by the enemy. At one meeting with these families, a bereaved Palestinian father interrupted an Israeli father's story of grief, shouting, "To tell you the truth, each time an Israeli child is killed I am happy that there will be one less soldier to hurt my child." The Israeli father rose, and clutching the heavy table, yelled, "To tell you the truth, I want to throw this table at you now for rejoicing at my child's death." Time stopped as the bereaved parents witnessed the rage and fear that perpetuates killing but will never be able to protect their loved ones. They joined in nonviolent action to create the Parents Circle Family Forum, one of hundreds of initiatives that allow ordinary people to take responsibility for ongoing injustice.

Acts of joint nonviolence happen every day, but they do not make headlines. Instead, the news is rife with reports of endemic cycles of violence as Palestinians and Israelis live the daily consequences of one of the most enduring conflicts of the past century. The official peace process has been a lachrymose trail of diplomatic failure. What can ordinary people do when faced with occupation and terrorism; economic, social, and political inequalities; ineffectual diplomacy; leaders hog-tied by their own interests; constituencies divided on the meanings of peace, survival, and justice; and vulnerability to extremist regional and international interests? How can they have an impact when so much is beyond their control? What can they do when consensus says the only choices are militarism and terror? How do they endure generations of killing, betrayal, and inequality?

The peoples of Israel and Palestine have responded to these questions with a kaleidoscope of grassroots joint nonviolent initiatives. We don't hear about these vital endeavors because the perpetuation of conflict depends in part on their marginalization. They don't fit the mainstream narratives of terror and despair, villains and heroes. They aren't organized into a movement but represent discrete approaches to specific aspects of conflict. They are safer to act in high-risk ways when they operate outside the limelight.

This volume is the first to present a panoramic history of Palestinians' and Israelis' joint activism. To my knowledge there has never been a persistent attempt to connect with an enemy in so many wildly diverse and creative ways by so many thousands of people. In each changing era Palestinians and Israelis have found new ways to challenge injustice, wrestle with differences, and confront inequalities undergirding conflict. Palestinian-Israeli nonviolent initiatives bear little resemblance to any other peace movement in history. Much is to be gained by chronicling the changing nature of their actions over time, in detailing what they have achieved and why their efforts have not yet brought peace.

This history bears witness to the efforts of ordinary Arabs and Jews who were not official leaders but took extraordinary actions. They persisted in making contact across prohibited borders despite their own justifiable rage, fear, and hatred. They did this even though their own people insisted that cooperation equals normalization of the status quo — or worse, collaboration with the enemy. Even the bloodstained consequences of the collapse of the Oslo talks in the first decade of this new century failed to derail them.

Joint nonviolence has existed since the inception of the Palestinian-Israeli conflict over one hundred years ago. This volume traces its development from the turn of the twentieth century to the first decade of the twenty-first century. During those years joint nonviolence was called by many names that appear throughout this volume, including coexistence, people-to-people programs, second-track diplomacy, citizen action, peace building, advocacy, solidarity, co-resistance, or simply work for equality and to end occupation.

Classifying these efforts as joint nonviolent initiatives reframes their role. It links them across the diversity of their goals, approaches, and ideologies. It connects them across decades of changing political contexts, borders, and leadership. It ties them across disciplinary boundaries of politics, arts, environment, education, sports, science, business, technology, and religion, and connects them to movements abroad. Nonviolent activist Lucy Nusseibeh makes a distinction between peace building and nonviolent approaches, arguing that the latter are "a prior step to peace building. . . . Sometimes you have to draw attention to injustice through nonviolence before you can even start to build peace."[3] This book includes initiatives that both address injustice and build peace.

The initiatives span a broad spectrum of goals, methods, and participant identities. A Palestinian lawyer creates the first Arab Holocaust museum. Palestinian and Israeli doctors operate on children's hearts. Committed killers turn into committed nonviolent activists. Arabs and Jews, children and elders, artists and activists, educators and students, garage mechanics and physicists, lawyers and prisoners meet in living rooms, theaters, olive groves, and hospitals; at protest rallies, concerts, festivals, and interfaith prayer gatherings; and in secret talks by self-appointed ambassadors. They make music, do business, play soccer, and plant and harvest crops. They protect the environment, demonstrate peacefully, advocate for justice and security, deliver babies, climb a mountain in Antarctica, and mourn together when their children are killed by the enemy.

Joint nonviolent activism occurs between two sides that are not equal. There is no symmetry, no mutuality. Israel is a state with an organized army. Palestinians are a stateless dispossessed people. Jewish Israelis are a tiny minority in an Arab Muslim Middle East and an outpost of Western culture that Westerners both back and condemn. This intertwining of two one-way inequalities demands a unique response that joint resistance provides by unwinding these strands of responsibility to take action. Activists oppose both Israeli military occupation and threats to Jewish lives; they reject force in order to ensure that there will be continued existence before coexistence.

Nonviolence doesn't avoid conflict; it rejects passivity and takes action.[4] It does avoid dehumanization of the self and others by acting with respect for all human lives. Weber and Burrowes argue that nonviolence "aims to arrive at the truth of a given situation (rather than victory for one side), and it is the only method of struggle that is consistent with the teachings of the major religions." They quote Aldous Huxley's assertion that "the means employed determine the nature of the ends produced" and Gandhi's teaching that "if one takes care of the means, the end will take care of itself."[5] Activists see that "a Manichean view of the Palestinian-Israeli conflict, with one side all light, and the other all darkness, is impossible to take."[6]

Palestinian-Israeli joint nonviolent activists reject the rejectionists and draw power "from the ability to resist the act, not the person in opposition."[7] Some of these initiatives engage in a kind of truth and reconciliation before a war officially ends, instead of after it ends as happened in South Africa after the fall of apartheid. Their work also resonates with the audacious work of women in Northern Ireland who reached across the bloody divide to end the Troubles.

The power of the work derives in part from the fact that despite both the obvious and hidden interdependencies of two peoples living in one land, most Jews and Arabs never meet. What they do see of each other confirms brutal stereotypes of soldiers or terrorists, of imbalances of power between the rulers and ruled, and of intent to harm. Over one hundred years ago, when the conflict began, it was not like this. Arab and Jewish farmers, neighbors, workers, homemakers, professionals, and self-appointed leaders of nascent nationalisms engaged in social, professional, and economic associations. But with each new chapter of history, segregation, inequality, occupation, and violence precluded possibilities for contact until the only way to meet was through these intentional encounters of joint nonviolent action.

This book is not about the activism of Israelis and Palestinians in their own separate societies. Some of the joint activists were already a part of grassroots peace or protest movements there. Nonviolent activists worked with their own peoples and critiqued their own leadership. Iconoclastic resistance to irreconcilable official policies was an important force of transformation. This book includes their work within separate societies only when it laid the groundwork for joint activism. Both joint and separate actions were indispensable forces for sociopolitical change.

This book is not about the official peace process. It is about the individuals and groups that engage with one another unofficially to address difficult issues. Boundaries between diplomatic and grassroots action are ambiguous, permeable, and synergistic. One cannot take the place of the other. All levels of action are necessary. Grassroots action can produce a groundswell of demands that prompt leaders to take diplomatic action. It can be a training ground for people who will eventually be involved in diplomacy. It can be a place to which leaders return when diplomatic action fails. Diplomatic action can propel or impede grassroots efforts, spur new projects or destroy old ones, spark the will to work together or drive a wedge of despair. Palestinian-Israeli grassroots nonviolence in this past century has managed to transcend diplomacy. Inter-Arab, intra-Palestinian, intra-Israeli, inter-regional, and East-West politics can undermine cross-group contact or put it on hold, but it has never been able to crush it.

The participants in these projects are not unbiased. There is no such thing as a nonbiased approach to the conflict. But to learn the unfamiliar and threatening narrative of the other's history is to hone critical skills of bias detection and to become attuned to distortions and contradictions in one's own and the other's assumptions. Biases are not inherently malevolent. They may stem from a deep desire to survive and to see one's children grow up in peace. Still, bias detection, like learning about one's own racism or anti-Semitism, is a worthy lifelong task. Cross-border encounters indicate that we are never free from the imperative to wake up to the reality of the other in ways that lance our distorted projections of who we are and who they are. We are here to challenge each other's blind spots and to take responsibility for the other's well being.

It is impossible to avoid the ideological and historiographical battles of dual and dueling narratives of Israel and Palestine, in the field and in this text. Every word written or omitted, every place name and historical date is a field of contestation that casts the narrator and the groups in question into ally or enemy orbits. Do they defend Zionism, believe Israel is a victory for all people, and celebrate the return of a displaced indigenous oppressed people to its ancient homeland? Do they attack Zionism as a colonial imperialist thief of the land and dignity of the indigenous Palestinian people? Is Zionism a national liberation movement, or an exclusive, racist, illegitimate movement that must be dismantled? Are Jews a nation or just adherents of a religion? Do Palestinians exist as a people, or is the

Palestinian people an invention of Arab political machinations? Are Palestinians, in Edward Said's words, "victims of victims," paying the price for the European-generated genocide and ethnic cleansing of Jews? Or are they terrorists carrying out the will of the Arab and Muslim majority to eradicate a non-Muslim usurper in their midst? Is Israel a homeland for the Jews or a nation for all its citizens? Is it an inspiring democracy or savage military regime? Was the Palestinian exile an inevitable consequence of a war initiated by Palestinians who rejected the United Nations partition plan, or was it the result of an intentional campaign by Israel to transfer the Palestinian population in order to achieve a Jewish majority for the new nation?

For the participants in joint nonviolent initiatives, the answer is yes. The groups' diversity spans all of these perspectives and beyond. Some groups bring together participants with opposing viewpoints. Others self-select for shared points of view to serve specific activist goals. Some groups judge other groups to be insignificant at best and seditious at worst. When groups do not function well, the work confirms individuals' worst fears and reinforces worn clichés that further entrench positions. When groups work well, individuals on both sides report the experience to be life changing.

Despite a surface discourse promoting peace, justice, and equality, underneath participants struggle with victim-villain dichotomies. There is so much evidence that the other's brutality demands one's staunch rejection or violent response. For the most part, the groups included here oppose violence, but they may have subtle or not so subtle messages that excuse it or indirectly participate in it. Underneath the rhetoric of promoting democracy, peace, or an end to occupation lurks a sense of existential and actual threat to each one's survival. In groups that work well, participants express these fears and find ways to work against oppression while honoring the aspirations of each people.

This book represents only a fraction of Palestinian-Israeli joint nonviolence. For every one of the over five hundred initiatives included here, at least two are omitted. Of course, inclusion of so many projects in one volume sacrifices depth for breadth. Some initiatives garner mention in only a sentence and others in a paragraph. Each one could fill its own monograph. Many groups have digital and print publications to consult for further information. I have omitted the names of many leaders and participants, in part to protect participants from unwanted exposure, in part because of space limitations, and mostly because so many of the people involved warrant a separate volume focused on their remarkable actions. Together these pieces form the details of a broad sweep of history never before gathered in one volume.

To select the initiatives that inhabit this book, I developed the following criteria for inclusion. Groups must:

(1) involve primarily Arab and Jewish participants who live in Israel and Palestine (many initiatives take place abroad and are included only if programs follow up at home);

(2) pursue nonviolent means of addressing injustices of occupation and the conflict, refraining from rhetoric that vilifies one side but does not turn away from injustice and inequality;

(3) show willingness to address power imbalances between participants by implementing, for example, nonexclusionary language, with meetings in Arabic and Hebrew translation or in a neutral language, and equitable leadership among Israelis and Palestinians; and

(4) already have a public media presence so this book does not out an organization or individuals.

Most groups do not fit all these criteria; some are exceptions to these rules; and some fit all the criteria, but are omitted anyway. One exception to all these criteria is the inclusion of allies: supportive individuals, and groups that include only Palestinian Arabs or only Israeli Jews but that work in their own sector on behalf of the other's well-being.

I describe each initiative in a brief account of its self-defined goals and aspirations. Most of the descriptions appear in chronological order, beginning with the group's founding. Others appear later than their founding or reappear to highlight changes at a particular historical moment. Some initiatives were founded jointly; some were founded by Palestinians partnering with Israelis or by Israelis partnering with Palestinians; others were founded by Arabs and Jews within Israel, and still others were founded jointly by Jews and Arabs in Israel and Arabs from the West Bank and Gaza. One group intentionally has equal representation from three groups: Israeli Jews, Palestinians from Israel, and Palestinians from the West Bank and Gaza. Some organizations have lasted as long as sixty years; others have risen and fallen in response to changing historical events.

The book does not deal with legal and financial aspects of the groups, but these details are often accessible in cited sources. Some groups are nonprofits or NGOs, and others are not legally constituted or even funded. Some register overseas when the Palestinian Authority or Israel balks at their binational character.

The striking diversity of ideologies and methodologies of the joint initiatives demands of you, the reader, what the encounters themselves demand of Palestinians and Israelis: that you sit with the discomfort of difference and open yourself to viewpoints that can sound like they are rooted in propaganda, naiveté, or treacherous lies. The reader, like the participants, will encounter an array of positions regarding Jewish nationalism, including Zionism, Marxist Zionism, right-wing and left-wing Zionism, religious and secular Zionism, anti-Zionism, non-Zionism, and post-Zionism, and an array of positions regarding Palestinian nationalism that are right-wing and left-wing, Marxist and capitalist, secularist and Islamic, pacifist and militant, moderate and radical, and Muslim and Christian. Some readers will see some initiatives as a thin veneer for ruthless aims. If you feel you can't bear to read any more, keep going anyway. It is possible that if you the reader, like the participants themselves, allow yourself to experience unbearable difference, to disagree with, be offended by, condemn, or reject this work, while continuing to listen to the multiple, contradictory voices of the text, you will gain a nuanced appreciation of both peoples' courage to be just allies.

## Constructs of Conflict

In *The Tiger's Wife*, Téa Obreht writes,

> But now, in the country's last hour, it was clear to him, as it was to me, that the cease-fire had provided the delusion of normalcy, but never peace. When your fight has purpose—to free you from something, to interfere on behalf of an innocent—it has a hope of finality. When the fight is about unraveling—when it is about your name, the places to which your blood is anchored, the attachment of your name to some landmark or event—there is nothing but hate. . . . Then the fight is endless, and comes in waves.[8]

Obreht's reference to the fall of Yugoslavia doesn't take into account what happens when the fight both has "purpose—to free you from something" and is "about unraveling—when it is about your name, the places to which your blood is anchored." For her, the "delusion of normalcy" connotes a longing for peace. But for Palestinians it is their worst fear that contact with Israelis will create a delusion of normalcy, acceptance of a status quo that does not redress structural injustices.

What are the sources of the protracted conflict between Palestinians and Israelis? The sororal births of Arab and Jewish modern political nationalism around the turn of the twentieth century laid its foundation. Changing global and local conditions precipitated a crisis of identity for Jews and Palestinians, incited by European imperialism, modern nationalism, orientalism, anti-Semitism, and geopolitics of the Middle East and World War I.

Nineteenth-century European liberal nationalists institutionalized the equality of its citizens and legally emancipated Jews from the ghetto. But modern anti-Semitism denied Jews' status as bona fide humans, attacked them as foreign nationals, blamed them for the disturbing consequences of modernity, and turned them into a Victorian-invented inferior "race" of "Semites" — drawing on nomenclature that previously had solely designated a language category. Second, European orientalism romanticized, denigrated, and dehumanized Arabs as part of this inferior race in the hierarchy of the West versus the rest. Europe defeated their Turkish rulers and took control of their lands.

The demise of the Ottoman, Austro-Hungarian, and Russian empires by the end of World War I and the triumph of British and French imperialism fueled forces of modern nationalism, capitalism, and the intertwined racisms of orientalism and anti-Semitism. The disintegration of political structures made untenable long-standing identities and severed connection to places, ideas, and centuries of life. Rashid Khalidi writes:

> If one takes identity as the answer to the question, "Who are you?" it is clear that the response of the inhabitants of Palestine . . . changed considerably over time. . . . How rapidly views of self and other, of history, and of time and space, could shift in situations of extreme political stress, which could be seen as watersheds in terms of identity.[9]

The origin of the conflict between Palestinians and Israelis was neither ancient nor religious. The modern crisis of identity rooted in physical and metaphysical dislocations also proffered a modern solution in nationalism. Modern national identity is, in Benedict Anderson's parlance, "imagined." Khalidi observes that "national identity is constructed; it is not an essential, transcendent given, as the apostles of nationalism . . . claim."[10] Its construction depends on the pretense of a pure, separate ancestral identity for which one is willing to die in conflict with nations seen as essentially different and menacing.

But in reality, members of the fledgling nations of Israel and Palestine constitute a palimpsest of interwoven identities engraved in endless iterations of peaceful migrations, religious conversions, and violent conquests. Linguistically, they share the etymology of their names in Semitic languages with the same letters, *Ivrim* (Heb. Hebrews) is A-B-R and *Al-Arab* (Ar. Arabs) is A-R-B, and both roots can connote nomads. Religiously, the Torah and the Quran both stress the importance of spiritual journeying and daily detailed ritual acts and blessings to connect with "the Merciful One of Mercy."[11] Scripturally, Christians and Muslims have both adopted the Hebrew Bible's Abraham as their ancestor and the Israelites' *Eretz Hakodesh* (Heb. holy land) as their holy place. Mystically, both Jewish Kabbalists and Muslim Sufis honed the monotheism of One God into "There is nothing but God," embracing the Other as a companion on the paradoxical spiritual journey of human beings, regardless of the Other's religion. Scientifically, genetic studies indicate that most Muslim and Christian Arab men and Jewish Israeli men share a chromosome pool dating to earliest prehistory.

Historically, the origins of Israel and Palestine are contested and entangled. Did the indigenous Hebrew tribes conquer Canaan and enter it peacefully, or did the inhabitants of Canaan initiate a monotheistic revolution? Did the Philistines (possible origin of the term *Palestine*) sail from Greece to conquer the coast in the twelfth century BCE? The Jewish Kingdoms of Israel and Judah that emerged in the tenth and ninth centuries BCE were destroyed and restored over the next thousand years as Israelites and Philistines intermingled with each other, with neighboring tribes, and with conquerors from Assyria, Babylon, Persia, Greece, and Rome. In the first and second centuries CE, during the Roman Empire, there were voluntary waves of conversions to Judaism and Christianity. When Rome defeated the Jewish revolt in 135 CE, it destroyed the Temple and exiled Jewish leaders. Two hundred years later, Romans converted most Middle Easterners to Christianity. Muslim Arab tribes invaded these lands in the seventh century, and by the eleventh century the majority of Christian and Jewish inhabitants had converted peacefully to Islam and learned Arabic. They lived under Turkish Muslim rule until 1917. For two millennia, there was neither a boundary nor a name that signified Israel or Palestine, even as the land remained a pilgrimage destination for three faiths.

By the twentieth century, Arabs and Jews met under new conditions that accentuated a gulf of difference in their respective historical development. Yet each one's transition to modern national identity presented contradictions and ambiguities that were sharpened in defiance of the

other. Joint nonviolence unfolded amid the violent clash of their two bur-
geoning nationalist movements. For the peoples that adopted the modern
identity of Israeli and Palestinian, peace was a luxury. Existence trumped
coexistence. Individuals could go elsewhere, but nowhere else could they
live as a people.

This is a chronicle of those who sought contact with each other to find
common ground for action. It begins with their lives under Ottoman and
then British rule, when quotidian contact was still the norm. Each passing decade deepened people's need and determination to throw off centuries of subjugation to foreign control and to live securely as a sovereign
majority. This, in turn, led to deeper segregation, enmity, and inequality
between them. Each passing decade also led to a trickle and then a torrent
of joint nonviolent initiatives. Much of the work was overtly political and
operated through negotiations or direct action, and much of the work was
cultural, economic, social, civic, scientific, or scholarly. Some acts were
dangerous, others were fun, and each one challenged what people believed
to be true about themselves and the other. They tested and lived the teaching of Martin Luther King Jr. that:

> The ultimate weakness of violence is that it is a descending spiral, beget-
> ting the very thing it seeks to destroy. Instead of diminishing evil, it
> multiplies it. Through violence you may murder the liar, but you cannot
> murder the lie, nor establish the truth. Through violence you murder the
> hater, but you do not murder hate. . . . Hate cannot drive out hate; only
> love can do that.[12]

The following chapters explore how thousands of Israelis and Palestinians took action in hundreds of joint nonviolent initiatives to stop
the "descending spiral" and to refrain from murdering the liar, even as
lies persisted. Could they learn to "murder hate" instead of the haters?
Could they find alternative ways to live their intertwined, interdependent
reality? Each chapter shows their unique responses to ever-changing historical conditions. The last chapter assesses the significance of their work
and asks why these good-will efforts have not yet managed to end the conflict or occupation.

## CHAPTER 1

# Quotidian Contact, New Conflict: Under the Ottomans, 1880–1918

*While we feel the love of homeland, in all its intensity, toward the land of
our fathers, we forget that the people living there now also have a feeling
heart and a loving soul. The Arab, like any person, is strongly attached to his
homeland. . . . When we enter our land, we must rid ourselves of all thoughts
of conquest and uprooting.*

*Our watchword must be live and let live.*[1]

YITZHAK EPSTEIN, ADDRESS TO THE SEVENTH ZIONIST CONGRESS, 1905

*All of us, both Muslims and Christians, have the best of feelings toward the
Jews. When we spoke in our resolutions about the rights and obligations of the
Syrians, this covered the Jews as well. Because they are our brothers in race and
we regard them as Syrians who were forced to leave the country at one time but
whose hearts always beat together with ours. . . . May our common country . . .
develop both materially and morally.*[2]

ABD AL-HAMID ZAHRAWI, PRESIDENT OF THE
FIRST ARAB CONGRESS, PARIS, 1913

One day in 1897 in Jerusalem, a Muslim midwife delivered a healthy baby
boy in the home of a wealthy Muslim family. The same week, that midwife delivered another boy to the family of a Jewish grocer. She brought
each baby to the other's mother to nurse. According to Arab custom, the
Arab and Jewish baby boys thus became foster brothers for life. The families became friends, and for the next thirty years they visited each other,
exchanged gifts on feast days, and gave each other congratulations and
condolences.[3] In another part of town, an Arab pharmacy owner hired a
Jewish pharmacist to work with him. Together they spent decades tack-
ling Jerusalem's illnesses and sharing family events. Around the corner, an

Arab mother hired a Jewish tailor to make clothes for her family, and the Jewish woman served her for many years.

For centuries nonviolent contact was the norm for Arabs and Jews. In ancient times they united even in war—for example, when a coalition of Jewish and Arab tribes fought against another coalition of Jewish and Arab tribes in pre-Islamic Yathrib in Arabia. When Muslim Arabs emerged from Arabia in the seventh century to conquer and settle the land now called Palestine and Israel, they guaranteed protection for the non-Muslims who constituted the majority until the tenth century. Jewish and Christian *ahl al-dhimma* (Ar. people of the book) maintained their own schools, courts, and prayer houses in exchange for paying an extra head tax and submitting to legal restrictions under Muslim hegemony. They lived in separate neighborhoods and had different religiously dictated food customs, but Jews, Christians, and Muslims interacted daily in shopping, trading, service provision, business partnerships, intermarriage, life-cycle celebrations, and mourning.

During the four hundred years of Ottoman Turkish rule (1516–1918) Arabs and Jews lived together mostly peacefully on the eastern shores of the Mediterranean. The populations were sparse, diverse, and contained in isolated villages, small urban centers, and semi-nomadic Bedouin encampments. The number of people in the region rose and fell with economic and political vicissitudes and natural disasters such as earthquakes. Sunni Muslim Arabs were the religious majority; Jews, Shiites, Druze, and diverse eastern Christian sects were minorities. The Ottoman millet system upheld the premodern Islamic practice of tolerance for non-Muslim autonomous communities. The economy was poor; the language was Arabic; the rulers were Turkish. Jewish and Arab lives fluctuated with shifting power matrices between local and central authorities.

Palestine and Israel did not exist in name; their lands were divided into smaller administrative districts within a larger territory of Greater Syria that encompassed what today are Israel, Palestine, Jordan, Syria, and Lebanon. Palestinians and Israelis, as we know them today, did not exist. Rashid Khalidi explains that it was difficult to find the specificity of Palestinian identity because it "intermingled" with so many other identities, including "Islamic or Christian, Ottoman or Arab, local or universal, or family or tribe."[4] In some ways this intermingling was the privilege of those who, even as peasants, were part of a dominant culture. The identity of the Jewish minority was multilayered but more externally fixed by the dominant culture, which tolerated their existence within limits.

Political changes demanded that the peoples of this land exert their agency in new ways that challenged premodern identities. Beshara Doumani notes that the interface of Palestinian elites and peasants with "commoditization of land" and "ongoing political, demographic, and economic changes" shaped their relations with the new Jewish immigrants, influenced the "pattern of Jewish settlements and land purchases," and contextualized both people's pursuit of political nationalism. This process was

> neither a linear march into the modern period nor predicated on a sharp break with the past. . . . Ingrained modes of social organization and cultural life, far from being shattered, proved highly resilient and adaptable. The meanings of modernity were redefined here, as they were everywhere, in uneven, contradictory, and internally differentiated ways.[5]

Ultimately the rise of two new nationalist movements put the two peoples on a collision course in one land. In this early period, only a minority on each side resonated with new nationalist identity as a strategy for coping with collective survival in a rapidly changing world. This chapter examines the earliest rumblings of Palestinian and Jewish nationalism amid the continuities and disruptions of age-old accommodations between Arabs and Jews, and joint nonviolent responses to new conflicts.

## A Tale of Two Nationalisms

Historical discourse is a battleground of conflict. The two peoples nurture narratives of the origins and history of their national struggles that interpret the same events in opposing ways. Many on each side have no idea of the history of the other side except in ways that confirm their enmity and the other side's illegitimacy as stewards of the land. Joint nonviolent initiatives provided an antidote to ignorance, with opportunities to listen and to learn of the other's survival struggles, dreams, and needs.

Up to the nineteenth century, the four hill regions of Palestine, al-Jalil (Galilee), Jabal Nablus, Jabal al-Quds (Jerusalem), and Jabal al-Khalil (Hebron) provided natural protection for Palestinian Arab peasants. These inland mountain peoples' experience was different from that of the Palestinian Arabs living in the plains leading to the Mediterranean, who were more vulnerable to periodic incursions by Ottoman or Egyptian forces, as well as to nomadic raids. The people of the hill regions enjoyed productive trade relations with the Bedouin, peasants, and town dwellers, as local leaders with some autonomy shaped indigenous society.[6]

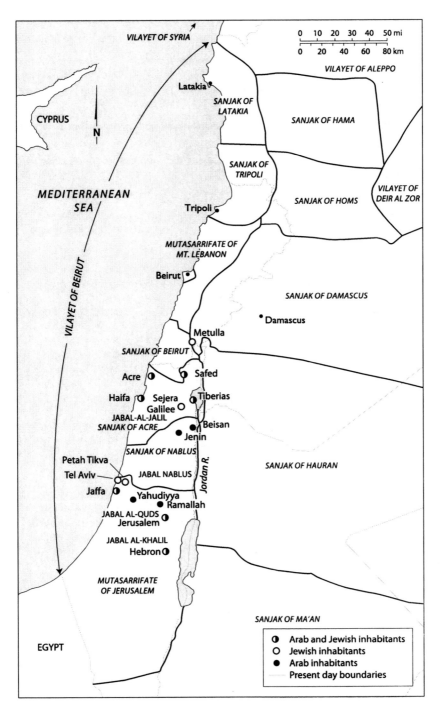

**Map 1.** Late Ottoman Syria to 1918

The peasants worked the land, lived in villages, and were loyal to family and *hamulas* (Ar. patriarchal clans), who protected individuals and shaped socioeconomic relations. Sheikhs collected taxes in olive oil to give to the Ottoman authorities.

New forces altered these socioeconomic relations. In the mid-nineteenth century Egyptian forces under Muhammad Ali and Ibrahim Pasha conquered and occupied these lands. The new rulers promised equality to non-Muslim minorities. That promise was one factor that provoked a Palestinian Muslim revolt against Egyptian rule that resulted in the killing, looting, and rape of Jewish and Christian people.[7] Subsequent reestablishment of Ottoman control and increasing connection to the global market provoked a shift to a market economy from subsistence farming in a "semi-feudal tribute-paying mode of existence."[8] Changes in land ownership, labor, Arab migration patterns, urban growth, governmental reforms, and European migrations all exerted influence.

Late nineteenth-century Zionists called the mostly Arabic-speaking Jews in this predominantly Arab milieu under Ottoman rule the "Old *Yishuv*" (Heb. settlement). Many were poor and dependent on charity from abroad. Ashkenazis (Jews of European origin), Sephardis (Jews of Spanish origin), and Mizrahis (Jews of Middle Eastern and North African origins) practiced varying expressions of Orthodox Judaism in their four holy cities of Jerusalem, Hebron, Safed, and Tiberias. As Ottoman subjects, they deferred to Turkish authorities and the Muslim majority while studying their primary texts, Torah and Talmud, and working as merchants, shopkeepers, and craftspeople.[9]

Under the Ottomans, joint nonviolent contact between Arabs and Jews was the norm, with daily encounters that were neither exceptional nor subversive. They owned businesses together; forged partnerships in wheat, livestock, and dairy farming; made shoes; sold spices; and owned the mills that ground wheat to flour. Muslims bought meat from Jewish butchers, rented ovens from Jewish bakeries, and bought cheese and jewelry from Jewish craftspeople. Jewish and Arab doctors covered for each other; Jews and Arabs rented space in each other's homes and often lived as neighbors. Families developed friendships and socialized within the limits of their religious dietary codes. Muslim men married Jewish women, though Muslim women could not marry Jewish men because patriarchal dictates required a woman to convert to her husband's religion, and conversion to Judaism was forbidden by Islamic authorities.

By the last decades of the nineteenth century, changes within and beyond the empire shook this long history of nonviolence. Historians Roger

Owen and Charles Issawi point to an acceleration of economic and social changes during this period.[10] Ottoman subjects interacted with expanding European imperialism, an uneven spread of modernization, the rise of modern nationalism, and progressive integration into the world market economy. To strengthen control in the face of European encroachment, Sultan AbdulHamid II expanded transportation, education, communications, and military presence. New laws privatized lands, enabling Muslim Arabs to acquire state lands on which peasants had usufruct rights (the right to farm the land and to pass that right to their children). Internal urban-rural and socioeconomic dynamics affected the lives of Arab merchants and peasants and began to give shape to a modern Palestinian identity.[11]

Expanding European involvement further ruptured the status quo of nonviolent Arab-Jewish relations. French Catholic traders introduced the European concept of blood libel. In 1840 Damascus, when a Christian child died, Christian Arabs accused Jews of taking the child's blood to make matzah (Heb. ritual unleavened bread), and used that supposed offense as an excuse to violently attack Jews. Over time Europeans settled in the area and extended their reach, in part by enriching and protecting the Christian and Jewish minorities with whom they traded. They pressed for Ottoman legal reforms to include equal rights for non-Muslim minorities, which led to Muslim riots and protests. One response to the rising privilege of Christian Arabs under European protection was the 1860 Muslim massacre of Christians in Damascus.

Other factors, however, led to closer relations between Christian and Muslim Arabs. Christians began to construct a new secular nationalism based on a shared culture of the Arabic language and spearheaded an Arabic literary revival in mid-nineteenth–century Beirut. Imagining a new nation as Arab rather than Muslim opened the possibility of the Christian minority gaining equal status with Muslims. Integration into the world market economy led to the rise of a middle class of Muslims and Christians who came together as landlords, tenants, shippers, bankers, and insurance agents.[12]

Ottomans selected newly wealthy Christian and Muslim Arabs to serve on the municipal councils. Arabs began formulating visions of a future that could set them free from tightening Ottoman control. Some dreamed of self-rule in a modern pan-Islamic nation; some articulated a new secular pan-Arab nationalism. Palestinian nationalism overlapped with and was distinct from both.

Forces stirring in distant Europe had an impact on Arab and Jewish relations in Ottoman lands. Mounting wealth from imperialism, pressures for equal rights, a rising bourgeoisie, and a nascent working class emerging from the Industrial Revolution all threatened traditional forms of power. One line of defense used by the antidemocratic forces of monarchies, churches, and aristocracies to oppose equal rights was the reimagining of modern anti-Semitism. If those in power could divert people's protest against their own oppression toward Jews, they could maintain inequality for all.

With equal rights on the ascent, however, severe restrictions on Jews lifted as ghettos were abolished. Throughout the nineteenth century, newly emancipated Jews gained rights to attend schools and work in European Christian society. But by the last decades of the century, traditional forces were defending their power and fighting against equal rights in part by fomenting pogroms and political attacks against Jews, such as the notorious Dreyfus affair, in which an innocent Jewish army officer stood accused of treason. Jews reacted to these dangers in three ways. They fought for others' rights in revolutionary movements, immigrated to America, or departed to form a new modern nation in ancestral lands.

This last group of Jewish immigrants who fled from anti-Semitic violence in Europe to the Ottoman Empire differed from the Jews who were already living there under the constraints of Muslim law in relative harmony with Muslim and Christian Arab neighbors. Like other colonized peoples, they had imbibed notions of freedom and individual rights from Europeans who refused to recognize them as human enough to share those rights. Also like other colonized peoples, they saw modern nationalism as a way to achieve and protect those rights. But like other colonizers, they internalized the racism of Europeans who gave lip service to equality but viewed the indigenous population as inferior. These new immigrants saw Arabs, and Jews from Arab countries, as primitives in need of modern development. Like other colonizers, they arrived in a land already inhabited by people who considered it theirs. For their part, Palestinian Arabs saw the new immigrants not as freedom fighters finally returning home, but as colonizers separate from the cultural landscape who ignored their norms and needs.

In 1882, the first *aliyah* (Heb. going up), or wave of Jewish immigrants, brought a new political vision of Jewish identity. The immigrants rejected the Napoleonic compromise of assimilation, which demanded that Jews renounce their national identity, and reduce it to a religion, in exchange for equal citizenship. National identity versus religious identity was a false dichotomy for Jews and for anyone whose identity was formed in premodern conditions in which land, government, peoplehood, and religion were synonymous. Hebrew *'Am* and Arabic *'Umma* mean peoplehood and nation.

The new immigrants also rejected their religious Zionist predecessors, who prayed thrice daily for centuries for messianic deliverance to return to Zion. Instead, 23,000 Jews entered the land determined to leave behind centuries of oppression in exile and to find freedom in an *Altneuland*—an "old-new" land.[13] They named this new, modern, political Jewish nationalism Zionism.

Zionists found a land ravaged by Ottoman rulers who had clear-cut forests to build railroads and had left the land desiccated and swampy. They saw a need for their European-style "civilizing mission" to improve the lives of Arabs, including Arab Jews, and they expressed the hope that their contributions to the development of Palestine would result in good relations with Arab neighbors and a new society based on equal rights that would free Arabs and Jews from age-old inequalities. Jews had not been allowed to own or work the land in Europe, so now they studied farming and invented and implemented agricultural techniques to raise the quality and quantity of food. They introduced new medicines to cure the Arabs of eye disease and cleared swamps to eradicate malaria.

Some of these early Zionists interpreted Arab hostility as a classic ploy of the greedy land-owning classes to divert the anger of their oppressed people away from their own reactionary policies. Arab violence seemed to mimic centuries of violent attacks by ruling-class persecutors who used peasants as pawns to attack Jews. When Jews had nowhere else to go, Arab attacks motivated them to learn how to defend themselves for the first time since their military defeat by Rome. The new culture of self-defense postulated that dying for freedom in the ancestral land was better than dying as victims in host countries turned hostile. Self-defense became a "major pillar of their ideology in Palestine."[14]

Equating Arab attacks with historical attacks on Jews resulted in a disregard for the legitimacy of Arab grievances over Jewish immigration and land purchases that threatened Palestinian dreams of political power in their own lands. By the late 1890s, Arab leaders could read about Zionist plans for a Jewish homeland in Palestine emerging from the First Zionist Congress in Basel. In response, the Egyptian journal *Al-Manar* warned Arabs that Zionism's aim was to take over Palestine. Yusef al-Khalidi, who was mayor of Jerusalem in 1899 and a scholar who lectured at the University of Vienna, wrote to the Chief Rabbi of France. He expressed support for the Zionist goal of relieving the suffering of Jews but argued that substantial settlement and an attempt to rule would provoke violence.[15] He urged Jews to find another place for the creation of a Jewish state. The British offered persecuted Jews a piece of Uganda.

Nagib Azuri, a French-educated Maronite Roman Catholic, left his Ottoman post for Paris, where he published a call for Arabs to secede from the Ottoman Empire, blamed Turks for the ruin of Arab civilization, and warned against the new Jewish immigrants' nationalist goals. During the Dreyfus trial, his writings reflected anti-Semitism and French Catholic reactionary views. He opened his treatise, *Le reveil de la nation arabe*, with this oft-quoted prophecy:

> Two important phenomena, of the same nature but opposed, are emerging at this moment in Asiatic Turkey. They are the awakening of the Arab nation and the latent effort of the Jews to reconstitute on a very large scale the ancient kingdom of Israel.[16]

Indeed, two new modern political identities were gestating in late-nineteenth- and early-twentieth-century Ottoman lands. Rashid Khalidi located the emergence of Palestinian nationalist identity in the same period as modern Jewish nationalist identity.[17] These identities arose from internal dynamics and exigencies, as well as in relation to Ottoman, Islamic, Christian, Arab, local Palestinian, Jewish, and European ideas and realities. Doumani shows how the active agency of both urban notables and "middle peasantry" determined the course of modern history for Palestinians. Historian Benny Morris shows that the urgency of a "growing number of desperate Jews seeking escape from persecution"[18] determined the course of modern history for them. Yet between 1880 and 1918, those who imagined a new future in a modern nation remained a small minority among both peoples.

## Workers, Peasants, Farmers

Palestinian populations grew, cities began to industrialize, commerce and tourist services expanded, and the import and export trades increased. In the cities lived *ashraf* (Ar. nobles), merchants, retail traders, artisans, and an urban proletariat. Unskilled wage laborers were growing in number, and many worked on farms of the new Jewish settlers—picking oranges, for example. Some *fallahin* (Ar. peasants) became sharecroppers on the lands of absentee Arab landlords. Small landowners lived above subsistence level, and a middle class of peasants, particularly around Jabal al-Quds, Jabal Nablus, and the Jabal al-Jalil, accumulated wealth. But indebtedness led to the fragmentation and loss of lands, which displaced *fallahin* from lands they had historically worked and sent them into the money economy, disrupting social relations.[19]

Zionists' introduction of new agricultural policies and practices further aggrieved the *fallahin*, who vented their anger on the Jewish settlers. Jewish socialists of the second *aliyah* decried the European colonial plantation model of living as masters over Arabs hired to do the dirty work. Instead, hard physical labor for Jews became a kind of religion of personal and national redemption that would free body, soul, and the nation while making the desert bloom. The anticolonial model of these Labor Zionists was *kibbush avodah* (Heb. conquest of labor), which insisted that Jews themselves work as farmers and manual laborers instead of hiring Arabs who wanted those jobs.

The newly constituted Jewish National Fund purchased land from absentee Arab landlords. These landowners often kept the peasants as tenants on the land and didn't tell them that they no longer had usufruct rights or title.[20] This meant that Jews, not the former Arab landlords, had to physically oust the *fallahin*. Already burdened by debt and displaced by Ottoman land laws, some peasants responded with violence. In 1886, *fallahin* from the village of Yahudiyya (derived from the Arabic root for "Jew(s)") killed Jewish settlers in nearby Petah Tikva (Heb. Opening of Hope). In subsequent years these patterns of attack continued until the *fallahin* could lease back land.[21] Settlers further aggravated tensions because of their ignorance of a local agricultural custom of *musha'a*, communal grazing rights, when they fenced off newly acquired lands in ways that interrupted habitual grazing patterns.

Some of the settlers forged good relationships with Arab neighbors and consequently developed ties based on mutual respect and help. In rural areas relationships between Jewish settlers and Palestinian peasants were enhanced in the Zionist settlements that employed more Arabs than Jews.[22] Arabs and Jews worked side by side fruit picking. In urban areas, they worked together in factories, in road building, on the docks, in construction, and on railroads. They joined forces to organize for better labor conditions. As workers, they manufactured together, ate together, suffered misfortunes at difficult jobs together, and were equally exploited in their workplaces.

In 1907, members of the Jewish workers party, Po'alei Tziyon (Heb. workers of Zion) acted independently without the backing of union leadership to help organize a strike among Arab workers in the Jewish-owned Petah Tikva's citrus groves.[23] Socialist Zionists cooperated with Arab "popular elements" as natural allies of the Jewish working class. Together they jointly opposed a hostile and defensive "Arab elite."[24] They were torn by the contradictory demands of their beliefs when they joined forces with Arab laborers but did not hire them for work they did themselves.

Most Zionist immigrants settled in the cities. They swelled the older Jewish neighborhoods and built new ones in Haifa, Jerusalem, and Jaffa. In the older parts of these cities Jews and Arabs lived in close proximity, developed good neighborly relations, watched over each other's children, and patronized each other's businesses. In the newer parts of the cities Jewish immigrants built neighborhoods and towns separated from Arab population centers. In the first decade of the new century, the immigrants founded the city of Tel Aviv (Heb. Hilltop of Spring) as an entirely new city on the Mediterranean coast inhabited by Jews.

Like colonial settlers everywhere, the new immigrants could not thrive without help from those who knew the land. Both Palestinian Arab and Middle Eastern Jewish women taught European and Russian Jewish women to survive. In Sejera, the first Jewish settlement to accept women workers, the Kurdish Jewish immigrant women from the lands of northern Iraq taught the women from Europe how to sift barley according to their traditional Middle Eastern agricultural methods.[25] In the first years of the settlement of Petah Tikva, the women and children spent long hours in the sun learning from neighboring Arab women how to bake bricks for their mud huts so they could move out of their tents before autumn rains. First, Arab women made the bricks while Jewish women and children carried the materials they needed. Eventually the Arab women taught the Jewish women to make the bricks themselves while their children carried the earth, lime, and straw. As Arab and Jewish women mixed these materials and added water, their children together stamped the mixture and kneaded it with their feet.[26]

Arab women saved Jewish women's lives in other ways as well. In one incident, members of a new Jewish settlement had no more food. The men had left to find food in a distant town, and rains washed out the roads, preventing their return. As the women and children began to starve, they defied the orders of the men, who prohibited contact with neighboring Arab villages. One little girl went into the tent of an Arab woman and watched her making barley cakes with meal and water. The woman offered her barley cakes and an onion and watched as the girl ravenously gulped it down. The Arab women kept baking barley cakes, preventing the Jews from starving before the men returned.[27]

In another incident, an Arab woman who had been selling eggs to Jewish women ran to their neighboring settlement to tell them that they had to take their families away into hiding. She warned that surrounding Arab villagers were angry and intended to surprise the village and kill everyone. The Palestinian woman feared that she would be killed for imparting this information to the Jewish women, but she said she was compelled to do so because of their relationship of mutual kindness, which had developed over time.[28]

## New Nationalist Leaders

In the last decade of Ottoman rule before World War I, Ottomans, Arabs, and Jews jockeyed for power. Arab and Jewish leaders sought contact with each other when they perceived a chance to further their own cause, and they dropped contact when the political winds shifted. But peace as a goal was eclipsed by budding nationalism. Leaders of both movements saw those on the other side as at best irrelevant and at worst enemies to their own sovereignty.

Nevertheless, there were Arabs and Jews who critiqued mainstream nationalists and sought rapprochement. Some Jews took an antinationalist stance in the hopes of living side by side with Arabs. Some were willing to renounce state power and accept minority status. Asher Ginsberg, also known as Ahad Ha'am (Heb. one of the people), developed ideas of cultural Zionism, calling Herzl's vision of statehood grandiose. He accused Zionists of mistreating Arab workers in the manner of European colonists and argued that the land was not vacant, so Jewish settlements must not dispossess Arab inhabitants. He urged that Palestine become a spiritual center for Jews but not a political state.

Yitzhak Epstein, an Arabic-speaking Palestinian Jew, defended the importance of coming to terms with Palestinian Arabs. At the Seventh Zionist Congress in Basel, Switzerland, in July 1905, he protested the eviction of Druze tenant farmers in Metulla in 1896. Epstein argued that these lands belonged to both peoples:

> The idea of the renaissance of our people on its soil [contains] a problem
> . . . equal to all others, . . . our relations with the Arabs. . . . There is in

our beloved land an entire nation, which has occupied it for hundreds of years and has never thought to leave it.[29]

In 1907 Epstein published an article that pushed Zionism to rethink its policy toward Arabs after almost three decades of settlement. He suggested there be joint Arab-Jewish binational development, no dispossession of poor peasants, a joint farming community, and bilingual schools. His vision was dismissed.[30]

Moshe Olgin saw Arabs as waging a people's war against Jewish conquerors. He accused settlers of building upon the "ruin of the Arabs":

Who are these Arabs? . . . Who is this mysterious enemy? Is he a tyrant who enslaved the country like the Czar of Russia? Is he an individual who rules through his money, like Rockefeller in Colorado? No. The Arabs . . . are the established inhabitants of Palestine, who lived there for hundreds of years before the arrival of the Zionist settlers.[31]

Some Arab Jews saw themselves in the unique role of bringing the two peoples together. Nissim Malul, a Safed-born intellectual from a Tunisian family, urged Zionists in 1911 to learn Arabic and "merge with the Arabs" in a joint "Semitic nationalism."[32] Shimon Moyal was a Jew from a Moroccan family living in Jaffa who studied medicine in Beirut and married the Arab journalist and early feminist Ester Moyal. They moved to Cairo and wrote articles in Egyptian newspapers about the need for close relations between Jews and Arabs. After returning to Jaffa, they founded an organization with Arab Jews called Ha-Magen (Heb. the shield) that declared the importance of creating peace between Jews and Arabs in the country and made contact with many Arab nationalists.

Malul and Shimon Moyal were Arabic-speaking Jews immersed in Arabic literature and the intellectual life of the Arab world. Both viewed Jewish knowledge of Arabic as the key to a future of peaceful coexistence. They even advocated assimilation with the Muslim majority. They saw many commonalties between Jews and Muslims but distrusted Christian Arabs, whom they blamed for instigating tension between them.

Arabs and Jews proposed fighting for their national rights together against Ottoman opposition. Sami Hochberg, owner of the newspaper Le-Jeune-Turc, unofficially represented Zionists at a meeting with the Cairo-based Decentralization Party and the anti-Ottoman Beirut Reform Society. Arabs adopted a resolution ensuring Jews equal rights under a decentralized Ottoman government.

In 1913, Hochberg attended the First Arab Congress in Paris where Arab and Jewish leaders promised support for each other's national movements. Abd al-Hamid Zahrawi, the President of the Congress in Paris, summed up the attitude of the delegates in the quote that began this chapter, saying that Muslims and Christians wanted to build a new Arab nation that included the Jews in the "rights and obligations" of "Syrians" and hoped that Jews would contribute "materially and morally."[33] The following year Arabs and Jews investigated more possibilities for mutual support. Ahmad Bayhum, Najib Suqair, Shukri al-Husayn, Said al-Husayni, Raghib Nashashibi, Said Shahin, Asad Daghir, Faris al-Khuri, and others met with Zionists Victor Jacobsen and Richard Lichtheim. Nasif al-Khalidi, Muhammad Kurd Ali, Abd al-Rahman al-Shahbandir, George Fakhuri, Shukri al-Asali, Muhammad al-Inglizi, and others met with Zionist Nahum Sokolov.[34]

Daud Barakat was an Arab editor of the Cairo daily *al-Ahram*. In 1913 he justified his argument for Arab-Jewish mutual support by drawing on familiar stereotypes of Jews:

> [There must be] entente between the Zionists and the Arabs because . . . the Zionists are necessary for the country; the capital they will bring, their knowledge and intelligence and the industriousness which characterizes them will contribute without a doubt to the regeneration of the country.[35]

World War I put a sudden halt to all efforts at rapprochement. The war ended the municipal council of Jerusalem that had operated under the auspices of the Ottomans, where six Muslim, two Christian, and two Jewish representatives had worked together.[36] The war scuttled the plans of Nasif al-Khalidi to work with Chaim Kalvarisky on the possibility of a joint Arab-Jewish nationalist conference.[37] It eclipsed Palestinians' meetings with Zionists to discuss aspirations in the spring of 1914, where they asked Jews to state their political ambitions, their willingness to open schools to Palestinians, and their intention to learn Arabic and integrate into the local population. It overshadowed the Palestinian press, in which Arab-Christian newspapers such as *Filastin* and *Al-Karmil* warned against a Jewish-Muslim entente that might exclude Christian Arabs from the newly emerging political configuration.

The war devastated the lands of the eastern Mediterranean, ravaged the peoples of the Ottoman provinces, and caused severe economic and political hardships. The Ottomans cracked down on Jewish and Arab nationalist activities. British and French representatives proposed secret and contradictory promises, with the aim of enlisting Arab and Jewish allies to fight the Ottomans. The Hussein-McMahon secret agreement promised the Arabs an independent nation of indeterminate borders if Arabs helped defeat the Ottomans. The Balfour Declaration promised Jews a homeland of indeterminate borders if Jews helped defeat the Ottomans. The Sykes-Picot secret agreement promised that the British and French would divide and rule the very same Ottoman lands promised to Arabs and Jews.

In the midst of the war Chaim Weizmann, a British Zionist leader, met with Sharif Hussein of Mecca and his sons, Faisal and Abdullah, as well as with Syrian notables.[38] The most famous of these negotiations occurred between Faisal and Weizmann. The latter's choice to negotiate with the Meccan leadership instead of Palestinians was not incidental. Faisal shared the view of Zionist leaders that upper-class Palestinian notables were "dishonest, uneducated, greedy, and unpatriotic" and accused them of siding with Germany and the Ottomans.[39] Faisal was a Bedouin leader encamped in the desert valley of Wadi Waheida, between what is now Jordan and Saudi Arabia. To Weizmann, he seemed an icon of the new breed of nationalist. At the Paris peace conference after the war, Weizmann wrote of Faisal with orientalist-inflected praise:

> He is the first real Arab nationalist I have met. He is a leader! He is quite intelligent and a very honest man, handsome as a picture. He is not interested in Palestine but . . . wants Damascus and the whole of North Syria. He talks with great animosity against the French. . . . He expects a great deal from collaborations with the Jews. . . . He is contemptuous of the Palestinian Arabs whom he doesn't even regard as Arabs.[40]

\* \*

The end of the Great War was also the end of the Ottoman Empire. Faisal and Weizmann pledged mutual national support to counteract European opposition to their recent promises of Arab independence and a Jewish homeland. The two leaders met at the Paris Peace Conference and secretly agreed "to harmonize the interests of Arabs and Zionists."[41] The British and French drew the borders of new Arab countries on a wall map in Versailles. In 1918 Faisal acted to make good Britain's promise by founding an independent Arab government based in Damascus. Weizmann and Faisal were acting on the belief that they could determine their own political destinies. Instead, the French marched on Damascus and took control of Syria. Faisal's brother, Abdullah, left Mecca with Bedouin troops to defend the fledgling Arab nation. Britain stopped Abdullah by creating Transjordan for him to rule. The French ousted Faisal and crushed Arab independence, while the British sent Faisal to be the puppet king of a newly created Iraq. Faisal withdrew his support for Jewish independence in Palestine and publicly denied ever making the agreement.

In the last half-century of Ottoman rule, two fledgling national movements emerged that imagined two different endings to a millennium of Turkish rule over Arabic-speaking peoples on the sliver of land by the eastern Mediterranean. A few Arabs and Jews explored the possibilities of compromise, coexistence, and mutual support. Others came together in social and business relationships—as laborers, farmers, and homemakers, living side by side within the fraying fabric of Ottoman hegemony. Each meeting, conversation, shared tea, draft proposal, and argument between Arabs and Jews forged an alternative narrative of possibility for joint non-violent action. Those who met, talked, joked, and listened took their place at the beginning of a long procession of Arabs and Jews who would come together in every generation over the next century to propose alternatives to the lethal collision of their national movements.

The Allied victors dissected the remains of the Ottoman Empire and distributed them among themselves, bending both the Arabs' and the Jews' dreams of political independence to their own imperial prerogatives. No matter how supportive or intransigent Arabs and Jews were toward the other's political aims, they would now have to pursue their nationalist ambitions while under the control of the largest empire in the world in a newly constructed Middle East.

CHAPTER 2

# Opportunities and Obstacles:
# Under the British, 1919–1939

*Jew shall not dominate Arab and Arab shall not dominate Jew.*
JUDAH MAGNES, FIRST CHANCELLOR OF HEBREW UNIVERSITY, 1925[1]

*[In] the railway workshops . . . Arab and Jewish workers were the*
*overwhelming majority. A kind of mutual understanding prevailed among*
*them. . . . The common language among them was Arabic. . . . The Jewish*
*workers regarded their Arab co-workers with considerable respect, for they*
*understood that the Arab workers possessed a great deal of professional skill.*
BULUS FARAH, A FIFTEEN-YEAR-OLD PALESTINIAN ARAB APPRENTICE
IN THE HAIFA RAILWAY WORKSHOPS, 1925[2]

Jaffa, 1921. Two mothers, one from an Arab Jewish family and one from
an Arab Muslim family, lived near one another. They often spoke to each
other in Arabic while their children played together. They traded daily
kindnesses and supported one another in the care of their families. During the Arab attacks on Jews in Jaffa, the Arab Muslim neighbor hid her
Arab Jewish neighbors. When attackers entered their home, the family
refused to give any information. As they beat the father, he declared to
his family that he would give up his own life rather than sacrifice the lives
of his neighbors.[3]

The homes of these two families had been located in what the Ottomans called Greater Syria. Britain and France had divided that territory
to create French Mandate Syria, out of which they carved Lebanon, and
British Mandate Palestine, out of which they carved Transjordan. Now the
homes of these two families were located in a land that Britain had politically unified for the first time in almost two thousand years, a land where
Jews lived, ruling on and off during the first millennium BCE as Israel

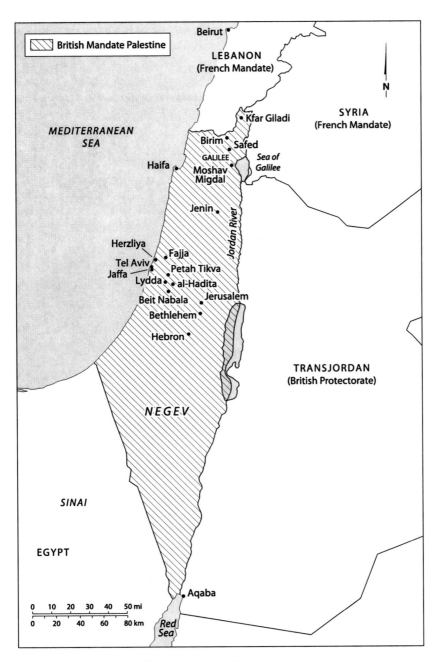

**Map 2.** British Mandate Palestine, 1920–1948

and Judah and that Greek and Roman conquerors called Palestine, the name Britain adopted. This chapter explores the repercussions of rule by the largest empire in history on Arab-Jewish joint nonviolence in British Mandate Palestine.

Arabs in Palestine were inspired to send representatives to Faisal Hussein's first independent Arab state, based in Damascus, in 1918. But soon the British and French disbanded the kingdom. Returning home, the Arab representatives organized the Arab Palestinian Congress of 1919. They emphasized the importance of both Palestinian independence and a connection to Greater Arab Syria. Beginning in 1920, the British officially ruled Palestine as a Mandate for most of the next three decades. During those years, Arab identity layered with Palestinian particularity, along with Muslim, Christian, and Syrian identities, in what Issam Nassar termed "interdependent narratives and consciousness." The National Arab Party's founding goals were "preserving Palestine for its people and establishing a constitutional government in it."[4]

The British Mandate officially sanctioned the Balfour Declaration, which gave Jews a national home in Palestine as long as it didn't "prejudice the civil and religious rights" of non-Jews. Palestinians were never mentioned by name. This generated hostility toward the Jews' presence and their goals, and it intensified structural differences. Jews were primarily urban, so their arrival spurred industrial growth. Arabs were primarily rural, and urbanization altered their society.[5] British divide-and-rule tactics exacerbated intergroup hostility. The British also set Palestinian elite factions against each other in order to rule them more easily and to defuse protest against Zionism's political aims. These policies backed Palestinian Arabs into what historian Rashid Khalidi terms an "iron cage."[6]

But these obstacles could not suppress opportunities for alliances among Arab and Jewish neighbors, women, workers, political leaders, and rebel intelligentsia. The drastic change in political rule catalyzed a range of nonviolent joint activity in mixed Arab-Jewish towns and neighborhoods. In Haifa, Jaffa, and Jerusalem, Jews and Arabs made contact in the marketplace, in urban friendships, through inter-village rural support, at cultural events, in workers' organizations, and in private homes. Aspiring Palestinian and Jewish leaders of rising national movements explored strategies of mutual support for dealing with British imperialism in pursuit of their own political goals.

## 1920s: Women and Workers

An Arab girl growing up in the Galilee befriended Jewish girls from Safed who invited her to work with them on Moshav Migdal, an agricultural collective founded by Russian Jewish immigrants near the Sea of Galilee. Her son writes of her work and friendship with Jews as an experience of discovery and pleasure. She took care of the children and picked almonds in the fields with no foreman above her, and she received a weekly paycheck. For the rest of her long life she defended her Jewish neighbors to her family and friends, including their right to fight back when attacked. She taught her children that Jews treated her as an equal. One son grew up to be the first Arab journalist in Israel to write in Hebrew critiquing the establishment and championing Arab rights.[7]

The combustible combination of British rule, Jewish nation building, and Arab rebellion against both fueled new alliances and hostilities during the first two decades of Mandate Palestine. Arabs and Jews of Palestine who came of age in the 1920s under British rule have rich memories of each other as friends, co-workers, customers, business partners, and romantic interests. Their memories are of amiable, intimate, entertaining, activist, and ordinary moments. They often express remorse at the severance of contact when British rule ended in the partition of Palestine in 1948.

Arab and Jewish women reminisce about their connections as mothers. A Jewish woman remembers the aid and wisdom of her Arab neighbors when she needed help with her children.[8] Sometimes these connections had political repercussions. Another Jewish woman's Arab friend moved to Beirut. When her friend was about to give birth, she summoned the Jewish woman to Beirut for help. Years later, when the Arab woman's family lost favor with the French regime, the Jewish woman became her refuge. She escaped to her home in Kfar Giladi, where the families lived together for months. When the British came to arrest the woman's husband, Jewish villagers refused to disclose his location.[9]

By 1920 new Jewish immigrants formed the Histadrut labor organization to support working men and women in a trade union and a cooperative organization that assisted them with health care and with physical and intellectual aspects of life. Socialist Zionism theoretically supported equal rights for women, but the reality did not match the ideal when women joined as workers and wives. The Histadrut also supported cooperation between Arabs and Jews in mixed workplaces. The strength of socialism and its checkered relationship with Zionism plunged the Histadrut into tumultuous internal struggles over whether the union should be a Jewish one engaged in joint actions with separate Arab unions, or whether it should become a joint Arab-Jewish union.[10]

In 1921 Arab and Jewish women established a workers alliance called the League for Arab-Jewish Friendship.[11] Women workers of all backgrounds collaborated in protests against oppressive practices in their factories. The owners of the Nur Match Factory, owned by the Weizmann family, preferred to hire women workers who were not unionized. The women received terrible pay and worked in filthy conditions. Six-year-old Arab children did some of the most dangerous work. Later in the decade one hundred women, about half of them Arab and the other half Jewish, organized a strike demanding improved sanitary conditions, a 50 percent increase in wages for the lowest paid workers, the end of dangerous work for children, payment during illness, and the hiring of a doctor to tend to the sick. Despite violent attacks by the police, arrest, and jailing, the strike lasted over four months.[12]

Whether male or female, Arab or Jewish, workers faced challenges that brought many of them together despite national differences. Historian Zachary Lockman provides a rich chronicle of Arab and Jewish workers' alliances. They found common cause where they labored for railways, telegraph and telephone systems, public works departments, and port authorities; in municipal governments; and on British and Allied military bases. They worked together in privately owned businesses such as the Dead Sea Potash Works and the Nesher Quarry and Cement Factory, and in the foreign-owned Iraq Petroleum Company in Haifa.

Arab railway workers opened their homes to their Jewish co-workers. They proposed the creation of a joint union for all railway workers. They specifically wanted to join the new Histadrut labor union. Many Jewish workers had been profoundly affected by revolutionary movements in Europe and believed that their only hope of improving things was to join with Arab co-workers.[13] Jewish railway workers invited Arab co-workers to the union, and they met together at local coffeehouses to discuss joint actions. By 1922 Jewish and Arab workers wanted to strike against layoffs and harassment. When David Ben-Gurion became secretary of the Histadrut, he promoted cooperation between Arab and Jewish workers. In 1922, Ben-Gurion addressed both Arab and Jewish workers arguing that:

> joint economic, political, and cultural work . . . [is a] necessary prerequisite for our redemption as a free working people and for the emanci-

pation of the Arab working people from enslavement by its oppressive exploiters, the dominant landowners and property owners.[14]

The internationalism of the workers' movement offered an alternative to nationalism. Two Palestinian Arabs, Ibrahim al-Asmar, a foreman in the freight-car department, and Ali al-Batal, a boilermaker, wanted to associate with a Jewish union despite threats against them by management. They attended the union congress in 1923 and heard leftist forces emphasize Jewish-Arab solidarity. After the congress, Arab workers wanted to join the union if it would alter its description, in which it referred to its workers as Jewish. One Arab worker, Ilyas Asad, explained this reasoning at the Arab railway workers council:

> I am striving to establish ties between the Jewish and Arab workers
> because I am certain that if we are connected we will help one another,
> without regard to religion or nationality. . . . If they take out the word
> [Jewish on membership cards] we will unite and work together.[15]

By 1924 unprecedented numbers of Arabs had joined the union, which eventually became half Arab and half Jewish. The influx of Arabs led to a restructuring so all elected bodies would be half Jewish and half Arab.[16] Palestinian Arab Bulus Farah was a fifteen-year-old apprentice in the Haifa railway workshops in 1925 and later became a leader in the communist and labor movements. He observed that Arab and Jewish railway workers had a special connection with each other. He delighted in the ways Jewish workers showed their respect for Arab co-workers by learning and speaking Arabic and by admiring their professional skills. [17]

For most of the Arab and Jewish workers in the railway industry, it was their first experience of direct contact with each other. Similarly, at the Nesher Quarry and Cement Factory established by a Russian Jew from Georgia, Arabs from Egypt supplied by a Palestinian Arab contractor worked side by side with Jews. In 1924 Jewish Palestinians defied the orders of their union when they joined a strike by Egyptian workers. In 1925, the management of the factory defied the Histadrut leadership to keep hiring Arab workers.[18] That same year, Jews, Egyptians, and Palestinian Arab workers went on strike together at another quarry.

In 1925, Philip Hassan, a Christian Arab tailor, founded a workers club for Arabs and Jews in Haifa. Club membership grew rapidly to 250 tailors and carpenters. They initiated a carpenters strike that reduced the hours of daily work from fourteen to nine. The club lasted seven years until its demise, which resulted from infighting and an influx of workers from Damascus.[19] Hassan declared: "The Arab worker has no one to depend on except the Hebrew worker." Palestinian Arab labor organizer Ahmad Hamdi proclaimed:

> Let not [distinctions between] East and West, Zionism and Arabism, Torah and Quran, cause divisions among us. When Arab workers approach Jewish workers, their enemies say to them, 'You are Zionists!' Others say, 'You are Communists!' So the Arab worker is confused. We must unite and present common demands to the [British] government, which ignores its obligation to the worker and instead sends in the police and puts him in jail.[20]

The fourth *aliyah* brought the population of Jews in Palestine from 95,000 in 1924 to 150,000 by 1926. Tension within unions increased, with fights between leftist political parties about whether or not to include Arabs in unions. But joint Arab-Jewish workers strikes in the tailors and carpenters unions continued. Po'alei Tziyon Smol (PTS) was the leftist Zionist workers party and promoted Arab-Jewish solidarity. Carpenter George Nasser, the Palestinian Arab leader of a group of Arab workers and a loyal adherent of PTS, said he supported Zionism

> precisely because I am a good Arab. I know and see with my own eyes that Jewish immigration improves the situation of the Arab masses. It contributes to raising the [Arab] worker's wages in Palestine and his standing in society. And since I seek the welfare of the Arab worker, I am ready to support Jewish immigration to Palestine. . . . All our comrades want to be members of one organization with you. They will pay dues and organize meetings everywhere.[21]

By 1926 Arab workers outnumbered Jewish workers. Jews quit railroad, post, and telegraph work because of the long hours and low pay as the number of Arab workers in the Histadrut increased. Ben-Gurion biographer Shabtai Teveth wrote that this expansion in the number of Arab workers "utterly transformed the union." Ben-Gurion defeated a binational labor federation, preferring separate Arab and Jewish unions united in a "league." He declared, "We have no shared program with the Arab ruling class. But we do share a program with the Arab workers." In the end, the Arabs left to found their own union.

### 1920s: Nationalism versus Binationalism

Internationalism was not the only reason for building a shared future based on common interests. One of the competing visions for implementing the Balfour Declaration was binationalism. At the first Zionist Congress after Britain issued the Balfour Declaration, philosopher Martin Buber, on the eve of publication of his seminal work on dialogue, *I and Thou*, called for coexistence between two nations based on mutual respect and goodwill. When the Congress rejected his proposal, he withdrew from mainstream Zionism and created a radical approach to Arab-Jewish coexistence.[22] For Buber, the relationship between Jews and Arabs was central to Zionism and Judaism because Zionism was the political test of Jewish ethics. Buber's biographer Paul Mendes-Flohr wrote:

> By seeking the liberation of Jewry from the fractured existence of the Diaspora, Zionism confronts Judaism *qua* religious faith and community with the mundane challenge of a normal life. . . . The fact that the ancestral home of the Jews . . . was also the home of an indigenous Arab population who had their own national aspirations—was according to Buber the preeminent challenge to Zionism and Judaism. Indeed, as a touchstone of Judaism and the Zionist enterprise, the Arab question . . . is an innermost Jewish question.[23]

Buber rejected Zionist resignation to Arab enmity, which resulted from the Zionists' pursuit of political power. He urged both sides to accept a binational state in which Arabs and Jews would live together with political and national equality. He urged Zionists to learn Arabic language and culture, to avoid being patronized by imperial powers, to remain a minority, and to seek to harmonize interests.[24] Neither side was interested.

In 1925, Buber helped found Brit Shalom/Tahalof Essalaam (Covenant of Peace), which spread the idea of peaceful coexistence through a binational state co-ruled by Arabs and Jews.[25] Its members included Henrietta Szold, who would become the founder of the Zionist women's organization Hadassah, and other leaders: Arthur Ruppin, Shmuel Hugo Berman, Hans Kohn, Gershon Sholem, and Ernst Simon, all Jews. Most Arabs and Jews rejected Brit Shalom's proposals, and the group eventually disappeared. But their idea of binationalism endured.

During the 1920s Shlomo Kaplansky was a leftist leader of Po'alei Tziyon who advocated binationalism with an Arab-Jewish parliament that would rule the country together. Rejecting Kaplansky's proposal, Ben-Gurion said: "I am unwilling to forego even one percent of Zionism for 'peace.' Yet I do not want Zionism to infringe upon even one percent of legitimate Arab rights."[26] Through increasing immigration and land sales, Zionist leaders continued to seek a Jewish majority as a foundation for eventual statehood.

Beyond internationalism and binationalism, fledgling nationalist leaders had a variety of motivations and visions for Arab-Jewish joint action. In Lausanne in 1922, Chaim Kalvarisky, from the Zionist Executive, met secretly with Musa Kazim al-Husayni, president of the Arab Executive Committee, the main Palestinian nationalist organization. It is possible that some of these Arab initiatives were motivated by a desire for funding from Zionists that did not materialize. Another basis for entente between Arab and Jewish leaders was the rivalry among the ruling Palestinian families. For example, the al-Husayni family attempted to form an electoral alliance with Jerusalem Jews that would help them defeat their rival clan, the Nashashibis.[27] In 1924 Kalvarisky met with Jamal al-Husayni, the cousin of Kazim, to discuss the possibility of a joint Palestinian legislative council. Leaders of the Yishuv (Heb. Jewish communities in Palestine) rejected the idea. Instead, they funded Kalvarisky's Arab-Jewish schools and clubs for young people.[28]

When Palestinians remained firm in their opposition to immigration and settlement, Zionists turned to Arabs outside Palestine to forge alliances for independence from colonial rule. Weizmann and King Abdullah of Jordan met secretly in London five times in 1922. There were also Arab-Jewish talks in Cairo and meetings between Zionist and Syrian leaders like Riad al-Sulh and Ittamar Ben-Avi.[29]

Some left-wing Jewish leaders were ready to let go of mainstream Zionist goals for political independence. Judah Magnes, founder and president of Hebrew University in Jerusalem, warned that "the fact . . . that Palestine has five or six times as many Arabs as Jews" meant that Jews could not claim free access to land and rights if they did not confer those rights on anyone else.[30] He saw Palestine as an international, not national, land and attacked Zionist insistence on achieving a Jewish majority:

> All that we Jews have a right to ask is peace, and the open door for our immigrants, and the opportunity without hindrance to live our spiritual and cultural life. This is all the Arabs have a right to ask for themselves, or any other people in this international land.[31]

Arab and Jewish attempts to forge alternative visions to mainstream nationalism could not overcome the determination of the British administration to establish hegemony in Palestine. British power depended on fostering perceptions that the two nationalisms were irreconcilable. Perhaps that is one reason each side swears by hard evidence that Britain favored the other side.

Jewish and Arab leaders met each other in hopes of advancing their own interests. Some of these leaders had official appointments or recognition by the British, but many were unofficial and self-appointed, with insufficient power and modest constituencies. If they showed any possibility of uniting the two sides, they were quashed by the British, undermined by their own leaders, or rejected by the other side. Neil Caplan titled the book detailing his research on Jewish and Arab attempts to resolve their differences through diplomatic means *Futile Diplomacy*.

## 1920s: Nonviolent Responses to Violence

Arab-Jewish negotiations hit a literal wall in 1929. The Western Wall, or Wailing Wall, is a remnant of the Second Temple, which the Romans destroyed in 70 CE, and is the holiest spot for Jews to pray. Hemmed in by buildings that encroached over the centuries, it had become a narrow, crowded space. For years Jewish women could not pray there because there was no *mehitza*, the requisite curtain for separating women and men in prayer. Finally, in 1929 a *mehitza* was erected in time for the Jewish High Holy Days so Jewish women could join the prayer.

In the early eighth century Arab conquerors had built, over this Jewish holy place, a mosque that became the third holiest Muslim site. Now Muslims protested the change in status quo represented by the curtain. Jewish and Arab negotiations broke down, and Muslims attacked religious Jews in Jerusalem, Hebron, and Safed. Ironically, the religious Jews they attacked were often as anti-Zionist as their attackers: they believed that only God, not secular nationalists, could restore the Jews to the Holy Land.

The attacks set off a chain of events that both separated Jews and Arabs and brought them together. The Zionist establishment, represented by Ben-Gurion, downplayed the violence as the work of "vandals" and "religious fanatics," rather than of nationalist protesters against Zionism. He viewed Palestinian Arabs not as a separate group with its own nationalist goals but as a branch of the larger Arab world. He reiterated "that the

Arabs of Palestine deserve full rights as citizens of the country, but they do not have the right of ownership over it."[32]

Three weeks later at the start of the academic year, Magnes insisted that Palestine was neither Arab nor Jewish but "the Holy Land of two peoples and three religions":

> If the only way of establishing the Jewish National Home is upon the bayonets of some Empire, our whole enterprise is not worthwhile. But the very attempt to build it up peacefully, cooperatively, with understanding, education and good will [is] worth having, even if the attempt should fail.[33]

In October 1929 Magnes met with St. John Philby, a British advisor to King Ibn Saud of Arabia, and Hajj Amin al-Husayni, the British-appointed mufti and liaison to the Arab Muslim communities in Jerusalem. Together the three men drafted a program for Arab-Jewish settlement. But Arabs rejected anything that gave the appearance of acquiescence to the Balfour Declaration. Jews rejected convening a legislative council on a democratic basis that would leave them outnumbered. By December Magnes laid out his ideas on binationalism, with a guarantee for Jewish immigration and settlement if Jews would give up the "Jewish state" and "majority."[34]

Lockman points out in his book *Comrades and Enemies* that the riots sparked by the *mehitza* at the Western Wall in 1929 did not spread to places where workers felt bound together. Arab and Jewish railway workers resisted polarization.[35] They did not see themselves as peacemakers but as laborers whose goals were better served through cooperation. In contrast, Ben-Gurion and Hajj Amin al-Husayni saw themselves as crusaders for peace that could be achieved only with defeat of the other's nationalism. Leaders' belief that they could succeed alone without support from the other side doomed official peace attempts.

## 1930s: Friends and Workers

Conditions deteriorated with worldwide economic depression, the spread of fascism, and continued rule by an increasingly defensive empire. Yet both Arab and Jewish nationalist movements made advances in Palestine. Their joint work persisted despite growing numbers of adherents to clashing nationalist visions for Palestine and despite the fact that Britain treated the binational work as a direct threat to its authority. Friends played, workers met in solidarity, an emerging elite spun alternative visions, and a renegade intelligentsia believed national security could be better served by coexistence. Arabs and Jews kept alive the spirit of alliance when they sensed that the other was inextricably part of their lives and not merely a threat to be overcome. And in the midst of it all, a Jewish midwife delivered an Arab baby boy who grew up to advocate for the rights of Palestinians: Edward Said.

Memoirs of Arabs and Jews growing up in 1930s British Palestine illustrate the rewards and challenges of coexistence. P. J. (Taki) Vatikiotis was born in Palestine, grew up in Haifa and Jerusalem, and became a scholar of the Middle East in the United States and England. His Greek Orthodox Christian family moved from Greece to Jerusalem in the nineteenth century. The family did not consider themselves Arab, which was still pejoratively associated with Bedouin nomads. As meaning and identity morphed in the twentieth century, Vatikiotis came to see himself as a Palestinian Arab who spoke Greek and Arabic. As a child he observed Jews and Arabs playing together on beaches and playing fields, and enjoying public entertainment and nature together. His Haifa landlord was a Persian Baha'i whose tenants were Greeks, Jews, Arabs, and Armenians. And he saw that Greeks intermarried with Arabs.[36]

Vatikiotis mourned the loss of this diversity as new Jewish immigrants built Jewish neighborhoods in the 1930s. He called the schools and public services that Jews founded exclusive, but did not use that label for Muslim or Christian neighborhoods. Wherever Jews were excluded in Christian lands, they were eventually accused of being exclusive. He reports on Christian beliefs that Jews were anti-Christian, that Muslims followed "a phony, mad prophet," and that Palestine was an Arab country in which "Jews were our dogs." Christian Arabs joined fascist youth groups in the 1930s. But Vatikiotis was drawn to Jews' modernization, with a public bus system, sports, and girls wearing shorts. He and his siblings were given music lessons by Jews and went to "Jewish concert halls" and art exhibits, and to Jewish-owned cinemas. They traveled on Jewish-owned buses driven by Jewish bus drivers, drank fresh pasteurized milk from a Jewish cooperative dairy, and competed with Jewish teens in an Olympic-size pool built by Jews.[37]

Elias Freij, who became mayor of Bethlehem, remembers significant interaction between Jewish and Christian Arab communities. "When I was young I had many Jewish friends at school and I could see how they were organized," he said. [38] Elias Chacour, who became a Melkite priest, recalls attitudes toward Jews in the Galilean village of Birim. Christians there heard about the terrible things that were happening to Jews in Europe. His family called them "our Jewish cousins," and his father would pray, "Lord, do not forget to liberate persecuted Jews from the hand of the cruel Hitler." [39]

Gideon Weigert came to Palestine from Germany in 1933 at the age of fourteen. He studied cattle breeding and went with Jewish agricultural students to visit Arab neighbors in Beit Nabala, al-Hadita, Midiya, and Lydda. The school's director, Siegfried Lehman, former principal of a Jewish orphanage in Berlin, taught that Arabs were co-citizens of the country. He organized *El-Hakfar* (Heb. to the village), in which Jewish and Arab folk dancers and singers performed together. While working on a new kibbutz in Petah Tikva, he befriended Nihada Jaouni, a teacher in the village of Fajja, who taught him Arabic. Their sixty-year friendship survived a nineteen-year separation after partition. An Arab family in Herzliya with whom he lived "adopted him as a son." [40]

Jewish and Arab workers continued their joint actions in the second decade of the Mandate. In May 1930, Ahavat Po'alim (Workers Brotherhood) promoted Arab-Jewish unity on the basis of the Arab masses' right to national development and of unlimited Jewish immigration and national development. British authorities dissolved that group and undermined others. But they could not stop Jews and Arabs from attempting to unify. Twice in 1931, an Arab-Jewish committee organized Arab and Jewish taxi, bus, and truck drivers in a strike led by Hasan Sidqi al-Dajani. The Arab Workers Club and Jewish Kupat Holim (Zionist health care organization) met for social activities and football games. [41] The Jewish labor movement defined Palestine as "not a Jewish state and not an Arab state but a bi-national country" for both peoples to live in equality, freedom, and independence, with a government of equal representation. [42]

Arabs and Jews cooperated in joint actions during the waves of layoffs in 1932 and 1933. In February 1935 hundreds of Arab and Jewish workers at the Iraq Petroleum Company in Haifa went on strike for higher wages, shorter hours, and better working conditions. In the spring of the same year other Arab and Jewish workers went on strike on May Day in Haifa. A joint delegation of Jews and Arabs met with the British high commissioner throughout May and June and made significant gains for workers. [43]

## 1930s: Compromise against the Tide

All political compromises failed in the shadow of rising Nazism, which turned Jewish immigration into a life-and-death issue, overriding Arab objections. Emerging political leaders continued to meet to explore common ground despite the yawning chasm between their political goals. Negotiators debated Jewish immigration, Arab land sales to Jews, Jewish support for Arab political independence, and Arab support for Jewish cultural presence versus political statehood. But this moment of extreme danger to Jewish lives sharpened determination to establish a refuge where Jews would not be a minority dependent on the mercurial good will of others. Arabs were equally adamant about not compromising their majority status.

Hajj Amin al-Husayni told Ben-Gurion that he opposed encroachment by Jewish foreigners. He proposed that Zionists stop Jewish immigration in exchange for the establishment of a Palestinian state that would safeguard the rights of a permanent Jewish minority. Ben-Gurion's party opposed these talks on the grounds that Arab leadership was feudal and that compromise was possible only with a democratic Arab government.[44] Ben-Gurion made al-Husayni a counterproposal for Arabs and Jews to fight the British together. Britain destroyed both these attempts with separate and contradictory promises to each side.

In 1935 the newly elected president of the Jewish Agency (the Zionists' decision-making assembly), Ben-Gurion, initiated talks with leaders in Palestine, Syria, Lebanon, Egypt, and Saudi Arabia. He cultivated a long-term relationship with King Abdullah of Jordan. He sought Arab leaders' approval for Jewish immigration to Palestine in exchange for Jewish support for Arab unity and independence from Britain and France. Together they advocated the formation of a Middle East union to safeguard Arab minority rights in Israel when Israel and Arab states gained independence.[45]

Ahmad Samah al-Khalidi, Palestinian director of the Government Arab College in Jerusalem, offered Zionists a different compromise. Divide Palestine into Zionist autonomous cantons and Arab cantons along the lines of the Swiss model. Al-Khalidi's plan was close to Ben-Gurion's, but the Khalidi family did not have enough power to influence the mufti. So Ben-Gurion turned to Musa Alami, who was related to the mufti by marriage. Alami was in his late thirties, hailed from a wealthy family, and was personal secretary to the British high commissioner and assistant attorney general for the British Mandate.[46]

Ben-Gurion tried to persuade Alami that Zionists sought social justice and equality for all and would "unconditionally [guard] the rights and interests of non-Jewish inhabitants of the country."[47] He told Alami, "We bring a blessing to the Arabs of Palestine." Alami shattered Ben-Gurion's assumptions about what Zionists brought to the Arabs, replying that Arabs "would prefer that the country remain impoverished and barren for another hundred years until we ourselves are ready to develop it" than have the Jews do it for them.[48] He charged that Jewish creation of economic opportunities gave Palestinian Arabs a sense of shrinking opportunities.[49]

Alami tried to get Ben-Gurion to see that Jewish acquisition of land was equivalent to Arab dispossession. Ben-Gurion countered that Jews cultivated only desolate, unpopulated areas that had never before been farmed, and that they created teacher colleges to train much-needed Arab teachers and built Jewish-Arab factories. Alami protested that the Jewish-only labor policy hurt Arab economic opportunities. Ben-Gurion answered that the policy prevented African-style plantation colonization based on "native" labor.

Alami wanted to know what would happen to Muslim holy places in a Jewish state and tried to persuade Ben-Gurion to restrict immigration for ten years. Ben-Gurion proposed open immigration to raise the level of Arab development. Alami saw this as impossible as long as Arab teachers did not have the same level of education as Jews. He said there could be no solution to their dispute within the borders of Palestine alone.[50]

When Alami relayed to the mufti the Jews' willingness to come to an agreement with Arabs, Hajj Amin was surprised. He was open to an agreement as long as the Arab nature of Palestine was safeguarded. Ben-Gurion learned from Alami that the mufti supported the fundamentals of an Arab-Jewish pact:

> The two peoples would recognize each others' national aspirations and would help in bringing about their full realization . . . without dispossessing the Arabs . . . The Jewish people's right to return to Eretz Yisrael and to settle there without numerical restriction would be recognized.[51]

Then when the Mandate ended, a Jewish state would join a larger federation of Arab states. This would safeguard Arab Palestine and a Jewish majority.

Neil Caplan's research shows that Zionists cultivated "grassroots" contacts between Arabs and Jews, made local accords with Arab villages, showed respect for Palestinian customs, and continued to participate in friendly conversations between Arab and Jewish leaders. Awni Abd al-Hadi, the Palestinian Istiqlal Party leader, and Omar Salih al-Barghouti, a Jerusalem lawyer, met to study Kalvarisky's "Platform for Judaeo-Arab Accord," which argued for binationalism and addressed fears of economic dispossession and hopes for creation of a federation of Arab states. Arabs accepted it as a basis of negotiation, but the Jewish Agency wouldn't endorse it. Magnes opposed the Jewish Agency's "militaristic, imperialist, political Zionism" and argued instead for "peaceful, international, spiritual Zionism." [52]

Even as nationalist goals set Arabs and Jews at loggerheads, they worked together in British-created municipal councils. Haifa's municipal council in particular provided conditions that promoted a productive relationship between the two communities. The councils "provided the sole political table around which Jews and Arabs sat together," a "common denominator" despite cultural, religious, and political difference. [53]

## Nonviolent Responses to Violence

The eruption of violence in both Palestine and Europe in the 1930s crippled nonviolent joint action. By mid-decade Magnes lamented the estrangement between Arabs and Jews: Arabs would not sit on a committee with Jews, and they declined to meet Jews privately, implemented a commercial boycott, and inculcated hatred of Jews in their children. [54] Awni al-Hadi met with Ben-Gurion to complain that Jewish settlement was undermining Arab existence and that Jews' purchase of land at high prices drove prices up. He said that if Jews could help Arabs achieve a nation they could settle as many millions as they wanted. Ben-Gurion agreed that the Jewish state could be a canton among independent Arab cantons united under a joint bicameral democratic state. [55]

With Britain facing mounting dangers at home and abroad they actively sought to undermine Arab-Jewish joint action that might oppose their rule and fan Arab and Jewish discontent. Palestinian Arab parties turned to the British rulers to demand a halt to Jewish immigration and land sales. Ben-Gurion turned to the British when Hajj Amin and Jamal al-Husayni sought an alliance with Nazi Germany against the British and the Jews. [56]

When Palestinians' political tactics of petitions, testimonies, public meetings, delegations, congresses, and resolutions failed, tensions exploded and turned into the sustained Arab Revolt.[57] This new militant rejection of Zionist presence and British rule lasted three years. Arab leaders called for a general strike against Zionists, a halt to Jewish immigration and land purchases, and the establishment of a parliament elected by Palestinians.[58] George Antonius, a Christian Lebanese pan-Arab writer, rejected a binational state or Jewish state but said he would support a Jewish spiritual center limited to 400,000 Jews. He suggested Jews move to Syria, Lebanon, Jordan, Turkey, and Egypt's Sinai desert.[59]

Intensification of violence made urgent Magnes's and Alami's determination to reach a compromise. They agreed on an annual quota for Jews, addressed Arab grievances over land sales to Jews, and proposed a larger role for Arabs and Jews in government. They drew up interim steps toward a binational Palestine in confederation with Jordan, Syria, and Lebanon.[60] When the British Peel Commission visited Palestine in 1936, Magnes sent them the agreement, but the Jewish Agency rejected it and no Arab group endorsed it. Arab leaders saw no need for compromise with Jews, and Jewish leaders rejected minority quotas.

Arab nonviolent protests called for a general strike like the one in Iraq that led to independence from British rule. Activists mobilized Arab laborers, transport workers, and shopkeepers, demanding that the British declare general amnesty and suspend Jewish immigration.[61] In response, the Peel Commission recommended partition of Palestine so Jews and Arabs could each rule themselves as independent entities. The Arab Higher Committee sent Magnes new proposals, but with no results.

Fuad Bey Hamzah, a Druze man of Lebanese birth who wore traditional robes and spoke fluent English, met with Eliahu Epstein and then Ben-Gurion to convey Palestinians' concern about Jewish immigration. In May, St. John Philby from London, a convert to Islam fluent in Arabic, delivered an Arab initiative for rapprochement with Jews. Kalvarisky met with Arab envoys, and Magnes met with two Arab groups. The mufti himself backed a plan that would make Palestine part of a Middle East federation with no more than 50 percent of inhabitants being Jewish, but the Jewish leadership refused limits to immigration as Nazi terror escalated.[62]

The year 1939 was one of the darkest moments in history for all three peoples in Palestine. Britain broke the resistance of Palestinians; defeated the Arab Revolt; banned political parties; and killed, imprisoned, or exiled the Arab leadership. Jews tottered on the brink of genocide as Nazi horror intensified. Britain marched toward World War II, soon to be a lone bastion of resistance against the perpetual victories of fascism.

Britain sought once more to rally the Middle East to fight on its side.

For the first time it invited Egypt, Iraq, Saudi Arabia, Transjordan, and Yemen to a conference in London with Palestinian Arabs and Jews. The Palestinian Difa Party's Raghib Nashashibi headed the Palestinian Arab Higher Committee. Jewish delegates came from the Jewish Agency and from around the world.[63] But Nashashibi could not take part because the mufti refused to sit with him. Arabs refused to sit with Jews, and Britain held separate meetings. Yet Elie Eliachar, a Jewish man from an old Jerusalem family who spoke Arabic, had "close relations with a number of Arab delegates."[64] All rejected British proposals.

Instead Britain won Arab compliance with the 1939 White Paper. It met Arab demands that Jewish immigration and land sales be stopped and that an independent state be established with a Palestinian Arab majority ruling the Jewish minority. Britain repudiated the Balfour Declaration and withdrew support for a Jewish homeland as all doors closed to Jews who faced massive slaughter. Some militant Arab guerilla groups called for a rejection of the White Paper and assassinated those who disagreed. Members of the Arab Higher Committee counseled acceptance of partition for a Palestinian state in part of Palestine. Rashid Khalidi observes that a small group of rejectionist rebels and the "damaging conflation of the national cause with the personality of an overweening leader" caused a mistake that made this the last decision Palestinians would take on their own for decades.[65] He explains that Palestinians could not see Jews

> as refugees from persecution, as they were seen by the rest of the world
> . . . [but only] as arrogant European interlopers who did not accept that
> the Palestinians were a people. . . . There was . . . stubborn insistence . . .
> on seeing Jews as members of a religion rather than a national group.[66]

Arab violence compelled Jews to learn self-defense, and the Arab boycott drove them toward economic self-sufficiency. The Irgun and other underground militias responded to Arab violence with random terror. Brit Shalom upheld binationalism, as did its next iteration, the League for Jewish and Arab Rapprochement.[67] In August 1939, the periodical *Darkenu* (Heb. Our Ways) pushed for mutual Arab-Jewish support.[68]

One remarkable thing about this period is how little violence occurred among workers who lived together for decades with the reality of cooperation. A total of eight Jewish workers were killed during the three years of the Revolt. The revolt hurt both Arab and Jewish workers economically, but despite being on opposite sides of the war, the workers' friendly relations and enduring alliances allowed them to avoid the hostility that engulfed Arabs and Jews throughout the country. Arab railway men protected Jewish co-workers from Arab violence. A joint delegation of Arab and Jewish workers negotiated with management. Lockman observes that ideology "nourished a unique sense of possibility among the workers."[69]

* *

Throughout the 1920s and 1930s Arabs and Jews had friendships, romances, and business partnerships. Everyday contacts were not always easy, but they were often regarded with delight. Muslim midwives continued their centuries-old practice of bringing children born at the same time to each other's mother to nurse, turning the babies into foster siblings. Joint labor activism enabled Arab and Jewish workers to take power together to gain basic rights at work. It was a relief to experience relationships of interest, caring, and mutual help across the gulf of cultural, religious, language, and national difference.

Each group sharpened its determination to achieve independence from foreign rule through its own sovereignty. Jewish immigrants built new schools, neighborhoods, and workers collectives. A new generation of Arabs competed for leadership, creating new political parties and organizations. Self-appointed political leaders from both sides negotiated in a frantic yet futile search for alternatives to violent confrontation.

In another British colony, India, Gandhi was working on behalf of the rights of the Muslim minority. He succeeded in bringing Hindus and Muslims together in a nonviolent movement to fight British imperialism that would eventually win political independence by enlarging the concept of who was Indian, beyond sectarian designations. Although the nonviolent movement succeeded in liberating both peoples from imperial rule, Gandhi could not prevent partition and the resulting tragic massacres of Hindus and Muslims.

In Mandate Palestine, nonviolent joint action could not achieve a common front against British imperialism, in part due to British manipulation of each side's desire for majority rule. But what would have defeated even Gandhi in Palestine was the fact that Arabs and Jews had a double enemy. They had to fight not only British imperialism, with its anti-Arab attitudes of orientalism, but also international anti-Semitism, a force that even the best organized powers of the world could not stop. The same anti-Semitism in Europe that originally sparked Jewish nationalism in the 1880s was on the rise again, sending waves of immigrants to Palestine. As usual, anti-Semitism claimed Jews only as its first victims. Its more pervasive function was to prevent oppressed peoples from uniting to confront oppressive powers. As long as Arabs and Jews saw each other as the main threat to political independence, Britain's rule remained intact. Anti-Semitism proved an enemy even more formidable than the empire that planted its seeds in Palestine and beyond.

Yet all Jews and Arabs who found their way to each other uncovered common ground, regardless of their conscious or unconscious motives as friends, students, lovers, business associates, shop owners, laborers, or aspiring leaders. When they stood together and organized, when they debated with and befriended each other, they placed on the agenda the most important questions for the future of their peoples: How could one people's push for safety and dignity not ride roughshod over the other? How could two different peoples live together in love with and in need for the same land? As Arabs and Jews in British Mandate Palestine wrestled with tough questions, they fortified for future generations a foundation of joint resistance to injustice.

## CHAPTER 3

# Catastrophe and Celebration: 1940–1967

*There cannot be a solution that would be good and just for one side. Forget about such a peace. Let it suffice us to have a peace that is a little good, a little just, not totally, but to both Jews and Arabs alike.*

ABDUL AZIZ ZUABI, PALESTINIAN HEALTH MINISTER IN ISRAEL

*That peoples can . . . [not] carry on authentic dialogue with one another is not only the most acute symptom of the pathology of our time, it is also that which most urgently makes a demand of us. I believe, despite all, that the people in this hour can enter into a . . . genuine dialogue with one another . . . Even . . . in opposition to the other, [one] heeds, affirms, and confirms one's opponent as an existing other.*

MARTIN BUBER, JEWISH PHILOSOPHER, "GENUINE DIALOGUE AND THE POSSIBILITIES OF PEACE"[1]

In a private home on a leafy side street in Tel Aviv, Palestinian and Jewish men and women climbed the stairs to attend a secret meeting. It was the early 1960s, and for almost two decades Israel and the West had denied the existence of a Palestinian people while Arab countries had erased Israel from their maps. There were almost no opportunities for Palestinians and Israelis to gather as peers. This meeting was one of the first of its kind, a safe haven for the two peoples to make contact, confront inequalities, and tackle taboo subjects. Just sitting in the same room with each other was subversive. Insights and friendships grew over years of meeting. Safety in secrecy allowed even a military colonel to attend, and have his life, beliefs, and actions transformed by the others' perspective.[2]

But in 1940, Arabs' and Jews' joint nonviolent work was reeling in re-action to two events of the previous decade. The first was the devastating result of Palestinians' nationalist uprising, the Arab Revolt (1936–1939). Britain defeated the revolt by imprisoning, exiling, wounding, or killing an estimated 10 percent of the Arab adult male population, while many leaders fled. The remaining Arab population of around 900,000 was profoundly weakened.[3] The second event was the Nazi persecution that propelled the largest influx of Jewish refugees to Palestine to date, more than doubling the population.

These two events transformed power relations between the British, Jews, and Arabs in Palestine and altered their respective fates in the land. Their consequences were amplified in the 1940s when World War II, the worst war in human history, left 50 million dead while ethnically cleansing the Jews from Europe: dynamic thousand-year-old communities were destroyed in the murdering of six million. The aftermath of the war witnessed the demise of the British Empire; the formation of the United Nations, whose members voted to partition Palestine into Jewish and Arab states; the celebration of Yom Ha'atzmaut (Heb. day of independence), with the birth of Israel; the *Nakba* (Ar. catastrophe), with military defeat of Arab Palestine; and conquest of the West Bank by Jordan and of Gaza by Egypt. These events generated three waves of human expulsions that produced over two million refugees: European Jews, Palestinian Arabs, and Arab Jews. This chapter looks first at the forms joint nonviolence took in the years leading to 1948 when both peoples were still stateless and Palestinians were still a majority. Then it examines Jewish-Arab encounters in the first two decades of Israel's statehood and Palestinians' exile.

* *

## Workers during World War II

Zachary Lockman presents a remarkable portrait of workers' joint actions in the 1940s. Citrus grove owners in Petah Tikva chose a joint Arab-Jewish delegation to present their demands to the British government. Railway workers resumed contact, with an unprecedented degree of cooperation and militancy. Arab and Jewish unions worked together on an informal basis throughout 1940 and 1941. A joint Arab-Jewish strike in December 1942 in the Haifa railway workshops defied the prohibition against strikes during the war.[4] Fifty thousand Arabs and Jews worked side by side on British military bases and camps in Palestine. And the Histadrut organized a strike during May 1943, in which thousands of Jews and Arabs participated.

When an Arab worker was injured, the leftist Zionist political party,

MAPAI (Heb. acronym for Land of Israel Worker's Party), called for a demonstration. Fourteen hundred Arabs and Jews came together. Their strike committee demanded wage increases, workers' compensation, and retirement benefits. Arab and Jewish workers spent the night singing and talking around campfires. An Arab union sent food that Arab workers shared with Jews, while a Jewish organization sent food that Jewish workers shared with Arabs. There was a living sense of how Arab-Jewish unity could augment workers' power. Arab and Jewish postal workers in Jaffa and Tel Aviv went on strike. That summer the postal workers organized a national conference and elected an executive committee composed of Arabs and Jews.[5]

Arabs and anti-Zionist Jews envisioned a safe haven for Jews in Palestine that would be achieved not by the securing of a sovereign majority, but by the promotion of joint interests. Usbat al-Taharrur al-Watani (Ar. National Liberation League) was part of the new Arab left that emerged during the war. Its newspaper, *Al-Ittihad* (Ar. union), saw joint Arab-Jewish strikes as "clear proof of the possibility of joint action in every workplace."[6] The left-wing Jewish youth movement, Hashomer Hatza'ir, the Young Guard, advocated mutually supportive relations with Arabs. They joined the League for Arab-Jewish Reconciliation and Cooperation. People from neighboring Arab villages and Hashomer Hatza'ir settlements worked and played together. Abd Allah al-Bandaq, a Communist Party leader from a prominent Christian family, worked with Hashomer Hatza'ir leader Aharon Cohen to promote political equality.[7]

The Arab left insisted on Arab-Jewish solidarity among workers and critiqued their own Arab nationalist leadership as "unrepresentative." Throughout the early 1940s Arab Communists preserved the ideological distinction between Zionists, whom they regarded as exploiters, and the Jewish Palestinian masses and workers who were natural allies of the Arab Palestinian masses. Some believed that Jewish workers could be won away from Zionism if the Arab national movement "adopted a clear democratic and antiracist stance and offered the Jews a secure place in the future independent Arab Palestine.... Arab-Jewish cooperation was key to achieving the independence of an undivided Palestine."[8]

The Arab-Jewish Communist Party's opposition to Zionism clashed with their desire to reach pro-Zionist Jewish workers. The party split in 1943 into separate Arab and Jewish parties. By the end of World War II the all-Arab Palestine Communist Party recognized the Jewish *yishuv* as a national community and Palestine as a binational democratic and independent Arab-Jewish country. Even after the CP dropped its Arab-

Jewish and internationalist mantle to become an Arab party, individuals like Khalil Shanir worked for the continuation of Arab-Jewish unity.[9] Yet the party lacked enough votes to run in future elections.[10]

In April 1946 there occurred the "most dramatic episode of joint action between Arab and Jewish workers in the history of Palestine." The Haifa Oil Refinery was one of Palestine's largest workplaces. In fall 1945, amid a threat of layoffs, Arabs and Jews cooperated to win demands for improvement. The strike planners were Arab and Jewish unionists who had worked together for years. The strike spread from Arab and Jewish workers to white- and blue-collar government employees, postal workers, railway workers, middle- and lower-level white-collar workers, 23,000 government employees at British military bases, and petroleum workers. It was the largest Arab-Jewish strike in history and a victory for both peoples.[11]

## Post-War Visions and Divisions

"Long live unity between Arab and Jewish workers!" "Arab and Jewish workers are brothers!" "Long live the Histadrut and the Jaffa Arab Workers Society!" These were slogans in Arabic and Hebrew at a British military workshop where Arabs and Jews held a seven-day strike in which they picketed together and organized a joint march. In 1947, Mufti Hajj Amin al-Husayni's men murdered the Arab labor organizer Sami Taha because he worked for Arab-Jewish unity.[12]

Fissures within Arab and Jewish communities eroded joint nonviolence. Al-Husayni's notorious turn to the Nazis divided him from other Arab leaders. Jews splintered into two opposing groups. In New York the 1942 Biltmore Conference marked the first time a representative Zionist organization publicly declared the need for statehood in the face of genocide. Locating the conference in the United States marked a turn toward a new source of imperial backing. In Palestine, however, Martin Buber, Judah Magnes, and Henrietta Szold opposed the Biltmore platform for statehood by founding the Ihud (Union) for Jewish-Arab cooperation in a binational state in an Arab federation.[13] Ihud blamed Jews, Arabs, and the British for failing to develop joint self-governing institutions. Arab leaders rejected Ihud to avoid legitimizing Jewish rootedness in Palestine.

Magnes met with Arab leaders without the approval of the Zionist political establishment. This kind of action would become a hallmark of subterranean Arab-Jewish negotiations for the rest of the century. Magnes blamed the failure of Arab-Jewish conciliation on the Zionist Organization's determination to achieve statehood but overlooked the lack of Arab willingness to compromise. He continued to meet with Arab leaders from all over the Middle East, including Egyptian author Taha Hussein in Paris and Iraqi Nuri Pasha in Beirut. He concluded that "the slogan 'Jewish state' . . . is equivalent, in effect, to a declaration of war by the Jews on the Arabs."[14]

By the end of World War II, each side had strengthened its national identity and institutions. A separate Palestinian national consciousness grew apart from pan-Arab loyalty, and new leadership emerged among wealthy urban families who had diverse responses to British domination and Zionist state building. As Palestine became increasingly integrated into the world market economy, this emerging Arab elite gained wealth, education, and opportunity. They built new political parties, schools, medical facilities, businesses, and homes. There were increased levels of civic awareness and participation in political discourse. More women entered schools, published articles, engaged in political protest, raised money for the national cause, and helped their less fortunate sisters. Palestinian Arabs accomplished all this despite power contests between leading families, Balfour support for a national home for Jews, Arab absentee landowners' sale of Palestinian peasants' land to Jews, and British and Zionist inability to see Palestinians as a people with legitimate rights.[15]

Jews transformed biblical Hebrew into a modern spoken language and created protonational democratic governing bodies, political parties, schools, universities, workers unions, defense organizations, homes, villages, collective communes, cities, factories, and farms. They reclaimed land through irrigation, introduced medical advances, built hospitals and clinics, and initiated scientific research and technological innovation. They integrated tens of thousands of new immigrants, many escaping Europe during the rise of Hitler. Women and youth mobilized as integral parts of nation building. Palestinian Jews achieved these things despite internecine fighting, poverty, disease, rejection of Zionism by most Jews worldwide and especially in the United States, and opposition by Palestinian Arabs and Britain.

By the time the war ended, two-thirds of European Jews had been wiped out, and the rest were sent to displaced persons camps, some at the sites of former concentration camps, while Western nations tightened immigration laws against them. Every day from 1945 to 1948 newspaper headlines blasted the bitter fate of dispossessed, stateless Jewish refugees. A brigade of Palestinian Jews that had fought in the British army tried to get the refugees into Palestine. Britain intercepted the boats and sent some Jews back to Germany and interned others in detention camps.

In 1947 the Arab Office in London asked whether the Jewish-Arab conflict could be solved through compromise, binationalism, or a federation of Jewish and Arab states? Could they allow more Jews to move to Palestine but safeguard Arab rights? Was partition possible? The British backed the Arab solution: Palestine as an Arab state with its first language being Arabic, which Jews would learn as they became "de-Zionized" and gave up ambitions to live an "exclusive" "separate life."[16] The epithet of Jewish exclusivity was again projected onto the Jews by those who had excluded them for almost a thousand years. The British and Arabs advised Jews to choose minority status under Arab rule and dependence on Arab goodwill rather than becoming a majority in their sovereign state.

Instead, Jews intensified their resistance to British rule. During the war they had fought on Britain's side against the Nazis, but now they fought a guerilla war against Britain for national independence. Underground terrorist groups, like the Irgun and Stern gangs, fought to oust British imperialists from Palestine. They bombed British administrative offices, police stations, airfields, and armories and carried out kidnappings to ransom back Jews who were in British prisons. Seventeen thousand British troops attempted to subdue them. The Royal Marines stormed illegal immigrants' boats to prevent Jewish refugees from entering Palestine. Their two-thousand-year disarmament having culminated in mass murder in gas chambers, Jews now fought back with hot steam hoses, firebombs, pistols, and axes. The British captured and sentenced to death Jewish gang members, and in retaliation the "terrorists" or "freedom fighters" blew up British headquarters at the King David Hotel.

The fledgling United Nations took the problem out of British hands. On 29 November 1947, the nations of the world, including the Soviet Union, voted to partition Palestine into two states, one Jewish and one Arab. Partition was in diplomatic vogue in these incipient years of the Cold War: India/Pakistan, East/West Germany, North/South Korea, and North/South Vietnam. Palestinian Jews celebrated with dance and song all night in towns and villages at this dream come true, despite the fact that the borders of the proposed Jewish state were noncontiguous, indefensible, and politically untenable. Palestinian Arabs were unwilling to accept Jewish rule in any part of Palestine, and a civil war erupted that raged for over five months. The Haifa Oil Refinery, which had been a locus of Arab-Jewish cooperation, became the site of a bloody massacre in the first month of Arab-Jewish fighting. Efraim Krisher, a Hashomer Hatza'ir activist employed at the Haifa railway workshops, had worked closely with Arab unionists and "owed his life to their quick thinking and personal bravery." He mourned as they became refugees.[17]

In April of 1948 Judah Magnes left a war-torn Jerusalem to embark on his last peace mission. He flew to New York to meet with American Jewish leaders, the State Department, and Muhammad Fawzi Bey, Egyptian delegate to the United Nations. He proposed that the United Nations govern Palestine with Arab and Jewish police in order to enforce a ceasefire. But time and will were at an end.[18]

Jews prepared for war as a people for the first time since they rose up against Rome. In the first four months of the conflict, the Palestinians were winning. When the tide turned, it was in part due to the flood of new immigrants from the refugee camps in Europe. They took up arms against the Palestinians with a fury that conflated Arabs with Nazi murderers. They fought against obliteration, having no place else to go. The British resentfully relinquished their mandate earlier than practical, ensuring more violence. As they exited Palestine, Israel declared independence on 14 May 1948 within the 54 percent of Palestine granted to it by the United Nations. On 15 May, five Arab armies joined the fighting on the side of the Palestinians, promising to rid the land of Jews. By the time the UN imposed a ceasefire at the beginning of 1949, Israel had contiguous borders in about 78 percent of Palestine. Two Arab armies occupied the remaining 22 percent when Jordan annexed the West Bank and Egypt asserted administrative control over Gaza.

### Lost Worlds of Three Exiles

The creation of Israel resolved one refugee problem and precipitated two others. In the next few years, 700,000 Jewish refugees came with nothing to the new State of Israel as citizens of their own nation. This immigration emptied more than half of the displaced persons camps and detention centers. At the close of the first Arab-Israeli war, 750,000 Palestinian refugees left homes, villages, and assets. Only 156,000 remained in Israel, where they were placed under martial law because of fears that they would constitute a fifth column aiding the Arab enemies of the new state. Palestinian refugees came with nothing to UN relief camps in the West Bank, Gaza, Egypt, Jordan, Syria, and Lebanon, where Arab host governments often kept them confined to refugee camps, refusing them work permits

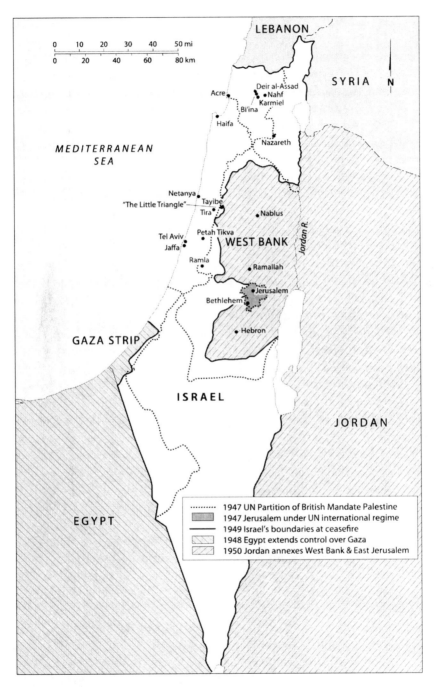

**Map 3.** Partition of Palestine, 1947–1950

and citizenship.[19] The enmity of Middle Eastern regimes toward Israel precipitated an exodus of Jews from Middle Eastern countries at various times over the next twenty-five years. The vast majority—750,000 Moroccan, Algerian, Libyan, Egyptian, Yemenite, Iraqi, Syrian, Kurdish, Iranian, and Turkish Jews—immigrated to Israel, leaving everything behind. This immigration decimated Jewish communities in the Arab world, some of which were over two thousand years old. Mizrahi Jews, whose mother tongues included Arabic, Farsi, Kurdish, and Turkish, came to constitute over half the Jewish population of Israel.

Homi Bhabha observed that the "nation fills the void left in the uprooting of communities and kin."[20] These three exiles marked the end of entire ways of life for Jews and Arabs. They were formative milestones in the construction of Israeli and Palestinian national identity as well as in practical state building protracted statelessness. In their effort to end one diaspora, Jews created a new one. A hostile international border separated Palestinian exiles from their homes. Countless personal stories attested to Arabs and Jews being uprooted by war and their homes being forever lost, their property confiscated, their comfortable lives impoverished, and their friendships broken. Palestinian villages were wiped off the map, and alienation, inequality, downward mobility, and physical and mental illness, even suicide, became ongoing threats for both peoples.

Memoir writers pine for friendships lost between Jews and Arabs who were separated by partition. Khalid al-Hassan, for example, was born into an Arab family in Haifa that was responsible for being the "keeper of Elijah's cave." Before partition, on Jewish holidays his father's house was "full of Rabbis."[21] Mustafa Natshe, who decades later became mayor of Hebron, recalls business contact with Jews in the 1940s, joint travel to Jerusalem and Haifa, and family orchards near Jewish Ramat Hasharon.[22]

Palestinian lawyer Raja Shehadeh remembers hearing of his aristocratic grandmother's life of luxury in Jaffa, where a Jewish seamstress from Tel Aviv made all his mother's clothes. When the Palestinian leadership fled after the partition vote, his parents left Jaffa with wealthy friends for "a two-week sojourn" to his grandmother's summerhouse in Ramallah. Raja grew up there listening to his grandmother's sorrow over lost splendors of the family home, which was traded for a house, town, and culture that were too small. He witnessed his father's anger at the Palestinian upper classes and his imprisonment in a Jordanian jail.[23]

P. J. Vatikiotis left his father in Palestine in 1944 for university in Cairo, where his best friend was a Cairene Sephardi Jew who spoke French, Ladino, Turkish, and Arabic. His father received a visit from two Palestinians with suitcases who "invited him to go along with them to neighboring Lebanon until the unpleasant business in Palestine was over. They assured him it would be like a two-week holiday, during which time the armies of the Arab states would clear the country of Jews."[24] When Palestinians instead lost the war against Israel, the holiday became permanent exile.

The younger Vatikiotis complained that young and strong Palestinian men had no intention of fighting. His multicultural youth had disappeared in Palestine and Cairo, and he left Cairo for the United States, sent off by three Jewish, five Arab, two Anglo, and two Greek friends.[25]

Edna Zaretsky's father reminisced about work and friendship with Arabs before 1948. At the end of the eight-day *matzah* fast for Passover, Arab friends always came to their house, bringing pita bread, green onions, yogurt, and olives. Edna, born in 1942, became a pioneer in bringing Arabs and Jews together twenty-five years after the birth of Israel. Willy Gafni grew up in Turkey until age eleven. With Nazis occupying neighboring countries and sending Jews in nearby Greece and Bulgaria to the death camps, his mother put him on a kinder transport to Palestine to save his life. He grew up among Arab neighbors and decades later founded the International Center for Peace in the Middle East.[26]

Joseph Abileah had immigrated to Haifa from Austria in 1923 at age seven. He and the Arab boys he grew up with called each other brothers. During his training as a violinist, he played music with Arab and Jewish Palestinians. As an adult, he played with the Haifa Philharmonic and dedicated himself to forming an Arab-Jewish initiative that advocated for an Israeli, Palestinian, and Jordanian confederation. The year Israel became a state, Abileah became the first conscientious objector, refusing to serve in the Israeli armed forces to fight his Arab friends.[27]

Israeli author Amos Oz remembers his uncle who emigrated from Poland and worked as a postal clerk in Jerusalem. A certain wealthy Arab businessman was a liaison at the time for French firms in the Middle East. When a large bank draft went missing, the French firm blamed the man's son, and the British arrested him. After trying many ways to rescue his son, the man begged the postmaster general to search for the missing bank draft. The receipt had vanished, and the postmaster reported that there was no hope of finding it.

Oz's uncle conducted his own investigation and discovered that the records had been destroyed. He found the teenage clerk who had stolen the money, and he returned the lost property. The man's son was released, and the family's honor was restored. When they received an invitation to the businessman's home, Oz's uncle's family prepared for the visit for days. They did not want the elegant Arab family to think they were "rough Jewish paupers."[28]

## 1950s and 1960s: Arab-Israeli Joint Nonviolence

After partition, joint nonviolent initiatives happened mainly between Israelis and Arabs who were not Palestinian. Arab countries would have no diplomatic ties with Israel, so they conducted meetings in secret. There was no official peace process. Arabs were determined to defeat Israel militarily. Israel was determined to build armed forces to prevent defeat. It would not relinquish land or permit Palestinian refugees to return. Egypt's Gamal Abdel Nasser named Israel its main enemy, attacked it with *fedayeen* (Ar. guerilla fighters), and closed the Straits of Tiran to Israeli ships. Britain and France were thus able to persuade Israel to join them in attacking Egypt in 1956 when Nasser nationalized the Suez Canal.

The Palestinians were conflated with all Arabs and appeared not to exist as a separate people. Rashid Khalidi delineates reasons for the apparent hiatus in visibility of Palestinians as a people in the 1950s and 1960s. First, small groups of clandestine activists were purposely invisible. Second, Palestinians, like other Arabs, identified with the "hegemonic ideology" of Arabism, which reached its apogee with Egypt's Nasser. Third, Palestinian leaders had repeatedly "lost" Palestine: in negotiations with Ottomans or British rulers, by selling lands to Zionists, in bloody rifts among themselves, in alienation from the younger generation of urban Palestinians, in defeats in the Arab Revolt and the 1948 war, and with delusional narratives of failure as victory.[29]

In Israel, the Palestinian minority that remained was treated as a fifth column of potential allies to Israel's enemies.[30] Their civic status developed in a country that strove to be Jewish and democratic. Palestinians were ignored in competing Cold War strategies as the United States and the Soviet Union courted Israel and the emerging Arab nations. The Arab League, formed during World War II with British assistance to woo Arab support, alternately ignored or gave lip service to Palestinians' cause. Arab leaders' anti-Israel rhetoric curried favor with their own peoples, who supported the Palestinians.

Palestinians saw themselves as part of an Arab world that would champion their cause and release them from Israeli, Jordanian, and Egyptian rule. Hanan Ashrawi remembers growing up in the West Bank under the

1948–1967 Jordanian occupation. Jordan forbade use of the words *Palestinian* and *Palestine*, referring to the Palestinians as Arabs instead. So the Palestinians waited for other Arab countries to liberate them.[31] Israelis also saw the Palestinians as Arabs, and they criticized Arab countries for refusing to help "their own" and for confining the refugees to UN refugee camps without work permits or regard for their human rights.

Inside Israel, Arabs and Jews worked together in political parties. The Communist Party provided a framework for contact between Arab and Jewish women. Even as the 1948 war raged, they organized the Democratic Women's Movement of the Communist Party (TANDI), a joint movement for women's rights, children's rights, and peace. TANDI was the first group to celebrate International Women's Day and to hold demonstrations and public events for both women's equality and Arab-Jewish solidarity.[32]

The leftist Zionist MAPAM (Heb. acronym for United Workers Party) attracted Arabs. In 1958, MAPAM's Third Congress had fifty Arab delegates representing 1,500 party members. Arab and Jewish members of the Arab Affairs Department disagreed on the return of Palestinian refugees and Palestinian self-determination. The party appointed seven Arabs and seven Jews with a more radical outlook to work together, but ended up marginalizing that department.[33] Arab citizens also played a role in the Histadrut. In 1959, Arabs citizens voted in Histadrut elections for the first time as equals and full members. The Histadrut dropped "Hebrew" from its name and became simply the General Organization of Workers in Israel.[34]

Throughout the Middle East, prominent Arabs spoke out for nonviolent initiatives. King Hassan of Morocco, for example, identified himself as the first Arab leader to call for peace with Israel, in Beirut in 1958, and to ask for Israel's admission into the Arab League because half the Jewish population came from Arab countries and 16 percent of Israeli citizens were Palestinian Arabs.[35]

Sana Hassan grew up in Cairo in the 1950s and 1960s amid upper-class Egyptians, Italians, Greeks, Armenians, Christians, Muslims, and Jews. They dated each other and occasionally intermarried. "We had many Jewish friends in Cairo but 'Zionist' was a dirty word. 'Israel' wasn't a word at all. We heard only 'occupied Palestine.'" Egyptian media called the Israeli government "the gangster regime of Tel Aviv." Then Hassan won a high-school competition allowing her to travel to the United States as the Egyptian delegate for a political youth forum. She befriended an Israeli girl her age. They got along great in private but publicly engaged in bitter arguments. The Egyptian press had taught her that this Israeli girl was a "blatant liar and hypocrite." A friend gave her the novel *Exodus* by Leon Uris, in which noble Jewish farmers till the soil under extreme hardship. That image clashed with the Arab media's portrayal of Israelis as murderous Zionist gangs who massacred women and children. Together with Israeli writer Amos Elon, she wrote *Between Enemies*, one of the first accounts of public Arab-Israel dialogue.[36]

The next generation of Palestinians and Israelis began to engage in nonviolent activism. In 1949, Uri Avnery, an Israeli from Germany, called for a "Pax Semitica" in which Arabs and Jews would form a regional organization. In 1950 Avnery acquired the magazine *Haolam Hazeh* (This World), which he turned into a voice of dissent in Israel. In 1954 he called for Operation Ismail to allow repatriation of Palestinian refugees. When Palestinians rebelled against Jordan in 1955, *Haolam Hazeh* urged Israel to support Palestinians with arms to set up their own state in Jordan.[37]

After the 1956 Suez War, Israeli intellectuals, artists, and writers formed Semitic Action. Their "Hebrew Manifesto" envisioned a federation between a Palestinian state, Israel, and Jordan in a "Jordan Union" echoing the UN's original partition plan.[38] Avnery helped form the first new party since Israel's inception, and in 1965, the New Force Movement won him a seat in the Knesset. He served for eight years and called for Israel to be integrated into the region instead of remaining a Western outpost.[39] He urged the creation of a Palestinian state in the West Bank and Gaza, freed from Jordanian and Egyptian rule.

Fares Hamdan, a Muslim Palestinian graduate of Al-Najah College in Nablus, also won election to the Israeli Knesset. He supported Arab-Jewish ventures in economic cooperation; spearheaded the first Arab-Jewish industrial enterprise, a cannery; opened the first Arab-Jewish Bank; and opened a regional health center for the 35,000 inhabitants of the cluster of Arab towns then called "the little triangle."[40]

Simha Flapan emigrated from Poland to Palestine in the 1930s as a member of the Hashomer Hatza'ir, which regarded Palestine as the homeland of two peoples. As a leader in MAPAM in the 1950s, he reached out to moderate and leftist Arab intellectuals in Israel and surrounding countries. He organized conferences on "New Paths to Peace" for Palestinians and Jews in Tel Aviv and Nazareth, and he participated in public encounters between Arab and Israeli officials that were organized by the mayor of Florence at the 1958 Congress on Mediterranean Culture.[41] Flapan founded the Arab-Jewish journal *New Outlook Magazine*, which reached Arab capitals as a voice of dissent from the Israeli enemy from

1957 to 1993. Its editorial board and sponsors included prominent Arabs who advocated regional cooperation and peaceful solutions, including Rustum Bastuni, Abdul Aziz Zuabi, Sabri Huri, Yusuf Khamis, Hisham al-Nash, and Jamil Shehadeh.[42] The editors described their offices as "a haven of humanity, friendship, good will."[43]

Zuabi was a thirty-year-old Palestinian from Nazareth who helped organize an Arab-Jewish conference in Haifa in 1956 with Flapan. He cofounded the Arab-Jewish Association for Peace and Equality at the conference. Bastuni was a thirty-two-year-old Palestinian architect from Haifa with a degree from the Technion. He ran for office with MAPAM and won election to the second Knesset. Greek Catholic archbishop George Hakim had a following among Palestinians in Haifa, Acre, and the Galilee and took initiative to create opportunities for Jews and Arabs to engage in dialogue.[44]

Willy Gafni had his first real contact with a Palestinian Arab when he lived in Tel Aviv in 1960. A friend asked if an Arab man from Nazareth could live with him in his apartment because no one would rent to him. Zuabi had been hired to edit an Arab newspaper and was to be in Tel Aviv three times a week. Gafni agreed, and the two became such good friends that Zuabi never left. When he got married, he brought his wife to live in the apartment. When Gafni got married, he brought his wife, and the two couples lived together. Whenever Zuabi came from Nazareth to Tel Aviv, his mother would force him to carry food for Gafni, "the Turk."[45]

Until the fighting broke out in 1947, Walid Sadik had never met a Jew. He grew up in the 1940s in the Arab village of Tayibe near the Jewish town of Netanya. The Israeli commander who took over his village seemed savage to a seven-year-old boy, but Sadik's image of Jews changed when he attended Hebrew University in Jerusalem. In 1959 there were only twenty-two Arab students, and they lived together in their own house. One day six Israeli Jews knocked on their door. The Arabs were afraid they were from the military, but they were from Hashomer Hatza'ir and MAPAM. The Jews spoke of equality and peace, and against military government and confiscation of land. At first the Palestinians thought it was propaganda, but gradually they saw beyond the stereotype of frightening, hurtful Jews and discovered that some Jews cared about Arabs. Sadik joined MAPAM and learned how deeply Jews felt about Palestine/Israel. In his second year at college he moved into the dorms with an Orthodox Jewish roommate, who learned that it was not true that Arabs were nice to your face but stabbed you in the back. Sadik learned Yiddish.[46]

Small dialogue groups sprouted in the early 1960s to make forbidden contact with the other in ways that had become impossible in daily life. Communication between Arabs and Jews was mostly nonexistent, and dehumanizing stereotypes of poor Arab workers and threatening Israeli soldiers prevailed. Participants tentatively and defensively reached across the chasm of segregation, inequality, willful ignorance, and distrust. These innovative and mostly secret joint nonviolent initiatives challenged stereotypes and fears of the other. Israelis learned of injustice towards Arabs, and Arabs learned of Jews' vulnerability.

Jews needed to learn the culture and language of their neighborhood, but options were limited. The progressive Kibbutz Artzi movement, affiliated with MAPAM, founded Givat Haviva in 1949 as an educational center. Givat Haviva's Institute for Arabic Studies encouraged Jews to learn the language and culture of their neighbors. It also provided Arabs and Jews with opportunities to meet in dialogue, joint study, and activism.[47] Over the next fifty years, Givat Haviva hosted a wide variety of initiatives in service to a "shared society," "resisting racism and all forms of discrimination, . . . educating for peace, democracy, coexistence and social solidarity."[48]

The first joint nonviolent protests by Palestinians and Israelis focused on land appropriation from the Palestinian villages Deir al-Asad, Biʿina, and Nahf in Galilee in the 1960s. The government confiscated olive groves in these villages to build the Jewish town of Karmiel. Hasan Amun of Deir al-Asad and Israeli activist Uri Davis went to the High Court. They were not opposed to the building of Karmiel, but they urged that it be constructed farther away to save the orchards of the Palestinian families in neighboring villages. They protested by planting tree saplings and by displaying banners in Hebrew, Arabic, and English.

In 1964, Jewish Israelis joined Palestinian Israeli farmers to illegally cultivate and harvest confiscated olive groves. Despite police blockades against Jews entering the villages, some got through and were arrested. In January of 1965, Davis resumed the protest by going on a hunger strike, and on the fifth day the Israeli military court in Nazareth sentenced him to prison in Ramla. Two weeks later, five hundred Jews and Arabs gathered from around the country to protest with the villagers.[49]

Abie Nathan was a renegade Israeli voice for peace. Born in Iran and raised in India, he flew as a Royal Air Force pilot in World War II and for the Israeli air force in 1948, and he piloted El Al planes throughout the 1950s. In 1966, he flew his personal plane, the *Shalom One* to Port Said, Egypt, on a one-man peace mission. Later that year he led peace marches from Tel Aviv to Jerusalem. After one more peace mission the Israelis jailed him for forty days. He then bought the *Peace Ship* and anchored it in international waters in the Mediterranean off the coast of Israel. From there he broadcast Voice of Peace radio programming throughout the Middle East.[50]

Months before the June 1967 war, Arabs and Jews of the Histadrut formed a study group that challenged prevailing notions of the conflict. The Jewish-Arab Circle for the Study and Clarification of Cultural and Social Problems argued that Israel must guarantee rights to its Arab citizens. The Circle represented the "good will of Jews and Arabs who felt that what united them transcended what divided them." The president of Hebrew University, Eliahu Elath, counseled Israelis to "cultivate the awareness that Jews are an Eastern people" in a Middle East that had always been pluralistic. They must study Arabic just as Arabs had learned to speak "impeccable Hebrew."[51] The Circle's platform was a mix of insight, naiveté, and euphemism. It was the last joint initiative before a new war altered the terrain of Arab-Israeli relations.

\* \*

The years before 1948 war were the last time Jews and Arabs worked together on joint nonviolent initiatives as two stateless nations under British rule. During World War II they enlisted in British armed forces to fight on the same side against fascism. They went on strike together, continued to seek negotiated agreements for mutual support, and critiqued their leaders, all while building separate nationalist communities bent on future sovereignty. With the birth of Israel, Jews were now free to return to a nation in their ancestral lands. The political defeat of the Arabs left Palestinians dispossessed and stateless. These new realities marked a nadir in a century of joint nonviolence.

For the first two decades of its existence, Israel created a social democracy with the barest of socioeconomic gaps by scrambling to meet three main needs of its people. It raced to construct shelter for hundreds of thousands of exiles and immigrants, who soon outnumbered the original inhabitants. They were holocaust survivors and refugees from Arab countries, often unskilled, illiterate, poor, sick, or old, survivors of ghettos, forests, and concentration camps. The government built *ma'abarot* (Heb. refugee camps) that eventually became towns, as well as cheap apartments and modular housing estates. Second, Israel urgently developed a food supply by building four hundred new *kibbutzim* and *moshavim* (Heb. pl. agricultural collectives, villages) near four hundred demolished Arab villages, doubling agricultural land use and tripling the rural population. Third, the government received Germany's reparations to Israel for Jews' slave labor and stolen property during the war and distributed them as loans to entrepreneurs to create industries to supply the people's needs.[52]

Palestinians in Israel were not the beneficiaries of these services. Those beyond Israel's borders had no right to return to abandoned homes and bulldozed villages. A new generation of Palestine leaders traded the suits of their predecessors for military fatigues and exchanged negotiations for guerilla warfare. They founded the Palestinian Liberation Organization (PLO) in 1964 with visions of direct armed conflict with Israel and political independence in a liberated Palestine. This appealed to dispossessed Palestinians and ushered in a new era of mass-based politics replacing notables' elite diplomacy. The young engineer Yasser Arafat would do more than anyone else to make visible Palestinians' right to statehood.[53]

Abdul Aziz Zuabi and Martin Buber, whose words launched this chapter of history, were ahead of their time. Their entreaties for dialogue and compromise were difficult to heed during the catastrophic destruction of European Jewry, the Nakba, Palestinian dispossession, euphoric Israeli celebration of independence, Arab Jewish exile, and the stringent exigencies of fledgling statehood. The next war created a set of conditions that would give new urgency to Zuabi's and Buber's pleas for dialogue and would lead to the implementation of unprecedented, innovative ways of connecting with the enemy.

## CHAPTER 4

# The New Dialogue: 1967–1980

*There are Israelis who are really human beings. They fight for the rights
of others as they have been fighting for their own rights and I tell you I feel
really touched by those people. . . . This is the only way that both Palestinians
and Israelis can make peace and survive and live as neighbors. I always try
to understand what makes the other side tick. . . . both the Palestinians and
Israelis really yearn for peace.*
HANNA SINIORA, PALESTINIAN NATIONAL COUNCIL[1]

*Unless the liberal and progressive values of Zionism are restored and
Palestinian rights to self-determination within a framework of peaceful
coexistence are recognized, Israel's search for peace is doomed to failure.*
SIMHA FLAPAN, ISRAELI HISTORIAN, *ZIONISM AND THE PALESTINIANS*[2]

Fifty Palestinians and Israelis sat together in a new dialogue group bound
by rules: keep confidentiality; one person speaks at a time; listen deeply;
share your life story; no political harangues; no cross talk; pain blocks
fresh thinking; release of painful emotion opens the mind; release occurs
when we receive openhearted attention. The personal, nevertheless, *was*
political and every sentence cut like a knife. So Israeli Jews and Palestinian
Arabs met separately to release anger and fear. Once reunited, they opened
their hearts to unbearable realities until an Israeli broke the rules, inter-
rupting a Palestinian's story: "Lies! Propaganda!" People turned their attention to her. "You don't know what expulsion means unless you walked
away like I did from my home in Egypt at age eight clutching the hand of
my six-year-old sister to cross the desert to Israel." After crying and detailing the attacks on Jews in Egypt, she began to hear the truth of the

Palestinian's story. And then as liberal Speaker in the Knesset, she challenged its policies.

New grassroots dialogues of the next decade were at once a form of resistance, an act of discovery, and a profound risk. To understand the significance of this form of joint nonviolence, one must grasp how the 1967 war radically altered the terrain of conflict. It closed the era of Palestinian invisibility, ripped open the borders between the West Bank, Gaza, and Israel, and brought Palestinians into contact with each other, Israelis, and the world. A growing minority stood on their predecessors' shoulders to risk innovative dialogue despite condemnation by their own people. This chapter traces the new dialogue through a variety of voices: individuals' experience; new cross-border contacts; unprecedented action by Arabs within Israel; emerging grassroots groups of Arabs, Palestinians, and Israelis; and early encounters between the Palestine Liberation Organization (PLO) and Israelis.

Israelis who had listened for a decade to Arab leaders' daily threats to throw the Jews into the sea were jubilant over their survival of the 1967 war, their swift six-day victory, and reunification of Jewish West Jerusalem with Arab East Jerusalem, where holy sites under Jordanian occupation had been forbidden to Jews. They won the Golan Heights from Syria, the West Bank from Jordan, and Gaza and the Sinai Peninsula from Egypt. The Israeli government passed two resolutions: to unite Jerusalem by annexing the eastern, Arab part of the city and to send a secret message to the United States that Israel was ready to trade land for peace. Arab regimes suffered humiliation, having staked their legitimacy on reclaiming Palestine for the Arabs, and many fell in the next few years. Soviet-backed Arab countries insisted that Israel withdraw from occupied territories as a precondition for peace; US-backed Israel saw peace negotiations as a prerequisite for relinquishing territories.

The Arab summit at Khartoum adopted three nos: no peace, no negotiations, no recognition of Israel. But in fact, moderate positions emerged, with Egypt's Gamal Abdel Nasser and Jordan's King Hussein open to political compromises that Palestinians considered a betrayal. Israeli rightwing groups urged annexation of the conquered territories for historic, religious, and defense reasons. Left-wing groups demanded return of these lands in exchange for peace. Arabs believed Israel sought expansion, not peace; Israelis believed Arabs still sought to destroy their country.

No one addressed the needs of the Palestinians. UN Security Council Resolution 242 ordered Israeli withdrawal from conquered areas but mentioned Palestinians only as refugees, ignoring their statelessness. Palestinians had pinned their hopes on Nasser, who effectively controlled the PLO. Over the next two years, the PLO wrested its cause from domination by Arab governments. They attacked Israel while also fighting Arab governments who repressed and discriminated against Palestinians refugees within their borders, and they often destabilized Arab regimes where they headquartered.[3] Yasser Arafat snuck into Israel, the West Bank, and Gaza in disguise to foment armed rebellion but failed. Respect for the PLO rose, however, when it withstood an Israeli attack in Karameh (Ar. honor) in Jordan.[4]

The 1967 war threw more than 250,000 Palestinian refugees into exile, some for the second time. It brought almost one million Palestinians under Israeli military rule, which replaced Jordanian occupation in the West Bank and Egyptian administration in Gaza. Palestinians who remained on their lands practiced *sumud* (Ar. steadfastness). Palestinian farmers became a spiritual symbol of preventing a repeat of the 1948 exodus. Some saw *sumud* as resistance to militarism, arguing that use of arms against Israel gave Israel permission to retaliate.

When Israeli prime minister Golda Meir declared, "There are no Palestinians," she reflected the attitudes of the status quo in Israel and the West. In retrospect, her remarks marked a turning point. Palestinians slowly and steadily gained recognition over the next two decades, not only as a people but also as the heart of the Arab-Israeli conflict. New dialogues contributed to this shift by exposing Israelis and Palestinians to realities previously assumed to be propaganda.

* *

## Frontiers of Perception

Open borders opened opportunities, however circumscribed, for Israeli-Palestinian encounter. New prospects for contact were primarily economic as Israelis frequented Arab markets and Arabs found jobs in Israel. These interactions made possible experiences of mutual respect, friendship, and humor that jockeyed with ongoing demonic stereotypes. Business encounters also underscored the economic inequality of those living in an economy supported by a state versus those who were stateless. Over time, more people on both sides than ever before came to see that the other would never disappear, neither by miracle nor by might.

In the midst of the violence of Israeli military occupation and Pales-

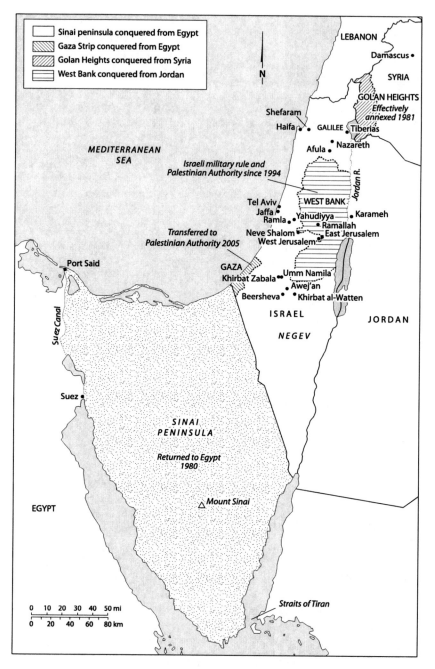

**Map 4.** Territories Conquered by Israel, 1967

tinian *fedayeen* assaults on Israelis, ordinary Palestinians and Israelis made poignant contact. Lawyer Aziz Shehadeh had been exiled from his home in Jaffa to Ramallah in 1948. After the 1967 war, his old Israeli colleague David Rosenblum was serving in the Israeli army's legal unit near Shehadeh's house. Rosenblum immediately visited Shehadeh and asked if he could do anything for him, then met his friend's request by taking him to his home by the Mediterranean. Shehadeh saw that Tel Aviv was no longer a sleepy suburb of Jaffa but a booming cultural center, and that Jaffa had become a "dead ghost."[5]

Israeli friends visited Shehadeh in Ramallah, and he returned their visits in Israel, where he met their sons, whose lives of freedom contrasted with his own son's. Aziz's sixteen-year-old, Raja, wrote, "The war began on Monday and ended on Wednesday. On Thursday [the occupation began]. . . . I had been brought up to think of Jews as monstrous and Israel as an artificial creation doomed to perish." But the first Jew who appeared in his house was polite, fluent in English, gentle, and civilized. Later, when Raja was a student at Birzeit University in the West Bank, his poetry was published in the *Jerusalem Post*, the Israeli English newspaper.[6]

Aziz Shehadeh developed a peace plan calling for forty Palestinian dignitaries from all over the occupied territories to convene a provisional independent government in mutual recognition with Israel, based on UN Resolution 181, the partition plan for Palestine. Israeli army reservists David Kimche and Dan Bavely took Shehadeh's peace plan to President Levi Eshkol. In local and international journals, Shehadeh advocated ending the conflict by way of the "peaceful establishment of a Palestinian state in the West Bank, Gaza, and East Jerusalem." Israelis rejected the proposal, and in 1985 the anti-PLO Abu Nidal faction assassinated Shehadeh.[7]

Hanan Ashrawi's father, Daud Mikhail, had been a medical officer in the Palestinian army in 1948 before moving his family from Tiberias to their ancestral home in Ramallah. The Jordanians forbid use of the word *Palestinian*, and they arrested and imprisoned Mikhail. Ashrawi believed that other Arab countries would liberate Palestine. When Israelis took control, she heard the word *Palestinian* but only with the word *terrorist*.[8] She recalls:

> Not long after I returned to Ramallah [with a doctorate in English from the United States], an elderly Jewish gentleman came to our home to visit my father. I was horrified. "How could you receive an Israeli in our home?'" . . . "We go back a long way," he answered. "Hear him out

first." The gentleman had been a prisoner of war in 1948. My father had been among the doctors who treated the Jewish prisoners. . . . "He was so human and kind to us," said the Israeli, "that we never forgot him. . . . His gentleness kept us alive. I've been looking for him for a long time to thank him."[9]

Ashrawi helped establish both a legal aid committee and consciousness-raising feminist groups. She joined the Balaleen drama movement for social change. Her husband, Emil, became involved with left-wing Israeli-Palestinian groups. Hanan helped form the first Palestinian-Israeli underground political organization. "Neither workers nor communists nor a league, we called ourselves the League of Communist Workers . . . [and wrote of ] our acceptance of the Palestinian Partition Plan of 1947."[10]

In July 1967, Dalia Landau was a nineteen-year-old Jewish girl in Ramla, a mixed Arab-Jewish town. Born in Bulgaria, she immigrated with her parents to Israel in 1948. They moved into an empty Arab house. Deeply identified with the Israeli story, she felt that the 1967 war was a miraculous rescue from being dumped in the sea. Soon after the war, three Arab men dressed in suits knocked at the gate. Dalia's parents were not home, but she did not hesitate to welcome them, imagining that it could have been her knocking on her parents' house in Bulgaria. Bashir al-Khayri had grown up in this house before 1948. The visitors told her that Bashir's father had planted the lemon tree that Dalia tended. The two families exchanged visits and hours of conversation that forced Dalia to reassess her history. In 1969, Bashir went to prison for fifteen years, charged with planting a bomb that killed civilians. Two decades later, Bashir and Dalia would turn their house into an Arab-Jewish center.[11]

In 1969, Palestinian Hanna Siniora became editor-in-chief of East Jerusalem's Arabic newspaper *al-Fajr* and formed professional relationships with Israeli journalists covering the West Bank. He participated in secret Palestinian-Israeli dialogue groups and discovered that Israelis were human and fought for Palestinian rights. He received death threats that strengthened his resolve to become a lifelong activist for joint nonviolence.[12] Siniora wrote: "Together with peace-loving Israelis who wish to help us we will bridge the gap that divides our two peoples. It is time to reach an agreement."[13]

Muhammad Abu Shilbaya, born in 1926 in the village Yahudiyya, grew up in contact with Jewish neighbors. He left in 1948 for East Jerusalem, where he became a writer and teacher, and he spent time in a desert detention camp for opposing Jordanian rule. After the 1967 war, Shilbaya renewed contact with Israeli friends. He wrote *No Peace without a Free Palestinian State*, which called for cessation of hostilities, mutual recognition, withdrawal of Israel from occupied territories, free elections for a Palestinian National Assembly, and abolition of the armed forces, which would be replaced by "an army of peace makers." Palestine, Jordan, and Israel would form a federation.[14] Palestinians sent death threats.

The novelty of nonviolent cross-border encounters did not catch the attention of the world media, but rising incidents of bloody terrorism did. Nasser fought a war of attrition against Israel in retaliation for their occupation of Sinai. Palestinians hijacked airlines, including El Al. The hijackings were mostly carried out by the Popular Front for the Liberation of Palestine (PFLP). The PFLP provoked a civil war against the Jordanian monarchy, whose troops massacred them in September 1970. A group named Black September was formed in their honor. It was responsible for the 1972 massacre of eleven Israeli Olympic athletes in Munich. The PLO sought to dismantle Israel. It proposed a peace plan for a single democratic secular state in the whole of Palestine, in which some Jews "liberated from Zionism" could remain. In popular media the word *Palestinian* became synonymous with *terrorist*.

This vortex of violence drew "internationals"—workers from international organizations—to formulate nonviolent strategies. The Quaker American Friends Service Committee traveled to the Middle East to listen to Palestinians, Israelis, Jordanians, Lebanese, Egyptians, and Syrians. Their policy emphasized dialogue: "No solution to the conflict can be found until . . . the outer world and the antagonists themselves really hear what divergent voices are trying to say"; violence never resolved "deep and continuing tensions"; the rights and needs of both must be met; Israel must withdraw from the territories, and Arabs must accept Israel; work on fear and hatred; fight anti-Semitism in the world; disengage militarily; develop economic ties; and stop delegitimizing and killing those who "seek a middle way."[15]

Bruno Hussar was a Catholic priest who moved from France to Israel. Born a Jew in Egypt and educated in France, where he converted to Catholicism, he was shattered by the virulence of French anti-Semitism during World War II. After the 1967 war, Hussar sought to unite Jews, Christians, and Muslims. In 1970, he leased ten hectares from the Latrun Monastery in a no man's land along the 1949 armistice line to create an "oasis of peace." He erected a tin shack on a thistle-strewn hilltop that had remained uncultivated since Byzantine times. The shack would become the cornerstone of a flourishing village, the first joint Palestinian-Israeli intentional village.

## The Rise of Arabs in Israel

Arabs and Jews in Israel lived in separate and unequal worlds. Since 1948 Arabs had lived as a minority under martial law and had been confined by travel permits, curfews, detentions, informer networks, and expulsions. Many of them were internal refugees. Their lands had been confiscated to build Jewish towns; the infrastructure where they lived was neglected; internal informers spied on them; it was illegal for them to assemble; and infant mortality and poverty rates were higher than the rates for Jewish citizens.[16] Israelis could not distinguish the Palestinians from the surrounding Arabs. And Palestinians could not see beyond the soldier, conqueror, usurper, and foreigner who treated them as second-class citizens. Israel ended military rule before the 1967 war, giving Arabs full citizens' rights and dismantling discriminatory laws.

The rise of the PLO and the end of Israeli martial law gave Arab Palestinians in Israel new confidence to protest inequality and to enter nonviolent alliances with Jews. They became politically active, exercising their rights to vote, run in and win elections, and form associations. They mobilized with Jewish citizens to redress inequality. The Covenant of the Sons of Shem was based on shared Jewish and Arabic ancestry: they were all descended from Shem, the biblical and koranic son of Noah whose name supplies the root for the word *Semitic*. The group was a "nonpolitical, fraternal" project to advance contact through social and educational programs for children and teachers. The half-Arab and half-Jewish membership spanned diverse political positions and forged thousands of family friendships.[17]

Arab students of Hebrew University in Jerusalem sometimes held their meetings at the Jewish students' Hillel House. After the 1967 war they wanted to address the uneasiness between Jews and Arabs, so they created One-to-One: The Arab-Jewish Project of Hillel House. They wanted a safe place to express themselves openly and to discuss taboo political subjects for the first time. Weekend retreats were co-led by an Arab and a Jew. Retreats were also held in the little shack on Father Bruno Hussar's Oasis of Peace, Neve Shalom/Wahat al-Salam.

Soon after the establishment of Haifa University, Jewish and Arab faculty founded a Jewish-Arab center in 1970. It examined the issues of the 20 percent of students who were Arab, fostered research on Arab-Jewish relations, and encouraged Arab scholars to join the faculty. In Jerusalem, Jewish and Arab students and scholars also worked together on joint research projects at the Truman Research Institute for the Advancement of Peace on Mount Scopus.[18]

The Association for Civil Rights in Israel (ACRI) was formed in 1972 to protect human rights and civil liberties, including freedom of speech, protest, association, religion, and movement, regardless of political views, race, ethnicity, or gender. They litigated, monitored, counseled, educated, and consulted on legislation for Arabs in Israel, the West Bank, and Gaza.[19]

Then in October 1973, Egypt and Syria launched simultaneous surprise attacks on Sinai and the Golan Heights during Ramadan, the holiest month for Muslims, and on Yom Kippur, the holiest day of the year for Jews. Egyptian and Syrian forces overran Israel Defense Forces (IDF) fortifications as Israel retreated. Palestinian women in Israel organized a buffet to feed Israeli soldiers at the Nazareth/Afula crossroads when Syrian rockets attacked Israeli Arab towns.[20] When the ceasefire became effective three weeks later, Israel had reclaimed all of its territory and was halfway to Damascus, but was deeply shaken. Fear gave electoral gains to the right-wing Likud in December, attenuating Labor's majority.[21]

The mood in the Arab world was jubilant. The Ramadan War lifted the Arabs' sense of humiliation from the 1967 Six-Day War. Sadat wanted to show Israel that security must depend not on territorial expansion but on relations with its neighbors. The Arab members of OPEC (the Organization of Petroleum Exporting Countries) imposed the 1973–1974 oil embargoes on the United States to protest its support for Israel in the October war. That action precipitated Henry Kissinger's shuttle diplomacy, in which he brokered disengagement treaties for Egypt and Syria with Israel that returned a bit of land to each by 1975.

The war advanced the PLO's standing. The 1973 Arab Summit recognized the PLO as the "sole legitimate representative" of the Palestinians. The following year Jordan agreed, even though West Bank Palestinians held Jordanian passports. By 1974 the PLO had, in cryptic language, eschewed dismantling Israel for an intermediate goal of a state in "liberated" parts of Palestine. Arafat called for building alliances with peace-oriented Israelis. The United Nations General Assembly invited Arafat to speak, voted for PLO observer status, and recognized Palestinians' "inalienable rights" to "sovereignty." In 1975 the UN almost abrogated Israel's membership and passed a resolution stating that Zionism was "a form of racism." A new generation of pro-PLO activists challenged older Palestinian notables tied to Jordan. Young people joined labor unions, quasi-political associations, and student movements that were beyond the reach of traditional elites.[22]

### Experiments in Grassroots Dialogue

Almost all meetings between Jewish and Palestinian citizens of Israel were first-time experiences for all involved. There were no other ways to meet as peers. Encounters occurred along a broad spectrum of political dialogue and activism, the arts, and social psychology. International facilitators brought experience with encounter groups, sensitivity training, and co-counseling, as well as practices for working on inequality resulting from structural oppression, such as racism, sexism, classism, and anti-Semitism. Participants engaged in authentic communication, confronted anger, and exposed asymmetries of power between Arabs and Jews. For people who had had almost no opportunity for contact in over two decades, these proliferating grassroots dialogue groups served as consciousness-raising boot camps to learn about the other's hardships, humanity, and humor.

Dialogue leader and scholar Mohammed Abu-Nimer points out that early dialogue initiatives could either expose or hide the imbalance of power, address or ignore injustice, and deal with emotional content or political problem solving. Martin Lakin worked with participants on communication skills and prejudice reduction. A. M. Levi and A. J. Benjamin worked with teens on steps for problem solving but learned the limitation of not having an Arab co-leader. A. Abdul Razak and C. Greenbaum led sensitivity training on stereotypes. Psychology professor Aharon Bizman ran three-hour prejudice reduction meetings that allowed for a more human view of the other.[23]

In the mid-1970s, Harvard social psychology professor Herbert Kelman, assisted by Stephen Cohen, led international workshops for Arabs and Jews that targeted leaders close to the mainstream. His third-party approach integrated Lakin and Bizman's psychological approaches with emerging conflict-resolution models. Semiofficial participants represented each national group and re-conceptualized the conflict in ways that opened the possibility of joint action to redress grievances. Workshops aimed for changes that could affect policy and power.[24]

But as important as it was to reach educated elites with access to policy makers, it was also crucial to challenge attitudes at the grassroots level to broaden the base that demanded policy change. In the 1970s grassroots social, political, and cultural joint nonviolence proliferated. A group of Jewish women from Tel Aviv, for example, began deepening friendships with a group of Arab women from Nazareth. They founded Gesher Le-shalom/Giser Assalam (Bridge to Peace) in 1974. At first they met for cultural activities, then for Arab-Jewish meetings with speakers on political issues. That led them to advocate for mutual recognition of the rights of both communities and to organize a peace conference with "recognized Palestinian representation."[25] In 1980, they formed the Israeli branch of the Women's International League for Peace and Freedom.

The Beersheba Municipal Theater, formed in 1974, was the first to serve the diverse peoples of the Negev, including Bedouin Arabs and the residents of Beersheba, who were mostly Jews from Arab countries and the Bene Israel and Cochin Jews from India. Many Jewish and Arab actors, directors, and designers got their start there. The theater ran programs for disadvantaged youth and Bedouin villages, performing for Arab and Jewish audiences.[26]

When I arrived in Jerusalem in the summer of 1975 to work with Palestinians and Israelis, I joined Shutafut/Mushaarakah (Partnership), which sought to turn adversaries into allies by developing common interests, trust, self-respect, and equality.[27] Rachel Rosensweig founded Partnership with Palestinian partners Nimer Ismair and Rushdi Fadila, teachers whose families had lost villages in 1948, and with Ibrahim Simaan, a Christian Palestinian Israeli Baptist minister. Rosensweig was born and raised in Germany, converted to Judaism, married an economist who was the son of the German Jewish philosopher Franz Rosensweig, and moved to Israel.

Partnership organized intercommunity mobile workshops in the Galilee, Central Israel, and the Negev that lasted three days: one on a kibbutz, one on a *moshav*, and one in an Arab village. Simaan helped Israeli teens overcome their fear of participation so they could learn that Arabs were not the cutthroats portrayed in media reports. Bedouin leader Nuri al-Uqbi partnered with Rosensweig to meet Negev Bedouin needs. Palestinian Arabs, Jewish Israelis, and internationals built a children's center by hand. Bedouin families fed us and worked by our side. Months later the government refused a permit and demolished the building.

I attended an *ulpan* (Hebrew-language immersion program) and enrolled in night classes for conversational Arabic at the Martin Buber Institute for Adult Education at the Hebrew University campus on Mount Scopus. Arabs from East Jerusalem and the West Bank came to study Hebrew at the same time that Israelis came to study Arabic. The highlight was a long coffee break to practice speaking to each other, with hilarious results in breakthrough first-time meetings with the other.

The first direct elections for mayor in the Arab town of Nazareth produced a Communist Party victory. The party's charismatic leader Tawfiq Ziad organized annual summer labor camps to mobilize Arab youth. Every year volunteers included Jews and Arabs from Israel, Arabs from the West Bank and Gaza, and internationals. We did backbreaking labor together under the hot sun to mend fences, pave roads, paint community centers, and restore schools. After work we browsed Arabic books adorned with images of Marx and Lenin, were fed by the townsfolk, and slept under the stars or on the cement floors of community centers.

European activists gathered young adults from Arab countries and Israel to meet for the first time. A Dutch group brought us to Cyprus to study a different conflict. Turkey had recently invaded Cyprus, taking 40 percent of the island, in response to a coup ordered by the military junta in Greece, which was seeking to annex the island. By the time we arrived, they had divided the island in two, with traumatic population transfers of Turkish Muslims and Greek Orthodox Christians from their ancestral homes to the other side of the ethnic partition. Cypriot realities stirred emotional arguments on Arab-Israeli issues, igniting friendships as well as heated debates. We crossed the new border into Turkish Cyprus, where small, beardless sixteen-year-old Turks brandished tall automatic weapons. The following year, a German group invited a different group of us to Frankfurt to participate in Israeli-Palestinian reconciliation work.

From 1975 to 1980, I led co-counseling workshops throughout Israel and the West Bank with Arabs and Jews. Co-counseling teaches compassionate listening to support another's release of emotional trauma from growing up with institutionalized oppression such as racism, sexism, and classism. With practice, people in the target (victim) role and the nontarget (oppressor) role learn to communicate, form alliances, and challenge inequality.[28] On the target side, for example, Palestinians worked on how Israel's power had devastated their lives; nontarget Israelis listened to how their country caused suffering and how to help end Palestinian oppression. On the target side, Jews worked on the ways anti-Semitism isolated, vilified, and destroyed their people; nontarget non-Jews, including Palestinians and others, listened to how they had unawarely dehumanized Jews and how to be allies against anti-Semitism. Each side worked on "internalized oppression," the insidious divisions among people on the same side. Participants learned to create conditions for emotional release that led to insight and action in recognition of their own and the other's humanity and dignity.

When the work got overwhelming, I ran away to the Sinai, which was under Israeli control at the time. Arab-Jewish contact in the Sinai desert made possible rudimentary access to the inaccessible heart of the peninsula. Haganat Hateva (Heb. Society for the Preservation of Nature), established in the first years of Israel's existence to preserve the natural flora and fauna of Israel, opened a base camp after 1967 at the foot of Mount Sinai. Bedouin inhabitants worked closely with Israelis to preserve this pristine mountain region. Intrepid tourists made the pilgrimage without roads, lodging, food, running water, or electricity. We slept on the ground under a blanket of stars for a few hours before starting up the mountain at 3:00 a.m. by the light of the moon to reach the peak of Mount Sinai at sunrise. Haganat Hateva drew up topographical maps and marked miles of walking trails through formidable desert *wadis* (Ar. dried river beds and valleys), oases, and mountains. The Bedouin drew maps in the sand to indicate routes through valleys snaking between black-streaked, pink granite mountains as they led us to secret springs for the water that enabled us to survive. To bake us pita bread, they filled a pigskin from a watering hole hidden under layers of floating sand, mixed the water with flour, plopped the wet dough in the sand, and buried it with more sand topped by the glowing red embers of a tiny branch from one of the thorny acacia trees that dotted the two continents of the African rift.

Up north in the Galilee on the first Land Day in 1976, Palestinians protested appropriation of land from Arab villages. The Israeli police killed six Israeli Arab citizens. An American Reform rabbi, Bruce Cohen, who had worked in US inner cities on violence, racism, and black-white relations, reacted to the violence by coming to Israel to found Nitzanei Shalom/Bara'am Assalaam (Interns for Peace). One participant recalled an arduous application process that included a psychological interview by the mother of a young Jewish man murdered as a civil rights worker in the US South.[29] Carefully selected interns underwent an intensive four-month training in community organizing. They formed teams of one Arab-Israeli, one Jewish-Israeli, and one international who would live for two years in an Arab village. They organized education, sports, arts, and industrial programs between Arab and Jewish villagers meeting for the first time after years of living as neighbors.

A year after I arrived in Jerusalem, the Arab-Jewish street theater troupe Tzoanim/Ghajar (Gypsies), composed of Arab actors from East Jerusalem and Jewish actors from Israel, invited me to sing and play guitar in their productions. We wandered from village to village performing the musical plays we composed for Jewish and Arab mixed audiences in Israel and the West Bank. Through metaphor and satire in the languages of Arabic, Hebrew, and English, and using slapstick comedy, pantomime, and music, we dealt with power imbalances, belonging, conflict, and resolution. The founders, who were known by their Sufi monikers Khusro and Shareen, were from San Francisco and had been Jewish before they became Sufi. They directed us in singing the American Shaker folk song "'Tis a Gift to Be Simple" in Arabic and Hebrew.

Right-wing Likud followers threw tomatoes at us in protest against what they deemed treacherous reconciliation with the enemy. Audience response to the shows became tense as the June 1977 election drew near and the Likud Party was rising in power. Israelis called the election a *mahpach* (Heb. revolution) because it was the first defeat in Israel's history for the socialist labor parties. Likud's support came in part from right-wing religious settler movement groups like Gush Emunim and in part from Jews from Muslim countries in the Middle East and North Africa as a rebuke against Ashkenazi hegemony and Israeli "WASPs" (White Ashkenazi Supporters of Peace).[30] Another first in Israel's history was the winning of two seats by the new party SHELI (Peace for Israel; Equality in Israel), a coalition of peace groups. That same year, the PLO National Council declared a willingness to accept the establishment of a Palestinian state in any part of Palestine, thereby implying for the first time an openness to a two-state solution.[31]

Then one day that autumn the inconceivable occurred. The president of Egypt, Anwar Sadat, flew to Jerusalem to present the Knesset with his vision for peace. The largest, most powerful Arab country recognized the State of Israel. Israelis flipped overnight from reflexive suspicion of Arab neighbors to incredulous, joyful welcome, waving thousands of Egyptian flags. On the initiative of the new US president, Jimmy Carter, Sadat and Israeli prime minister Menachem Begin entered into intense negotiations at the US presidential retreat Camp David. The talks became so acrimonious that at times Begin and Sadat sat alone in separate cabins.

By March of 1978, the talks were on the verge of collapse. Over three hundred officers of the Israel Defense Forces who had fought in the Yom Kippur War signed a letter in support of peace and launched the largest grassroots peace movement in Israel, Shalom Akhshav (Heb. Peace Now). By the end of the month there were 10,000 signatures. In April, Peace Now held its first demonstration, involving 40,000 people in Tel Aviv, including ten Knesset members. By the summer, the officers' letter had gained 100,000 signatures.[32] In September, when Begin met Sadat at Camp David, Peace Now brought 100,000 Israelis into the streets for a demonstration in support of a peace treaty.[33] A 1979 pamphlet titled *Peace Is Greater than Greater Israel* declared: "A people which rules over another people is not free."[34]

Roller-coaster negotiations at Camp David produced an agreement to return all of the Sinai, including the oil fields and military bases, in exchange for a formal peace treaty that would be signed in March 1979. Israel and Egypt exchanged visits of political and labor leaders, industrialists, university professors, and journalists; set up tourism channels; planned joint agricultural projects; and, in 1980, exchanged ambassadors. Arab leaders condemned the peace agreement as compromising with the enemy and abandoning the Palestinians. Israeli right-wingers attacked it as surrendering territory to the enemy. Begin won their support by expanding Jewish Israeli settlements in the occupied West Bank and Gaza.

Up north, in the Galilee, Arabs and Jews created political, religious, educational, and cultural encounters. In 1978, Elias Jabbour of the Lower Galilee Palestinian town Shefaram, in Israel, founded the first Arab-initiated peace center in Israel. He taught the use of *sulha*, a traditional Arab form of conflict resolution, to listen to grievances, deal with anger, and restore "wholeness and integrity."[35] House of Hope was a 200–year-old building in the center of town. Palestinians of Muslim, Christian, and Druze backgrounds gathered from surrounding villages to meet each other, as well as Israelis and internationals. The center sought to replace hostility bred in segregation with alliance bred in joint activity.[36]

The first feminist groups in Haifa mobilized Arab and Jewish women around gender and political concerns. The Bridge was founded in 1974 by a Haifa teacher who lost her son in the Six-Day War and Jihan Sadat, wife of the Egyptian president. They met in educational and political meetings, and together they critiqued the impact of militarism on women's lives. The Haifa Shelter for Battered Women was started in 1977 to address issues of violence affecting an estimated 10 percent of Israeli Jewish and Arab families when the subject was still taboo. The women took refuge and learned to support each other in a little five-room apartment on a quiet street in Haifa until they pressured the government to buy them a building.[37]

The New Israel Fund was established in 1979 by American Jews who developed partnerships with Arab and Jewish Israelis to promote social justice, pluralism, and tolerance through grassroots joint nonviolent initiatives. It took its mandate from Israel's Declaration of Independence, which called for a state "based on freedom, justice, and peace, . . . complete equality of social and political rights for all its inhabitants irrespective of religion, race, or sex."[38] They raised funds to support political, social, educational, and legal initiatives that strengthened equality and justice for all Israel's citizens. The New Israel Fund became one of the most effective supporters of civil and human rights for Israeli Arab and Bedouin citizens, immigrants, and women, along with environmental advocacy in the coming decades.

The exchange of Ambassadors between Egypt and Israel took place shortly before the Jewish holiday of Passover in the spring of 1980. The Passover Seder (ritual meal) teaches the possibility of freedom from slavery by recounting the Hebrew slaves' liberation from Pharaoh's Egypt. The word *Egypt* in Arabic (*Misr*) and Hebrew (*Mitzrayim*) means "narrow place," in reference to the geographically narrow civilization that bloomed on the banks of the long Nile River. But in the Hebrew Bible, that narrowness of Egypt became a metaphor for confinement under immoral power. Freedom meant serving God through compassionate action and fighting injustice. These stories took on new meanings when I sat with both Jews and actual, not metaphorical, Egyptians at a private home in Tel Aviv for the first Egyptian-Israeli Seder. A month later I boarded one of the first buses to cross the border overland through Gaza and Sinai into Egypt. There I reunited with my Cairene friends from the Arab-Israeli meetings in Cyprus.

## PLO and Israeli Peace Activists

The PLO felt betrayed by the bilateral peace. Palestinians correctly feared that the peace treaty would result in tightening control in the West Bank and Gaza. Israel remained opposed to recognizing the PLO and forbade contact with what they saw as a terrorist organization. Some Palestinians attacked those who engaged in joint nonviolent actions with Israelis. People on both sides stubbornly disobeyed these warnings.

Some of the earliest alliances arose with the left-wing parties, such as the anti-Zionist Jewish Matzpen, Siah (New Israeli Left), and Moked. Their meetings with the PLO signaled the existence of independent voices on both sides. In the late 1970s the Communist Party of Israel joined with SHELI and Shasi (Israeli Socialist Left) to establish "autonomous [Arab-Jewish] campus organizations" promulgating a two-state solution and daily joint nonviolent action. Palestinian academics at Birzeit University initiated private, informal contacts with Israeli peace activists. Professor Daniel Amit, a physicist at Hebrew University, formed the Committee for Solidarity with Birzeit University and the Committee for a Just Peace.[39]

The Israeli Council for Israeli-Palestinian Peace brought Labor outcasts like Matti Peled, Lova Eliav, Uri Avnery, and Moked together with progressive Palestinians like Said Hammami and Issam Sartawi. Anglican bishop Riah Abu el-Assal worked with Jews advocating Palestinian rights.[40] They hammered out principles of mutual recognition, a two-state solution, and dialogue with the PLO.[41] Their symbol combined an Israeli flag and a Palestinian flag.

Said Hammami was born in Jaffa, where his father had many Jewish friends. The family left for Jordan as tensions mounted before 1948. He graduated from university in Syria, worked as a journalist and teacher, and joined the PLO soon after its inception. He was the first high-ranking PLO leader to make an official speech with a substantial peace plan. The London *Times* published Hammami's plan calling for mutual recognition. Avnery publically recognized Hammami as a "pioneer of Israeli-Palestinian dialogue." In January 1978, when Hammami was in his London office, where he served as PLO representative to the United Kingdom, he was shot to death.[42]

Like Hammami, Issam Sartawi went through many stages from "terrorist" to "champion of peace." He grew up in Acre and Haifa, moved to Iraq in 1948, and graduated from medical school in the United States with plans to become a heart surgeon. He joined Fatah and fought in the battle at Karameh against Israeli forces. In 1976, Sartawi drew up a multipronged peace proposal. He spoke to Moroccan notables to urge them to recognize Israel, and he proposed that Americans aid a Palestinian state linked to Syria and Egypt in mutual recognition with Israel.[43] Sartawi told Avnery about a time when an anti-Semitic French leader entered his office in Paris to offer an alliance, but Sartawi threw him out because anti-Semites are "the greatest enemies of the Palestinian people."[44] His work for Palestinian independence and recognition of Israel ultimately cost him his life.

\* \*

Both societies staunchly rejected those who connected with the enemy, accusing them of naiveté or treason. Palestinians risked their lives to tell Israelis their experience of exile and destroyed villages and homes, love for Palestine, and daily life under conditions of occupation and statelessness. Israelis risked condemnation to listen to Palestinians' hardships and to tell them about genocide, exile, love for this ancestral land, and daily life under deadly threats from neighboring countries. These encounters heralded a mutual recognition that dissolved decades of delegitimizing the others' political existence. They generated a connection of caring that cultivated participants' aspirations to end harm.

The events of this period mark a watershed for joining nonviolent initiatives: the 1967 and 1973 wars, the end of military rule over Arab citizens of Israel, the beginning of Israeli military occupation over a million Arabs in the West Bank and Gaza, the first Israeli government led by he rightwing Likud party, the first peace treaty between Israel and an Arab country in exchange for return of the Sinai to Egypt. The borders were now open between Arabs in Israel, the West Bank, and Gaza, and between Israelis and Palestinians.

These dramatic changes demanded new responses from a new generation. The rightwing settler movement began to build communities in the West Bank and Gaza in hopes of permanently expanding Israel's borders. Jewish activists formed a peace movement to oppose expansion and demand exchanging newly conquered territories for peace. Arabs in Israel entered universities, the Knesset, and joint ventures with Israelis in commerce, dialogue, as feminists, and as activists against injustice. Arabs in the West Bank and Gaza formed new grassroots organizations with emerging local leaders. Organizers from Europe and the United States introduced initiatives for joint activism, communication, confrontation, compassionate listening, and healing.

Peter Demant writes that "low-key private encounter groups" were "moving or transformational" for the participants. But their lack of coordination with each other muted their influence on larger constituencies.[45] This fragmentation, however, turned out to be a virtue as well as a vice. Increasingly diverse nonviolent initiatives opened doors to a broader base of people from both sides. Diversity also led to disagreement between groups that differed on ideological and tactical means and ends. Nevertheless, the desire to challenge cyclical violence and inequality from many angles would in the next decade trigger an upsurge of joint nonviolent initiatives as Palestinians and Israelis branched out into new fields of human endeavor together.

## CHAPTER 5

# Grassroots Breakthroughs: 1980–1988

*Sooner than all our combined enemies think, peace shall and must reign between the Palestinian and Israeli states and their peoples.*
ISSAM SARTAWI, ADVISER TO YASSER ARAFAT[1]

*In reality, dialogue is one of the most profound human and political instruments. . . . We have suffered a host of defeats and setbacks. But we have also encountered human perseverance, dedication to an ideal, and courage in the face of adversity. People have given their lives, many have faced daily danger for years, not for war, but for peace.*
URI AVNERY, ISRAELI PEACE ACTIVIST, *MY FRIEND, THE ENEMY*[2]

On a barren hilltop punctuated with purple thistles and a sweeping vista of gently folding valleys stood a single shack where young Palestinians and Israelis listened to each other for the first time. Sitting face to face with the enemy was the hardest thing they had ever done besides enduring the consequences of violence: lost loved ones, exiled families, and destroyed villages. At risk was everything they had ever learned about themselves, their land, and their enemy. During the encounters they hurt each other with unconscious stereotypes, and they felt defensive about or saddened by discoveries of the other's hardships, guilty about their people's part in the other's suffering, relieved to meet the taboo enemy, surprised at similarities and differences, and joyful to form friendships. This was Neve Shalom/Wahat al-Salam, Father Bruno Hussar's "Oasis of Peace."

This small act anticipated a dramatic shift in nonviolent initiatives in the 1980s. Previous achievements had occurred under the constraints of the myth in Israel and much of the West that there were no Palestinians. Belief persisted that the conflict could be resolved with treaties between

Israel and other Arab countries, exemplified by the Egypt-Israel Peace Treaty in 1979, which ignored the Palestinians. When Palestinians did garner notoriety, it was as terrorists or resistance fighters, depending on the observer's point of view.

The vast majority of Israelis and Palestinians refused to acknowledge the other's existence, much less talk directly with the other. But a new generation of nonviolent activists joined forces on an unprecedented scale. The Israeli invasion of Lebanon in 1982 weakened Palestine Liberation Organization (PLO) military capacity and unwittingly strengthened internal peace and protest movements between Israel and the Palestinians. The PLO raised awareness of Palestinians' plight, and a new generation of "revisionist" Israeli historians exposed Israel's responsibility.

As Israel's occupation of the West Bank and Gaza entered its second decade, simple meetings were radical acts. Palestinians gunned down Palestinians for meeting Jews; Israelis were arrested or harassed as traitors for meeting Palestinians. But years before their leaders publically met, more people than ever before came together to learn, create, protest, teach, and take action in increasingly creative ways.

## In a Single Year: 1980

After five years, Oasis of Peace became the first intentional Palestinian and Israeli village when four families moved there to live side by side in mutual respect while preserving their distinct cultures, languages, and religions.[3] They founded the School for Peace, where Arabs and Jews could meet. More families joined them and founded the first binational bilingual Arab-Jewish school for children. Over the next thirty years, the community welcomed 35,000 people from Israel, the West Bank, Gaza, and beyond, and the school taught 250 Arab and Jewish students each year in kindergarten through eighth grade.

That year, dozens of Jewish Israelis from the now prominent organization Peace Now traveled to Beit Sahour, a Palestinian village near Bethlehem, to visit a Palestinian man temporarily deported to Jericho due to his son's role in riots. Another group went to Hebron to protest harassment of Palestinian widows by Jewish settlers. Arabs from Beit Sahour and Jews from Jerusalem began weekly meetings, visiting each other's homes. Jews invited Palestinians to public dialogues to expose Israelis to the unimaginable: moderate Palestinians. *Moderate* meant willing to consider the national existence of the other as something not necessary to destroy.

**Map 5**. Israel and Palestine

Peace Now refused to speak to Palestinians in the PLO as long as they refused to publicly recognize Israel and engaged in acts of terror. But Dedi Zucker and Yael Tamir broke ranks in October 1980 to meet Issam Sartawi, one of many meetings that would constitute a living example of Sartawi's vision expressed in the opening words of this chapter. The meetings provoked a crisis in Peace Now.[4]

Sartawi congratulated the Israeli Council for Israeli-Palestinian Peace (ICIPP) on their fifth anniversary in 1980 for maintaining ongoing dialogue with the PLO. Zionist Israelis had formed the ICIPP to challenge the PLO to make peace on the basis of Israeli withdrawal from territories occupied in 1967. Sartawi seemed to understand that Zionism was synonymous with patriotism in Israel. The Israeli government, nevertheless, arrested ICIPP members for wearing their symbol, composed of an Israeli and Palestinian flag.[5] Yet the new Law of Associations, passed in 1980, portended the flowering of over a thousand Israeli-Palestinian nongovernmental organizations (NGOs) in the coming decades.[6]

* *

## Lebanese War Turning Point

The intensification of grassroots encounters was due in part to the policies of Israel's leaders. In the second decade of occupation of the West Bank and Gaza, Israel's prime minister Menachem Begin continued to support the expansion of settlements and to oppose Palestinian-Israeli dialogue. In November 1981, the Israeli army demolished three Palestinian houses in an act of retaliation when students threw firebombs at Israeli soldiers. Israeli activists mobilized pressure on the government to alter its tactics in the territories. Fifty Israelis traveled to Beit Sahour to support the Palestinian families.

When Jews at the Yamit Gaza settlement tried to prevent Israeli withdrawal from Sinai in accordance with the Israeli-Egyptian peace agreement, Peace Now demonstrated in Tel Aviv with 100,000 marchers. Begin's minister of defense, Ariel Sharon, had to forcibly evacuate the settlers.[7] That same month, Palestinian Birzeit University and the Israeli Committee for Solidarity made front-page news. Palestinian demonstrations at Birzeit and Ramallah resulted in a government shutdown of the university. Hundreds of Israelis sneaked onto campus to symbolically reopen it. Another fifty Israelis were arrested for demonstrating at Bethlehem University.

Israel's 1982 war in Lebanon was a turning point for both joint and separate nonviolent initiatives. The invasion of Lebanon weakened PLO military capacity to harm Israelis and headquartered them at a safer distance in Tunis. But until the Lebanese war, most Israelis believed that its military existed to defend them against attacks by Arab countries. Crossing the Lebanese border was tantamount to crossing an ethical line. The war gave rise to a new level of Israeli public outcry that ironically fortified the Israeli protest movements, which eventually demanded Israel's recognition of the PLO as a negotiating partner. After Lebanese Christian Falangists massacred Palestinians in the refugee camps of Sabra and Shatila with General Sharon's tacit agreement, Israeli grassroots groups mounted the most massive protest in their history. In September 1982, 250,000 Israelis came out to demonstrate.[8] That was one sixteenth of the population, equivalent to 14,000,000 demonstrators in the United States.

The rise of nonviolent activism in separate Israeli and Palestinian societies often preceded and eventually supported joint action. In Israel, Jewish protest against the war took many forms. On the day of the invasion, the Committee for Solidarity with Birzeit University had coincidentally planned a demonstration to protest the fifteenth year of occupation with 5,000 people in Tel Aviv. In response to the invasion, it turned itself into the Committee against War in Lebanon and held another demonstration in June with 20,000 protesters.[9] Soldiers against Silence formed to protest the immorality of the war. Parents against Silence organized vigils and protests.[10]

That summer, for the first time in Israeli history, Yesh Gavul (Heb. there is a border, or limit) supported those who refused to serve in the army in the occupied territories. They had no problem with young men and women serving inside the Green Line to defend Israel, but rejected being an occupying force.[11] They declared, "There can be no military solution to the problem." The government sentenced 168 soldiers to military prison, some repeatedly, for refusing to serve in the armed forces. More people refused than were arrested, but rising numbers dissuaded the army from prosecuting most of the refuseniks.[12]

Jewish activism opened doors to dialogue with Palestinians. Jeremy Milgrom was an American-born Conservative rabbi and an Israeli army reservist who got involved in Yesh Gavul and became a refusenik. In jail he went on a hunger strike. When he returned to Hebrew University, Arab students began attending his interfaith dialogues and invited him to their homes. The Arab mayor of Umm al-Fahm, an Arab village in Israel known for radicalism, organized interfaith dialogues with him there.[13]

Palestinians cultivated nonviolent activism in their own society to re-

sist occupation and meet the needs of the population. When Raja Shehadeh returned to Ramallah after completing his law degree in London, he
saw the human rights abuses that were occurring under occupation. As a
result, he founded Al-Haq in 1979 to promote human rights and the rule
of law by documenting violations. By the mid-1980s his book *Occupier's
Law* was published, and Al-Haq expanded its focus to include women's
and labor rights.[14] The organization grew to forty staff by the end of the
decade and also began covering the Gaza Strip. In the 1990s it focused on
human rights under the new Palestinian National Authority.[15]

The Palestinian-American psychologist Mubarak Awad returned to
his birthplace on a tourist visa and established the Palestinian Center
for the Study of Nonviolence (PCSN) in 1983. The Center culled information about reconciliation and nonviolence from Arabic literature and
Islamic texts to raise awareness amongst Palestinians of these ideas in their
own heritage. Among over 120 practices of nonviolent resistance, Awad
worked with twenty Palestinian intellectuals who led sit-down strikes and
cultivated local food production. He roamed the West Bank by scooter,
led seminars, and worked with Palestinian human rights lawyer Jonathan
Kuttab. In 1988 Prime Minister Yitzhak Shamir accused him of fomenting civil disobedience in the intifada (Ar. shaking off, uprising) and deported him.[16]

The seeds Awad planted blossomed. When the Israeli government
wanted to take over Palestinian farmers' land for new settlements, they
uprooted hundreds of olive trees. Palestinian and Israeli nonviolent activists gathered together to plant new olive trees. When the government built
a fence in front of shops in Hebron as a security measure for right-wing
Gush Emunim settlers living above the shops, Palestinians and Israelis
organized shopping expeditions.[17]

One legacy of Awad's work was the Library on Wheels for Nonviolence
and Peace in Jerusalem and Hebron. Nafez Assaily studied with Awad and
developed the mobile book-lending service in conjunction with the PCSN
in 1986. The library touched thousands of families over the next three decades, teaching traditions of nonviolence and peace in Islam to empower
participation in social change. It cultivated ties with libraries around the
world, working for social justice and training young leaders in nonviolent
communication.[18] Assaily argued:

> Only the Palestinians can give [Israelis] peace. The US can give them
> money and weapons but not peace. And the only people who can give
> us peace are the Israelis. The Arabs can give us money and weapons,

but they cannot give us peace. We must act on these two facts. More nonviolence.[19]

Hussein Issa, a friend of Awad, studied psychology and worked with Palestinian refugee children. In belief that nonviolence could gain Palestinian freedom, he founded the Hope Flowers School in Bethlehem in 1984. He invited Israeli kindergarten children and their families to the school and taught Palestinian children Hebrew. Incensed that he taught the language of the occupiers, Palestinians burned Issa's home, car, school bus, and finally the school itself. But he rebuilt everything and persisted.[20]

## The Audacity of Mutual Recognition

Joint activists grappled with the near unanimous refusal of their societies to recognize each other. No Palestinian leaders used the word *Israel* in public. Instead they referred to Occupied Palestine. No Israeli leader recognized PLO leaders as legitimate representatives of their people. Instead they called them terrorists. Activists struggled together over mutual recognition and explored a two-state solution when it was anathema to the vast majority of their people. It was so taboo that they often had to meet beyond the borders of Israel and Palestine in neutral territory, away from media condemnation. A peace group in Amsterdam, for example, invited Israelis and Palestinians to talk to each other. Uri Avnery came from Israel, and the PLO sent Imad Shakur, an Arab citizen of Israel who had left Israel after being arrested several times. When they all heard about the Sabra and Shatila massacre, Shakur expressed Palestinian determination to keep the dialogue alive despite efforts to destroy it, declaring, "We shall not let them."[21]

Arafat moved the PLO headquarters to Tunis in part due to conditions of the cease-fire, which forbade him to go to any country bordering Israel. In Rome he toasted the Israeli Peace Movement's demonstrations against the war. He expressed readiness to meet with Israeli Labor Party representatives. In 1983 Avnery met with the PLO in Paris and Tunis, and with Elias Freij, the mayor, in Bethlehem. Freij recommended that the PLO recognize Israel unilaterally. Avnery conveyed this recommendation to Arafat so the Americans might support a peace process that recognized the PLO, but it was not yet time. Arafat, however, gave Avnery permission to publish photos taken of them together.[22] Abu Iyad, a Palestinian hardliner, came out in favor of a two-state solution. Sartawi met Avnery in London and talked about his plans to create a Palestinian Peace Party. When Sartawi showed up at the Socialist International conference held in Lisbon that year with Israelis in attendance, he was assassinated, silencing his voice for peace.

In 1983, the UN held an international conference on Palestine in Geneva. It was boycotted by the United States, West Germany, and Israel. The ICIPP sent representatives, and the PLO sent two pro-Syrians, Farouk Kaddumi and Yasser Abed Rabbo, who were at that time against peace with Israel. Back home in Israel, the ICIPP was attacked for attending. At the conference Palestinians publicly dismissed the ICIPP. Palestinian delegates who were friends with the Israelis could not speak out against PLO rejection. Yet behind the scenes, Kaddumi proposed peace and lauded the Israeli peace camp.[23]

The Hungarian Peace Council invited Arabs and Israelis to their country. When Walid Sadik, the Palestinian Arab trade unionist from Israel, entered the conference, he saw Palestinians from the West Bank and Gaza on one side of the room and Israeli Jews on the other. As an Israeli and a Palestinian Arab he did not know which side to choose, as either choice would cut out part of his identity. Instead, the group made him chair, and he took a seat in the middle.[24]

Back home, Israelis learned of Palestinian perspectives through cross-border meetings with Mayor Freij of Bethlehem, Gaza mayor Rashad Shawwa, journalist Ziad AbuZayyad, and *al-Fajr* editor-in-chief Hanna Siniora. Within Israel, peace activists Galia Golan, Lova Eliav, and Matti Peled met with Arab trade union activists Walid Sadik and Nawaf Masalha, and with intellectuals Majid al-Haj and Sami Mar'i from Haifa University. Together they created the Arab-Jewish Educational Council, in which educators worked to improve schools in Arab villages in Israel.[25]

In 1984 the Communist Party of Israel joined with the Democratic Front for Peace and Equality to win four seats in the Knesset. It attracted Arab and Jewish Israelis to its call for a two-state solution, an end to occupation, and recognition of the PLO in an international peace conference. The Labor Party ran on the policy of ending the occupation, as did Shulamit Aloni's Civil Rights Movement, Amnon Rubenstein's Shinui (Heb. change), and MAPAM.[26]

These parties clashed with another new party founded by sixty Jewish Israelis and sixty Palestinian Arab Israelis, called the Progressive List for Peace (PLP). The formation of the PLP marked the first time Israeli Arabs and Jews were fully integrated into one political force. The founders were the Arab Israeli lawyer Muhammad Miari and Jewish Israeli general Matti Peled. Miari was a Palestinian nationalist who had worked with Al-Ard (Ar. the land) movement in Israel, and later with the Committee for the Defense of Arab Land. Sadik and Riah Abu el-Assal were also members of the PLP, which won seats in the Knesset in July 1984.[27] Their platform called for coexistence of the State of Israel with a State of Palestine composed of the West Bank and Gaza, and complete equality for all Israeli citizens, including Arabs. The Communist Party attacked them from the left and the Labor Party attacked from the right.[28]

The PLP recognized and held talks with the PLO. Israel's law forbidding contact had not yet passed, but phone tapping harassed Israelis who met with PLO representatives. Philip Mattar, of the Institute for Palestine Studies, brought together five Israeli Knesset members and five Palestinians associated with the PLO to draft a mutually acceptable document for cooperation. Away from the public eye, a few dozen Palestinians and Israelis came together over the next few years to work out the details of the agreement. In 1986 Faisal Husseini, the grandson of Musa Kazim and relative of Hajj Amin al-Husayni, helped establish a joint Israeli-Palestinian peace group called the Committee against the Iron Fist in response to tightening repression in the West Bank and Gaza. The Israelis who joined at first were mainly anti-Zionist, but Faisal widened his contacts over the next year so that, according to political analyst Reuven Kaminer, his outreach became "an important link in the chain of Israeli-Palestinian joint action."[29]

Shimon Peres, Israel's foreign minister, tried to skip over Palestinian leadership to make an Egypt-type peace deal for the West Bank in secret negotiations with Jordan.[30] But the PLO's influence continued to grow. It reached out to Israeli Arabs, appointing Ahmad Tibi, a gynecologist from Tayibe, an Arab town in central Israel, as Arafat's "expert on Israel," while Imad Shakur and Mahmoud Darwish pushed for a peaceful solution. The PLO also cultivated representation by Hanna Siniora on the West Bank, and Fayez Abu Rahme, president of the bar association in Gaza.

By 1986, the Likud Party was so incensed with the escalation of meetings between the PLO and Israelis that the Knesset passed a law outlawing contacts. To the Likud, the PLO was a terrorist organization officially committed to Israel's destruction. The new law precipitated Mizrahi Israeli peace activists' creation of the Committee for Israeli-Palestinian Dialogue (CIPD). Siniora published their platform and welcomed them. Even Likud member Moshe Amirav met with Husseini in Jerusalem and stood his ground when Likud renounced him. The government did not put Amirav on trial, but did try four Israeli leftists for meeting with the PLO in Romania.[31]

Israelis and Palestinians held a press conference to declare: "No power in the world can prevent the dialogue between the Israeli and Palestinian peace seekers which will continue at all times in all places." Mordechai Bar-On noted that frequent meetings and planned joint nonviolent activities broke the "wall of enmity." This was an understatement. These "elite-level" meetings were part of a paradigm shift and an assault on the rejection of mutual recognition. They broadened acceptance for a two-state solution and conflated the one-state democratic secular solution with a threat to Palestinian Arab or Jewish Israeli independence, at least for this point in history. From Bar-On's vantage point as a leader in the Israeli peace movement, Arab-Jewish activism seemed confined to "elite circles."[32] But this was not true. Palestinian and Israeli nonviolent activism was expanding to include women, young people, clergy, scientists, and teachers who dared to learn about the other's reality, struggles, and political needs.

## Forces of Feminism

Women were at the forefront of nonviolent action within their respective separate societies long before they found ways to work together. The General Union of Palestinian Women, formed in 1965 in the West Bank and Gaza, mobilized for a national struggle that usually excluded the struggle for women's rights.[33] Israel ended women's disenfranchisement in the West Bank after 1967, so Arab women had their first experience of direct democracy in the municipal elections of 1972 and 1976. They entered higher education in unprecedented numbers. Suha Hindiyeh, Palestinian professor of sociology at Bethlehem University, cofounded the Palestinian Women's Resource Center, enlisted women to gather information on Palestinian and Arab women's movements, published a women's magazine, organized markets for cottage industries, and assisted battered women. The Palestinian Federation of Women's Action emerged in 1978 as the first grassroots women's committee in the West Bank. It started with educated, urban, middle-class women, but 90 percent of its membership came to be composed of village and refugee camp women. These women established kindergartens and nurseries to increase literacy.[34]

As independent thinkers and activists, some Palestinian women expressed "a need to form channels to Jewish/Israeli society to reach more women and to increase the number of women who believe and act upon a two-state solution."[35] In 1981 they formed the Union of Women Workers Committees to support women's rights and an independent Palestinian state. Some Palestinian women proposed that two nations could live together, learn from each other, and take joint actions to end the occupation.[36]

The Union of Palestine Women's Committees in Gaza and the West Bank was a women's rights advocacy group calling for civil democracy and full human rights. Israeli repression of Palestinian causes stimulated women's committees to provide everything from job training to birth control advice. Historian Joel Beinin wrote that "by the mid-1980s, 10,000 women were organized through these committees, out of a population of a million." Beinin suggests that these committees had direct impact later on the intifada as key elements of a "social revolution." When schools were shut by Israel, for example, Palestinian women would step in to teach young people and encourage them to stand up for their rights.[37]

Nabila Espanioly was one of the Palestinian women activists who emerged in Israel at this time. She grew up in the Galilee when it was still under military rule. Espanioly founded and directed Al-Tufula Pedagogical Center, which focused on early childhood and women's empowerment in Arab communities. In the next three decades she organized joint nonviolent initiatives with Jewish women, founded Jewish-Arab Women for Peace, and cofounded the Haifa branch of Women in Black to protest the occupation. She was a founding member of Mosawa (equal rights), a joint Palestinian-Israeli organization based in Haifa. She campaigned against an Israeli law that barred Palestinians from the West Bank and Gaza from acquiring Israeli citizenship when they married Arabs in Israel. After decades of activism, Espanioly was named one of the "1000 Peace Women around the Globe" who were collectively nominated for a Nobel Peace Prize in 2005.[38]

Before the Lebanese war, Israeli women had participated in peace groups as individuals. After the war, they formed women's groups for peace. Women against the War and Mothers (then Parents) against Silence began when a mother of a soldier sent a letter to three main daily newspapers protesting "the accursed war" as Israel's first "war of choice." Jewish women became active in issues of peace and national security in ways that had been closed to them.[39] Jewish women publicized the plight of Palestinians after the invasion of Lebanon. In 1984 they demonstrated at Neve Tirtza, a women's prison, to protest the treatment of Palestinian women.[40]

In 1983, Arab and Jewish women in Israel joined together to form a new organization, Isha l'Isha/Amarah il-Marah (Heb./Ar. Woman to Woman). They promoted both peace and the rights of women and girls. Over the next three decades they helped organize the fight for health care and against trafficking in women. They created a

supportive environment . . . regardless of religion, ethnicity, or cultural background . . . to address their needs, provide room for self-expression, . . . [and deal with] violence against women, reproductive rights, discrimination in work and society, sexual identity, . . . [and] Israeli-Palestinian conflict.[41]

## Religious Militancy and Civil Society

The mid-1980s saw a rise of Jewish and Muslim religious militancy that melded ultranationalism, racism, and the restriction of women's rights. Both groups categorically opposed peace and a two-state solution, each believing that they were the only legitimate citizens of Greater Israel or the whole of Palestine. In 1983 a right-wing religious Mizrahi Jew killed a left-wing secular Ashkenazi Jew. The victim, Emil Gruenzweig, was a member of Peace Now. In response, nonviolent religious activists founded progressive action groups such as the Mizrahis' East for Peace and the Orthodox religious Jews' Netivot Shalom (Heb. Paths of Peace), joining with the progressive religious group Oz v'Shalom (Heb. Strength and Peace).[42]

Meir Kahane led a religious, right-wing, rejectionist group in Israel. He was repeatedly jailed by Israeli authorities for planning armed attacks on Palestinians in revenge for their killing of Jewish settlers in the West Bank. Kahane founded an ultranationalist party that gained a seat in the Knesset elections of 1984 on the basis of a racist platform calling for annexation of the West Bank and Gaza and expulsion of Arabs. In response, the Israeli government passed the Anti-Racist Law banning parties with racist platforms from elections.

Hamas was a Palestinian religious, right-wing, and rejectionist offshoot of the Muslim Brotherhood that Egypt had brutally repressed in its occupation of Gaza. It campaigned for women to don the hijab (Ar. head/chest covering) in public, stay at home, and keep segregated from men—thus moving Palestinian society in a socially conservative direction. It promised to use military means to defeat Israel, a promise that would become manifest in the coming decades in suicide bombings and rocket-mortar attacks.

Peter Demant points out that these were the years before religious political "opposition to secular nationalist leadership . . . reached its subsequent strength."[43] But nonviolent joint activists were nevertheless quick to respond to rising racism and polarization. Naftali Raz, one of the founders of Peace Now, started a new organization called Adam (Heb. human) to deal with racism and to hold seminars on democracy and tolerance.[44] Arab and Jewish high school teachers created curricula with Arab and Jewish students in Israel and the West Bank, in Arabic, Hebrew, and English. Palestinian and Israeli teachers worked together in hundreds of schools, community centers, and youth movements, with thousands of teachers and students in grades K–12, to teach democratic principles and practices, minority rights, and how citizens effect government.

Shatil (Heb. seedling), founded by the New Israel Fund, dealt with polarization and inequality in Israel by promoting empowerment, democracy, tolerance, and social justice in an attempt to strengthen civil society. Shatil seed-funded thousands of social-change organizations, supporting consulting, training, advocacy, media, coalition building, resource development, and volunteer management for many decades. They promoted Jewish-Arab equality and nonviolent joint action, serving Arab and Jewish populations in areas around Haifa, Beersheba, and Jerusalem. Shatil's multicultural staff worked with activists and grassroots groups on social, economic, and environmental justice; human and civil rights; respect for religious and cultural differences; poverty; and leadership. Their projects advanced the right of Palestinians in Israel, Bedouin Arabs in the Negev desert, Ethiopian immigrants, and women. Oded Haklai, a researcher of Palestinian nationalism in Israel, found that by dealing with marginalized populations in Israel, Shatil cultivated "a more pluralistic discourse and greater public space for civil society to check the influence of the central state."[45]

Palestinians in Israel mobilized to strengthen civil society. In the northern Arab town of Shefaram in Israel, four Arab health care professionals founded the Galilee Society, also known as the Arab National Society for Health Research and Services, to address inequalities in health, environment, and socioeconomic conditions. They created the first data-bank on Arab communities to correct the gross inadequacy of knowledge about them. The Galilee Society worked with citizens groups, village and municipal councils, the Arab mayors association, international health groups, and the Arab Group for the Protection of Nature. Arab doctors, scientists, engineers, and social workers developed sewage plans for villages, pollution prevention and monitoring systems for an industrial zone, drinking water for unrecognized Arab villages, and the first regional research and development center in the Arab sector, affiliated with Haifa University and funded by the Israeli Ministry of Science.[46]

### Youth against Inequality

Joint nonviolent youth initiatives must have been making an impact because by mid-decade an Orthodox rabbi wrote in a religious Jewish newspaper, "We should relate to the issue of Arab-Jewish youth encounters as one of the most dangerous threats we face in the state today."[47] Yet the meetings were fraught with mistrust and hostility, in part due to young Israelis' political, social, and class privileges. The cultural and economic differences between Jewish and Arab towns within Israel were vast, let alone the difference between Jewish citizens of a state and young Palestinians under military occupation.

The Israeli government allocated 10 percent of its budget for social services to the 16 percent of its citizens who were Arabs. Economic inequality produced striking differences between the youth of the two populations in Israel. The traditional authoritarian social structures of the Arab communities shaped education and widened the gap. Between 50 and 75 percent of Jewish youth held negative images of Arabs and thought they were disloyal to the state. Arabs continually expressed more willingness to meet with their Jewish counterparts than Jews did to meet with Arabs, despite the sense among Jews that there was no one on the other side who cared to talk.[48]

Israeli Arabs began to demand that the government address inequality and racism. The Ministry of Education launched democracy and tolerance programs in the Israeli school system. New programs included Youth Sing a Different Song and the Institute for Education and Coexistence between Arabs and Jews. They also put together Arab-Jewish intervention programs.[49] But there were limits to how far these government-sanctioned initiatives could go. Mohammed Abu-Nimer suggests that government involvement bent initiatives "to the principles and assumptions" of Israeli society, so efforts would be aimed only at "reforming defects in the social order" instead of transforming them. They operated in ways that "directly or indirectly contributed to preserving the status quo . . . imposed on Arabs in Israel."[50]

Independent NGOs were less beholden to government biases in addressing inequalities. The Van Leer Institute, for example, founded in 1959 by a Dutch Jewish family, became an intellectual center for Arab and Jewish scholars dedicated to strengthening civil society in Israel and advancing pluralism. In the 1980s their nationwide education program on Arab-Jewish relations produced twenty textbooks and trained two thousand teachers to address imbalances of power.

Sadaka-Reut (Heb./Ar. Friendship) brought together young people outside school to foster respect for diversity and strengthen alliances. In branches throughout Israel, Arab and Jewish youth participated in weekly meetings, topic seminars, youth exchanges, volunteer projects, and even a year of service. The group believed that "conflict stems from miscommunication on a cultural level . . . [that is remedied by] lengthy interaction between the two peoples."[51]

Sadaka-Reut could have ignored structural causes of inequality but they did not. For three decades they worked with thousands of young people in small groups of mostly teenagers in yearlong after-school programs facilitated by trained Arab and Jewish leaders. In the first few weeks, participants engaged in introductions through games and interviews; in the next few weeks they focused on Arab and Jewish cultures; and in subsequent weeks they examined stereotypes, identity, politics, and moral issues facing their society. "One Year of Life for Coexistence" trained Arab and Jewish high school graduates to lead Sadaka-Reut, live together, solve day-to-day problems, work in poor communities, and lead educational activities for local youths.

Friendship's Way began in 1983 when Arabs and Jews volunteered to tutor children in their homes in Jaffa. It grew into the Jewish-Arab Association for the Child and Family, which targeted at-risk Jewish and Arab children, ages six to twelve, and their families in an integrated after-school program in Jaffa. Because the project lacked funding, volunteers worked as private gardeners in Tel Aviv and used their earnings to rent space. Eventually Arabs and Jews built an organization that met physical, emotional, and educational needs of Jaffa's inner-city children in a loving, homelike environment. Children received assistance with homework; were instructed in Arabic, Hebrew, English, and math; and participated in sports, drama, music, dance, science activities, and health education.

For more severely endangered children, the Neighborhood Home offered a daily, after-school enrichment program for fifty Jewish and Arab children who otherwise would be placed in boarding schools or foster homes. They received hot, healthy lunches and dinners, had daily contact with families, and were protected from substance abuse, malnutrition, neglect, and violence. Programs cultivated tolerance and awareness of stereotypes, and they celebrated Muslim, Jewish, and Christian holidays through multicultural song, dance, and stories. All materials were in Hebrew and Arabic. The staff included professional volunteers, Arab and Jewish university students and professors, parents and community activists, and international volunteers who made a one-year commitment.

Perhaps it was inevitable that some participants in these encounters fell in love with one another. Enormous pressure on both sides against Arab-Jewish romance kept most relationships secret. Trouble developed when the young people wanted to marry. Most Israelis and Palestinians saw such marriages as scandalous, even though they were not illegal under Israeli law.[52] But love loves to trespass boundaries, and couples did marry. Some moved in with their Arab families in Israel or the West Bank. Others left for more tolerant societies in the West. In some cases both sets of parents were supportive. Tal Bar-On, for example, is the Jewish daughter of Mordechai Bar-On, who dedicated his life to peace between Jews and Arabs. She married Daher Zeidani, a Palestinian Arab Muslim from a prominent Jerusalem family. Tal's father rattled the social taboo when he proclaimed that his son-in-law "is one of the nicest persons I have ever met and I love him dearly."[53] The Zeidani family accepted Tal into the family due to the dominance of Daher's mother, who loved Tal and "authorized" the marriage. The children, nevertheless, broke their parents' hearts when they left for Europe.

* *

In the 1980s, Palestinians and Israelis cautiously or raucously tested the possibilities of joint work in record numbers. Some Palestinians in the West Bank and Gaza took initiatives that challenged the PLO. Some Israelis disregarded their leaders' attempt to outlaw their contact with Palestinians. Demant sees the period between the First Lebanese War in 1982 and the first intifada in 1988 as a time of expanding unofficial contacts and dialogue that "put the Palestinian question at the center of public consciousness, . . . erod[ing] a bit further the anti-Palestinian dogma in Israel."[54]

Not all nonviolent joint actions succeeded in doing this. Much of the work was unprecedented and many mistakes were made. Many hurdles existed. Some were on the physical level of how to cross borders, others on the emotional level of how to allow in information that shook their assumptions. There was a high degree of mistrust involved in meeting individuals whose people had openly oppressed or willfully murdered one's own people. There was ignorance about how political and economic power imbalances played out between Palestinians and Israelis on political and in interpersonal levels. The seemingly breathless pace of grassroots breakthroughs in these years must not disguise how daunting the encounters were: the painful personal and political challenges, the backlash of each society against joint work, the consequences of really listening to the other that revealed the magnitude of the changes needed.

Most Palestinians refused to participate out of the conviction that participation would normalize injustice and take the place of necessary diplomatic negotiations. Most Israelis refused to participate because it meant talking to individuals whose loyalties were to leaders who were still calling for an end to Israel. Some participants' worst fears were confirmed, and they never met again. Others were intrigued or even profoundly moved despite or because of the shattering of preconceptions regarding self, society, and the other. Collectively the joint work addressed the chasm of sorrow, rage, impotence, and stonewalling silence between neighbors, allowing people to expose and address inequality.

The decade of the 1980s opened with a few Arabs and Jews meeting in a lone shack atop the barren hill of Neve Shalom/Wahat al-Salam. By the end of the decade that hilltop had become a thriving intentional community, half of the residents Jews and the other half Arab Muslims and Christians. They lived daily with the tensions inherent in the ongoing conflict, buffeted by each eruption of violence beyond their village borders. But by 1988 they were surrounded by hundreds of Jews and Palestinians in Israel, the West Bank, and Gaza: academics, politicians, scientists, artists, workers, physicians, educators, students, clergy, homemakers, men, women, and children who engaged in nonviolent joint action to touch the impossibilities at the heart of conflict.

CHAPTER 6

# First Intifada: 1988–1992

*Israeli women's rights activists merged their feminism with the quest for equal rights for Palestinians. Israeli women began denouncing violence against Palestinians exclaiming, "We've had enough of the legitimization of brutality, of violence" against women and against Palestinians.*

NAOMI CHAZAN, KNESSET REPRESENTATIVE[1]

*As a result [of Palestinian and Israeli women's meetings] a new language emerged, . . . taboos were broken, . . . long held antagonisms and fears were uncovered. Gradually, we came to . . . distinguish the sacred from the profane, the meadow from the minefield, the scar from the wound, and the human being from the stereotype, . . . [to gain] a mind-set, commitment and political will for inevitable and painful compromise.*

HANAN ASHRAWI, PALESTINIAN LEGISLATOR, *THIS SIDE OF PEACE*[2]

Dalia met Bashir two decades before the intifada. He was forced out of his house in Ramla in 1948. She grew up in that house with her immigrant Bulgarian family, exiled after the Holocaust. Dalia was confined to a maternity hospital for the birth of her son when, at the start of the intifada, she learned that Bashir was in detention and facing deportation. She protested with her "Letter to a Deportee," which was published in the *Jerusalem Post*. In Bashir's response, he revealed that when he was six in Gaza he found a shiny toy that blew up in his hand, crushing all but his thumb, and believed that Zionists intended children harm. Despite deep ideological differences and disparate lives, during the intifada, Dalia and Bashir dedicated their house to serving both their peoples. Open House became the first Arab preschool and community center for Palestinians and Jews to study, make music, celebrate holidays together, and support each other.[3]

Media portray the first intifada as a path of violent provocation. One narrative begins with the stabbing death of an Israeli shopper in Gaza on 6 December 1987, followed by the killing of four Arab residents of Jabalya refugee camp in a traffic accident rumored to involve an Israeli truck driver out for revenge. On 9 December a Palestinian teen threw a Molotov cocktail at an army patrol, and an Israeli soldier shot him dead. Mass rioting spread from Gaza to the West Bank and East Jerusalem and turned into sustained demonstrations and strikes by tens of thousands of men, women, and children.

Rock throwing, road blocking, and tire burning followed. In the next four years, Palestinians threw 3,600 Molotov cocktails and a hundred hand grenades; they made six hundred armed assaults on soldiers and civilians. Israelis killed over a thousand Palestinians, made mass arrests, and closed Palestinian schools. Palestinian death squads killed 1,100 Palestinians suspected of collaborating with Israel or of being from opposing political factions. Hamas and Islamic Jihad increased the number of civilian murders of Palestinians and Israelis.

The most gripping news, however, did not make headlines. It was the explosion of nonviolent tactics used by Palestinians and Israelis separately and together. Research by the Palestine Center for the Study of Nonviolence documented that during the first year 92 percent of actions called for by the intifada coordinating committees were nonviolent.[4] These nonviolent actions, like the violent actions that eventually eclipsed them, arose from the deeper reasons for the uprising. In the second decade of occupation, Palestinians were experiencing Israel's increasing control over their lives, Likud's determination not to let them go, appropriation of land to build illegal settlements, informant networks, and increasing disruption of daily life that offset economic rewards. The uprising brought Israelis and Palestinians together in new acts of solidarity.

* *

### "No Taxation without Representation"

Palestinian and Israeli activists worked separately in their respective societies to address injustices. In the West Bank and Gaza, Palestinian non-violent activists founded civic organizations to broaden an infrastructure for independence, peace, human rights, and democracy. Hanan Ashrawi, for example, founder of the English Department at Birzeit University and daughter of a PLO founder, had spent a decade advocating for human and legal rights. The intifada was a turning point for her as she joined its Political Committee and served in international peace negotiations over the next decade.

Nonviolent organizations proliferated among Palestinians. Al-Watan (Ar. homeland) resisted occupation through "civic education, nonviolence, and conflict resolution."[5] After the intifada they spread their nonviolent teachings to reach over 8,000 children. The Arab Association for Human Rights, based in Nazareth, served the Palestinian minority in Israel.[6] Panorama formed in Jerusalem and eventually opened offices in Gaza and the West Bank as the Palestinian Center for the Dissemination of Democracy and Community. Over the coming decades it sought to create an egalitarian, pluralistic society based on citizenship, accountability, transparency, and good governance.[7] Muwatin (Ar. citizen), the Palestinian Institute for the Study of Democracy, sought transformation of Palestine into an independent state.[8] The Palestinian Center for Peace and Democracy worked on governmental, legislative, and grassroots levels to alleviate hardships under occupation.[9] The Gaza Community Mental Health Programme aimed to improve the well-being of children, women, and victims of human rights violations while combating the stigma of mental illness.[10]

When the Israeli government closed down schools in the West Bank in response to the violence, mayors in Beit Sahour and Bethlehem initiated independent educational networks. Palestinian educators established CARE, the Center for Applied Research and Education, to organize teacher, student, and parent councils and trainings about democracy, civil society, and human rights. Palestinians participated in mass demonstrations, displayed Palestinian flags illegal under military law, closed shops, boycotted Israeli goods, and went on strike. In the first year, the intifada's leadership called for an escalation of nonviolent resistance to a level of "total civil disobedience."[11] Grassroots nonviolent resistance nurtured confidence in Palestinians' ability to show the world life under military occupation and to publicly resist without waiting for action from leaders in Tunis.

"No taxation without representation" was the slogan from the Unified National Leadership of the Uprising coalition, urging people to stop paying taxes. "Military authorities do not represent us, and we did not invite them to come to our land. Must we pay for bullets that kill our children or for . . . an occupying army?"[12] The people of Beit Sahour organized a city-wide tax strike. Israeli military authorities placed the town under curfew, blocked food shipments, cut telephone lines, and imprisoned residents.

The Palestinian Center for Rapprochement promoted grassroots dialogue and invited Israelis to join them in Beit Sahour. Israelis by Choice, an immigrant peace group, sneaked through roadblocks, pretending to visit a Jewish West Bank settlement. Seventy-five of them, mostly observant Jews, spent Shabbat (Heb. Sabbath, Saturday) in Beit Sahour. The army tried to remove them, but they were forbidden to travel on Shabbat.[13] Twenty-five families brought babies and kosher food to celebrate Shabbat in Arab homes. After a shared dinner, Arab and Jewish children went out to play. The army forced them to leave the next day.[14]

The Israeli group Dai Lakibush (Heb. Enough of the Occupation), born six months before the intifada to protest the twentieth year of occupation, now organized weekly visits to villages, refugee camps, and hospitals, going to the "heart of the intifada" to meet local Palestinian leaders and families of those killed, wounded, or arrested. Arab students in Dai Lakibush "served as guides . . . into the 'interior' of the occupation." In house meetings, Israelis visited Palestinian activists who reported on life under occupation. Mobilizing many sections of the organized left, dozens of activists gathered in decision-making forums, and hundreds participated in public activities. These included weekly vigils of forty to fifty people in major cities and a visit to Beit Sahour with three hundred Israelis.[15]

Each new action was a revelation. Cracks appeared in what had seemed like an impenetrable wall of mistrust, powerlessness, and segregation. Palestinians met Israelis whom they could count on to risk their lives to stand with them in protest. Israelis learned of humiliating and dangerous conditions that echoed their own Jewish past. They took their places, as Jews had done in the 150 years since their release from ghettos, to defend the rights of others whose struggles resonated with their own. Israeli activists in Twenty-First Year (established on the fortieth anniversary of Israeli independence, which was the twenty-first year of the occupation) demonstrated against military service in the Occupied Territories. Witness the Occupation protested Jewish violence toward Palestinians and boycotted goods produced by Jewish settlers.[16] All groups rallied to protest the rising number of Palestinians in jail.

Yesh Gavul, formed in 1982 during the First Lebanese War, now renewed support for soldiers who refused to serve in the Occupied Territories. By 1989, 150 soldiers had gone to jail rather than serve in the West Bank or Gaza, and thousands more found ways to avoid serving.[17] Refusing to serve often meant going to jail for a month, losing a month's salary, and being subject to social stigma at work and with family. Reuven Kaminer argues that Yesh Gavul expanded the debate over the morality of occupation like no other group.[18] The Red Line, founded by an Israel Defense Forces (IDF) colonel, brought Arabs and Jews from the Galilee together to organize a peace festival with thousands of people in Tel Aviv. Other groups included Ad Kan (Heb. Until Here); the Council for Peace and Security, which included high-ranking reserve officers; and Horim Neged Shkhika (Heb. Parents against Violence).[19]

Activists from the Palestinian Human Rights Information Center and the Jerusalem Media and Communications Center connected with their emerging Israeli counterparts. B'Tselem, the Israeli Information Center for Human Rights, focused on abuses in the West Bank and Gaza. The group's Hebrew name referred to biblical story of the creation of all humans "in God's image," but it could also mean "in the shadow" of the occupation. Founders included Knesset representatives and leftists Dedi Zucker, Yossi Sarid, Edy Kaufman, and Zahava Golan.

HaMoked was a hotline in Israel for victims of violence in the West Bank, East Jerusalem, and Gaza. The organization eventually expanded to handle detainee and residency rights, family unification, freedom of movement, security force and settler violence, and house demolition. The Israeli Committee against Torture confronted Israelis with information that was difficult to face. The Israeli lawyers Leah Tsemel, Ruhama Marton, and Avigdor Feldman worked to ameliorate conditions under occupation.[20]

A new Palestinian-Israeli peace group, Kav Yarok (Heb. Green Line) protested harassment and a month of 5:00 p.m. to 5:00 a.m. curfews. Thirty activists demonstrated at the Deheisha refugee camp and handcuffed themselves to a fence. Palestinians held a parallel demonstration inside the camp. Muslim, Christian, and Jewish religious peacemakers joined them in the West Bank.[21] Kav LaOved was a workers hotline to help protect the rights of Palestinians who crossed the green line every day to work inside Israel. They formed a legal aid service that handled hundreds of cases in the first year.[22] The hotline grew over the decades to protect the rights of more disadvantaged workers employed in Israel, including Palestinians, migrant workers, subcontracted workers, and new immigrants as part of a larger effort to bolster international law on human rights.

## Academics, Artists, Doctors, Rabbis, Businesspeople, Joggers

Leading Israeli and Palestinian scholars and professionals found ways to translate their skills into activism that challenged the status quo. Sari Nusseibeh declared, "Marry us or divorce us." He hailed from a prominent Jerusalem family, held a doctorate from Harvard, and taught philosophy at Birzeit University and Islamic philosophy at Hebrew University. Months before the outbreak of the intifada, Nusseibeh asked Israel to give Palestinians rights equal to those of Israelis or else let the occupied territories go: The intifada called for independence, not equal rights, so Nusseibeh worked on Palestinians' declaration of independence and helped create two hundred political committees and twenty-eight technical committees. Palestinian leaders presented fourteen points to the Knesset peace caucus. Nusseibeh and Faisal Husseini met with Likud cabinet minister Ehud Olmert to press demands.[23] Hanna Siniora launched a civil disobedience campaign, citing Gandhi's independence movement and King's civil rights movement. He advocated strikes and boycotts of Israeli products as means to reduce dependence on the Israeli economy and loosen Israel's control.

Husseini's Arab Studies Society worked with the Truman Institute for the Advancement of Peace at Hebrew University to form the Israeli-Palestinian Peace Research Project. They hammered out policy on federal frameworks, economic support, settlements, Jerusalem, democracy, and water allocation in published papers.[24]

Arab intellectuals in Israel established Al-Qasemi College as an institute for Sharia and Islamic Studies certified by the Council on Higher Education in Israel. They provided degrees in religious and secular subjects with Jewish and Arab faculty, and partnered with academic institutions in Israel to foster "dialogue between religions, cultures, and traditions." The college saw "Arab Islamic culture as an active partner in the cultural heritage of humanity." Its covenant emphasized "the dignity of humans," "freedom of choice and expression," and the development of Arab society in Israel.[25]

The Israel-Palestine Center for Research and Information (IPCRI) formed a think tank and activism center. The founder, activist Gershon Baskin, codirected IPCRI with Birzeit University history professor Adel Yahia to foster an ongoing peace process that recognized the legitimacy of Palestinians' right of self-determination and Israel's security concerns.[26] Binational research groups created and promoted policy on business, economics, water, and Jerusalem. In the following decades they addressed environmental concerns, public media distortion, track-two diplomacy, and the nitty-gritty details of a just peace. IPCRI modeled equal partnership as Palestinian co-CEOs Zakaria al-Qaq, Ghassan Abdullah, Khaled Duzdar, and Hanna Siniora teamed with Baskin.

Palestinian artists from the occupied territories joined Israeli artists to portray poignant political realities in fresh ways. In August 1988 Israeli and Palestinian painters launched an exhibition that focused on young Palestinians killed in the intifada. Suliman Mansur was an artist from East Jerusalem who had studied at the venerable Israeli art institute Bezalel in West Jerusalem and chaired the Palestinian Artists Association.[27] Gazan and Israeli poets, writers, and filmmakers produced works that exposed injustice.[28] Palestinian and Israeli painters mounted joint exhibitions. Jewish and Arab writers formed the Committee of Creative Arts, and their dialogue produced a full draft of a peace treaty. Israeli and West Bank musicians trespassed national, class, and gender boundaries to form Alei Hazayit (Heb. olive leaves). "In spite of border closures that prevented band members from getting together for rehearsals or gigs," they played Israeli, Ladino, and Arabic folk music for twelve years.[29]

Doctors formed the Association of Israeli and Palestinian Physicians for Human Rights to maintain contact, protect Palestinian doctors from arrest, send Israeli volunteers to Palestinian clinics, and hold conferences for the improvement of health.[30] Jewish and Arab medical professionals opposed occupation as a violation of medical ethics and worked to change Israeli government policies.

Psychiatrists, psychologists, and social workers established Mental Health Workers for the Advancement of Peace. They organized a conference on Psychological Barriers to Peace. Five hundred participants met for two days to analyze the psychological consequences of occupation for both Palestinians and Israelis and to discuss the addiction to an outside enemy. Munir Fasha from Birzeit University reported on the intifada.[31]

Arab and Jewish social workers who created Ossim Shalom: Social Workers for Peace and Welfare insisted that social welfare could not be separated from peace. When Arabs murdered two Jewish teenagers and Jews retaliated against Arabs in the neighborhood, Ossim Shalom secured the trust of the municipal government and people in the neighborhood to develop a professional intervention program to defuse hostility. They worked with right-wing Jewish militants because for "ethical and pragmatic reasons, retaliation by Jews against innocent Arabs had to be prevented" as a first step.[32]

Jewish clergy formed Rabbis for Human Rights to challenge the domination of the religious right. They received endorsements from a thousand North American rabbis but none from Orthodox rabbis in Israel.[33] Israeli progressive rabbis Levi Kelman and David Forman went to "visit the sick," which is a mitzvah (Heb. good deed, act of connection to God), in the West Bank when those who were ill could not get medical treatment due to military curfews.[34]

The Interreligious Coordinating Council of Israel formed to counter religiously based violence. They drew on teachings from the three Abrahamic faiths to "transform religion's role from a force of extremism into a source of reconciliation." In the next two decades they united over seventy-five Muslim, Christian, and Jewish institutions in religiously based solutions through dialogue and action.[35]

Arab and Jewish businesspeople in Israel formed the Center for Jewish-Arab Economic Development with the conviction that joint economic activity would add to everyone's prosperity. They addressed structural inequalities like unemployment, unskilled Arab labor, and lower employment of Arab women. In the coming decades the center developed non-discriminatory work plans, diversified hiring practices, and trained Arab women to enter the workforce. They worked to shift tax revenues to be shared equally in joint industrial parks, promoted businesswomen, made credit and loans accessible, and gave incentives to Jewish-Arab-owned businesses. The center teamed with the Palestinian Media Institute in the West Bank and the Jerusalem Women's Association to attract Palestinian, Israeli, Jordanian, and Egyptian businesspeople who worked in "textiles, construction, tourism, plastics, foodstuff, and software."[36]

Even runners joined the fray with a Joggers for Peace run from the West Bank and Israel. They had to go to the High Court of Justice to fight the IDF's curtailment of their right to jog together.[37] They jogged through Jewish neighborhoods, Palestinian villages, Jerusalem, and Bethlehem, wearing trilingual T-shirts with the colors of both the Israeli and the Palestinian flags. The T-shirts read: "We Want Peace between Palestine and Israel." Each run ended with a talk in someone's living room.[38]

## From Covert to Overt Action

At this point, people in official public roles began to cultivate unofficial secret relationships. The PLO's Bassam Abu-Sharif, mastermind of terrorist attacks, met with Uzi Mahnaimi, former Israeli intelligence officer turned left-wing journalist. Abu-Sharif supplied Mahnaimi with inside information about Arafat's growing willingness to renounce violence and recognize Israel, and Mahnaimi wrote about it. Their relationship grew out of a conviction that compromise was imperative. Their people denounced them.

When Abu-Sharif started faxing information to Mahnaimi on PLO stationary, other reporters wanted nothing to do with it. But Mahnaimi's editor-in-chief backed him. Abu-Sharif's peers criticized him for giving secrets to the enemy's newspapers. Mahnaimi wrote about the intifada as a "revolution" after twenty years of occupation and received repeated death threats. They met twice in 1988, with another journalist in attendance so Mahnaimi could say he was at a press conference if he was arrested by Israeli authorities. Abu-Sharif put forth a peace plan that got a big reaction at the Arab Summit and met with disbelief in Israel. "It was the Oslo agreement, almost word for word, five years before the event," they wrote in their joint memoir.[39] The PLO called Abu-Sharif a traitor, but Arafat defended him.

Throughout 1988 the PLO and Israel were involved in covert, indirect contact. Rita Hauser, an American Jewish lawyer-activist at the US Council on Foreign Relations, met in Stockholm with the chair of the Palestinian National Council's Foreign Relations Committee, Khaled al-Hassan. Through a "secret, deniable channel" they agreed that the PLO would recognize Israel and foreswear terrorism in return for a two-state solution. Arafat announced to the UN a new peace plan, but it did not meet enough conditions to gain US approval.[40]

The following June, US president George H. W. Bush's Secretary of State, James Baker, was in dialogue with the PLO, which publicly recognized Israel's security requirements. In July, King Hussein of Jordan made a major move, renouncing Jordan's irredentist claim to the West Bank and declaring that it belonged to Palestinians. That removed the possibility of Israel bypassing the Palestinians to make a deal with Jordan.[41] In November, the Palestinian National Council announced a Declaration of Independence signaling acceptance of a two-state solution within a framework of mutual recognition. In December, Arafat announced to the UN Assembly in Geneva that the PLO renounced and denounced terrorism.[42]

For the first time, Israeli peace groups invited Palestinian speakers to rallies. Ahmad Abu-Asneh from the Council of Arab Mayors and Zakariyya al-Agha, chair of the Association of Physicians in Gaza, attended rallies. Al-Agha was arrested two days later. Peace Now waited until Bassam Abu-Sharif published his support for a two-state solution in the international press to invite Faisal Husseini and Radwan Abu Ayas, head of the Journalist Association in the Occupied Territories. The Israeli media portrayed Husseini as a leading Fatah activist, but he supported cross-border dialogue, opposed violence and terror, and was optimistic about a two-state solution. Two days later Israel arrested him and closed down the Arab Studies Society, which he had founded in 1979. Peace Now held a vigil at the Russian Compound where Husseini was imprisoned. Three thousand demonstrators marched past Rabin's residence in protest. Peace Now would not support negotiation with the PLO but organized two mass "expeditions" across the border to mark the twenty-first anniversary of occupation, calling on leaders to "Free Israel of the West Bank."[43]

Peace Now met publicly with Palestinian leaders to press for open dialogue.[44] Hundreds of Israelis met with whole Palestinian villages. Over the next few months, 2,500 Israelis and 1,000 Palestinians held peace meetings in six locations in the West Bank. The "state" of Palestine extended a semi-official welcome to Israelis who were willing to negotiate with their national leadership.[45]

"We want peace" read Palestinian graffiti that the Israeli military authority ordered erased. The Association for Civil Rights in Israel asked the High Court if it was illegal to call for peace. Peace Now activist Hillel Bardin got a Palestinian friend to ask families in Jabal Mukabbir to put peace stickers on their homes. Two hundred agreed. In January 1989 Israelis and Palestinians held a public meeting in a village that straddled East Jerusalem and the West Bank. They addressed the crowd and ceremonially put up a sticker that read "We want peace between Israel and Palestine, both free and secure" in the colors of both peoples' flags. Together they went to villages to distribute stickers.[46]

In February, Dai Lakibush hosted a meeting with Husseini in Levi Kelman's Reform Jewish temple, Kehilat Kol Haneshama (Heb. Every Soul/Breath), in Jerusalem. In May 1989, the activists of Twenty-First Year sent twenty-seven protesters to Qalqilya in the West Bank to nonviolently resist destruction of Palestinian homes. They expressed solidarity with thirteen occupants, including ten children, whose petition the High Court had rejected. Protestors sneaked into an area declared closed by the IDF and were arrested. Among them was the prominent Israeli academic and activist Daphna Golan.[47]

In response to the military curfews in Gaza, Israelis formed convoys in a project called Food for Children of Gaza. They collected food from all over the country, but Israeli settlers from Gaza waited to block them before they reached the border. So they got out of their cars, "lugging bags of rice and baby formula" toward Erez Checkpoint. Settlers grabbed the rice and dumped it on the ground, but others succeeded in getting the food through to the Gazans. In the West Bank, Israelis supported self-sufficiency for Beit Sahour by delivering tree and vegetable seedlings. Students and faculty demonstrated near the Knesset to reopen Palestinian universities in the occupied territories.[48]

## Arabs and Jews in Israel

The intifada emboldened Arabs within Israel to create both separate and joint nonviolent initiatives in record numbers. After 1948, 156,000 Arabs remained in Israel; by 1990 their population had grown to 700,000. The confluence of the uprising across the border, their own demographic growth, Israelis' visible support for Palestinians, and ongoing inequalities galvanized Arabs in Israel into action.

The Abraham Fund was formed to address the inequality of the Arab minority in Israel. American Jewish philanthropist Alan B. Slifka was troubled by the socioeconomic gap between Arab and Jewish communities, so he launched this fundraising organization, which itself became an Arab-Jewish joint action organization. It initiated countless concrete nonviolent projects to redress inequality and racism and to support activists in the field. By the end of the intifada, the Abraham Fund had published the first listing of almost three hundred joint nonviolent groups in the six-hundred-page "Directory of Institutions and Organizations Fostering Coexistence."[49]

Sikkuy (Heb. opportunity), the Association for the Advancement of Civic Equality, formed as a Jewish-Arab advocacy organization combating discrimination in "government budgets, resource allocation, hiring policy, land usage, and access to government services" and working for equality, shared citizenship, and human dignity. They practiced joint and equal leadership at every level to transform "relations between the state and the Palestinian Arab minority." They worked with the prime minister's office, government agencies, and local officials to form the Jewish-Arab Mayors' Forum for Regional Cooperation to alter policies detrimental to Arab towns, enable local taxes to benefit towns, and get services to Arab residents.[50]

Jews and Arabs founded Citizens for the Environment in the Galilee to protect the air, water, and soil of their lands. The organization and its seven hundred members shared leadership on all levels. The next two decades witnessed many successes: lobbying for laws to stop pollution, closing a polluting fifty-year-old factory, cleaning up natural areas, cultivating youth and women's leadership, conserving water resources, preventing illegal dumping, and forming sustainable industries.[51]

Jewish and Arab children and their families from neighboring communities met to explore each other's folklore in long-term programs at the Center for Creativity in Education and Cultural Heritage.[52] One Palestinian school principal from the West Bank reported that his students expressed surprise after their first encounter that Jews were not demons but "made of flesh and blood," and Israeli children saw Palestinians not as terrorists but as people with shared dreams and fears.[53] On a forty-acre, four-thousand-year-old farm turned into the Ein Yael Living Museum, Jewish and Palestinian children studied their common heritage. They explored farming, mosaics, baking and preservation, archeology, and nature in Jewish-Arab summer camps that also served children with special needs.[54]

Low-income residents of the Wolfson neighborhood in Acre founded a Jewish-Arab Community Association to provide education, services, leadership development, and advocacy for equal opportunity. Arabs and Jews created interreligious early childhood, youth, and women's programs. They founded the Network of Organizations for Jewish-Arab Partnership, which exposed stereotypes and structural causes of inequity. Nearby, the Galilee Foundation for Value Education in the communal village Moshav Shorashim (Heb. roots) built new intergroup connections that modeled the diversity of Israeli civil society.

Long-established joint initiatives expanded. At Givat Haviva, founded in 1949, Arab and Jewish young people taught each other Hebrew and Arabic through art, drama, literature, and music. During school vacations they attended communication seminars and went on tours to Arab villages that Jews would never enter on their own. Three-day live-in workshops brought 2,700 Arab and Jewish eleventh graders together in 1990. An Arab-Jewish art center for sculpture and painting brought together eight hundred Arab and Jewish students, who also studied Middle East history and current politics.[55]

In Jerusalem, the Van Leer Institute created the Pairing Project to bring sixteen Arab and Jewish schools with 150 teachers to study together. They organized international conferences on Israeli-Palestinian relations. In Haifa, Beit Hagefen (Heb. House of the Vine), founded in 1963, was Israel's largest Arab-Jewish community center, where high school students participated in an Arab-Jewish folk dance troupe, an Arab mobile theater, and an annual Arab Culture and Book Week.

Haifa was supposedly a successful "mixed" city, but its two peoples had only superficial contact, often marked by inequality. The Leo Baeck Center in Haifa, founded in 1938 as a school for German Jewish immigrant children, expanded to include disadvantaged Ethiopian and Mizrahi Jews. In 1991, it opened an Arab-Jewish summer camp for children at risk. Arabs and Jews supervised the training each year of youth leaders for community service and the arts, helping each other decipher Arabic and Hebrew instructions.[56]

Neve Shalom/Wahat al-Salam organized an Arab-Jewish festival of the arts that was attended by thousands of students. Its School for Peace brought four hundred Arab and Jewish students together each year. The village education system continued to grow and was still the only Arab-Jewish bilingual school. Elsewhere, Midreshet Adam led encounters between Arab and Jewish schools that taught children to recognize nondemocratic elements in their society and to understand pluralism.[57] Project Encounter brought together 4,000 Arabs and Jews, secular and religious, urban and rural, primary and high school students and 1,200 teachers.[58]

## Women and the Intifada

The intifada provided Palestinian women with opportunities to engage in joint nonviolent activism with Israeli women. Hanan Ashrawi characterized the encounters as "unobtrusively changing the discourse." Palestinian and Israeli women traversed "uncharted terrain, armed with a map of joint gender concerns and a dedication to save, rather than sacrifice, lives."[59] Amal Kawar, author of *Daughters of Palestine*, brought Palestinian and Jewish Americans into the Dialogue Project. Ashrawi notes that as a result of the meetings between Palestinian and Israeli women, understanding improved dramatically, but this was not enough to make peace. What was needed was the "mind-set, commitment and political will for inevitable and painful compromise."[60] Sociologist Nahla Abdo asserted: "The Palestinian women's movement has shaken up the Jewish feminist movement in Israel and abroad," politicizing Jewish feminists.[61]

The Israeli feminist scholar Simona Sharoni observed that the intifada gave impetus to women's joint initiatives as a "primary catalyst" for cross-border contact.[62] Feminist theorist Sandra Harding said that in order for the Israeli women to do solidarity work with Palestinians, they had to cast off expectations and withstand being seen as traitors. Knesset member Naomi Chazan described how "Israeli women's rights activists merge[d] their feminism with the quest for equal rights for Palestinians."[63]

Ashrawi formed a working relationship with the Israeli defense attorney Leah Tsemel. As head of a university legal aid committee, Ashrawi worked with Tsemel for Birzeit University students arrested for protesting. She says that Tsemel was a "fierce yet gentle Israeli woman who early on took a moral and legal stand against cruelty and injustice."[64]

Women in Black held weekly vigils at the start of the intifada. The women wore black to signify mourning and held signs that demanded a two-state solution, an end to occupation, and a start to negotiations with the PLO as a partner.[65] They stood on hectic street corners at the busiest time of the week, Friday afternoon before sundown, when all shops, offices, restaurants, and entertainment closed for the twenty-five hours of the Sabbath. They vowed to keep the vigil going until the occupation ended. Despite right-wing backlash, groups spread across the country and throughout the world.[66] Palestinian and Jewish Israeli women stood together in twenty-six vigils in Jerusalem, Eilat, Rosh Pina, Tel Aviv, Haifa, Nazareth, and Acre. Women from the occupied territories joined on special days.

Feminist Israeli writers Barbara Swirski and Marilyn Safir observed that before the Palestinian intifada most Jewish feminists in Israel did not deem issues of peace as intrinsic to feminist concerns.[67] Ayala Emmett said that "for the first time in the history of the State of Israel, women . . . [chose] to take a public position regarding the Middle East conflict in organized women's protest groups, thus establishing a women's peace camp."[68] The group SHANI (Heb. acronym, Seven Women Together) protested occupation and called for a two-state solution through direct talks with the PLO. They visited Palestinian women's centers and featured Palestinians in thirty lectures. When the first international Jewish feminist conference in Jerusalem ignored the intifada, SHANI organized a postconference of three hundred Jewish and Arab women to forge a feminist response to occupation.[69]

Whereas most Israelis saw women political prisoners as enemies, feminists and radicals saw sisters. The new Women's Organization for Women Political Prisoners handled one hundred women's cases in the first six months of its existence. Israeli women adopted prisoners, made appeals to the High Court, and gathered data. At the Russian Compound, where Palestinian men, women, and young political prisoners were held, activists assisted Arab families in dealing with Israeli authorities, finding out where children were held, getting legal help, and providing for material needs.[70] Kaminer notes that "sisterhood can and did transcend the conventional bounds of national discourse."[71]

Na'amat was a long-standing movement of working women affiliated with the Israeli labor union, the Histadrut, and the largest women's movement in Israel. Arab and Jewish women workers traditionally confined their focus to women workers' concerns. Now Jewish and Arab women all over the country voted to put peace on the agenda.[72]

In May 1989 the Belgian Jewish Susskind family helped convene a Palestinian-Israeli women's peace conference in Brussels. Palestinian women's organizations drew up a list of participants and named Hanan Ashrawi spokesperson. The Israelis sent Knesset representative Shulamit Aloni, founder of the Citizens Rights Movement Party, as their spokesperson. Ashrawi reported that at the conference "a path of mutual recognition and identification was charted . . . both internally within each side and externally between both."[73] Chazan, founder of the Israel Women's Network, and Ashrawi drafted a joint political statement, but it was defeated. The Israeli Labor Party representative wouldn't sign its call for "Palestinian statehood." They rewrote a joint statement that met with unanimous approval and was celebrated that night, as Palestinian Rita Giacoman played women's, Arab, and Jewish music on the piano and they all danced.

Palestinian and Israeli women's joint nonviolence spread to Prague, London, Paris, New York, Stockholm, Jerusalem, Milan, and Helsinki, where dialogue groups argued the fine points of the agreement. The Brussels peace conference led to a new Palestinian-Israeli women's network that would aim to forge consensus for the agreement. Zahira Kamal, founder of Palestinian women's groups, took the agreement back home to show that there were Israelis working to end occupation. Israeli women went to the West Bank to help monitor injustices, and thousands stitched a peace quilt.[74]

On December 29, 1989, a coalition of Palestinian and Israeli women's groups organized an International Women's Peace Conference with 1,500 women from Israel, Palestine, Europe, and America. The focus was on ending occupation, negotiating with the PLO, and supporting a two-state solution. Palestinians and Jewish Israelis represented Women against the Occupation, Women for Women Political Prisoners, Peace Quilt, Bridge for Peace, the Haifa Women's Group, Women in Black, the Women's International League for Peace and Freedom, Community of Feminist Lesbians, the Organization of Democratic Women in Acre, and Yesh Gavul. Also in attendance were Arab and Jewish women who had been imprisoned together.[75]

In the afternoon, three thousand women joined the vigil of Women in Black in Jerusalem. From there thousands marched from Israeli West Jerusalem to Palestinian East Jerusalem, where hundreds of Palestinian women joined them until five thousand people were marching and chanting songs of freedom, justice, and peace in the largest women's peace march in the history of Israel and Palestine.[76] The women had to remove their conference buttons because they displayed the symbols of the Israeli flag and the still illegal Palestinian flag. The next day on 30 December 1989, over twenty thousand Israeli, Palestinian, and international representatives joined hands to form an unbroken six-mile human chain for peace around the Old City of Jerusalem in an atmosphere of exuberance and unity.[77]

A few months later, Masha Lubelsky, Yael Dayan, Shulamit Aloni, and Zahira Kamal kicked off Reshet (Heb. network) with a Palestinian-Israeli rally on the boundary between East and West Jerusalem to mark International Women's Day and to advocate for a two-state solution. It was the first time Jewish women leaders from the Zionist establishment formulated policies with the Palestinian women's movement.[78]

In June 1990, Jewish women from religious peace movements came together to form Nashim Datiyot Lemaʿan Shalom (Heb. Women's Religious Network for Peace). They based their work for peace on Jewish values rather than secular or revolutionary tenets. Over a hundred religious women gathered in Jerusalem to support a Palestinian state and land for peace. They created a new point on the spectrum between secular left and religious right, understanding and surpassing Jews and Muslims who saw the land as indivisibly God-given.[79] Veronika Cohen, an Israeli Orthodox Jew and musicologist from Hebrew University, organized over ten dialogue groups that met in Jewish homes in Israel and Palestinian homes on the West Bank during alternating weeks until travel restrictions during the Gulf War prevented Palestinians from leaving their homes.[80]

In the month before Iraq's invasion of Kuwait, four hundred women gathered in Kafr Yasif, an Arab town in northern Israel, for a peace conference. It was the first time this many people met for Arab-Jewish contact on Palestinian turf in a northern Arab village in Israel. It was the first time Kafr Yasif women had Israeli women guests sleep under their roofs. It was the first time most of the Israeli Jewish women visited an Arab village. Just showing up broke down long-held taboos. Palestinians came from the West Bank, and the proceedings were in Arabic, Hebrew, and English. Women in jeans sat next to women in veils listening to Arab women speak of racism, life as a minority, and their alliance with Palestinian and Jewish Israelis.[81]

On the eve of the Iraq's invasion of Kuwait, 130 women and five men gathered in Tel Aviv for the conference Peace and Identities in Israeli Society: The Place of Mizrahi Women in Political Activities. Mizrahis complained that they were invisible to Ashkenazi Israelis who privileged Palestinian equality over Mizrahi rights, and that they had not been invited to Brussels. The Israeli left had stereotyped Mizrahi women as indifferent or opposed to peace. One Mizrahi woman claimed not to "follow" coexistence: "There is only existence, or non-existence."[82]

### Iraqi Invasion of Kuwait and the Madrid Conference

Iraq's invasion of Kuwait in the summer of 1990 created a crisis for joint nonviolence, exposing the work's vulnerability to regional upheaval. Palestinians were portrayed on international television as cheering on their rooftops when Iraq dropped forty Scud missiles on Tel Aviv while Israelis huddled with gas masks in plastic-sealed rooms due to threats of chemical warfare. In reality, Palestinians' relationship with Saddam Hussein was more complicated. They opposed Iraq's invasion and occupation of Kuwait as well as the US-led war against Iraq, but also had been victims of Saddam's support for Abu Nidal's murder of PLO officials.[83] But Palestinians' televised stance split the peace movement. Some insisted that there could not be peace with those who celebrated threats to Israeli lives. Others argued that Palestinians had no real connection to Saddam.[84]

Kaminer wrote that Israelis now saw the peace movement as dead and peace advocates as dupes of Palestinians who rejoiced at Iraq's attack on Israel.[85] But the war also led to new grassroots opportunities and diplomatic maneuvers. Palestinians took more initiative to build alliances for a politically negotiated solution. At the peak of the Gulf crisis, Palestinian women came from all factions to join the Women and Peace Coalition.[86] Women in Black, the Israeli-Palestinian Women's Network, Physicians for Human Rights, and Peace Now persisted in joint nonviolent actions.

Peace Now organized a public meeting with Palestinians to argue the issues, sent "squads" to "rescue Palestinians under attack," organized dialogues with the Arab municipalities, and gathered five thousand Jews and Arabs along a ten-kilometer stretch of Wadi Ara Road to call for peace and condemn anti-Arab racism.[87] The Women's Coalition formed a convoy to Jalazun refugee camp to deliver supplies to Arab towns under curfew. Taghrid Shbeita, a Palestinian woman from Tira, collected supplies that Arabs and Jews delivered by bus, including milk for babies in Qalqilya and Gaza.[88]

The regional perception of Palestinian support for Saddam Hussein diminished funding from the Gulf states. The PLO took new measures to retain viability. Palestinians agreed to meet Israelis for official public negotiations for the first time in history, in Madrid under US and Russian auspices. But the United States and Israel refused to negotiate with the PLO and chose other representatives who nevertheless remained in constant contact with PLO leadership. In 1991, Haider Abdul Shafi and Elyakim Rubenstein engaged in the first official diplomatic Palestinian-Israeli handshake.

Peter Demant argues that Palestinian-Israeli joint nonviolent initiatives made Madrid possible. Cultivation of cross-national networks had an impact far beyond the projects themselves. Likewise, the Madrid talks stimulated new joint initiatives. The Truman Institute of Hebrew University and Husseini's Arab Studies Society started joint research projects.[89] Peace Now gathered tens of thousands of Israelis in support of the talks.[90] Raja Shehadeh, a lawyer with personal and professional Israeli contacts, now joined the Palestinian negotiating team as its legal advisor.[91] Fifty Israeli and fifty Palestinian high school students met in Gaza, on a kibbutz, in Ramallah, and in the West Bank settlement Reihan. Peace Now organized bus tours to East Jerusalem and the West Bank to protest the government's use of funds for new settlements, and they gave legal help to Palestinians in East Jerusalem displaced by Jewish settlers buying homes.[92]

Arafat's supporters in Gaza organized a peace demonstration. They handed Israeli soldiers olive branches and tied balloons to soldiers' jeeps. When Palestinian negotiators returned from Madrid to the West Bank, they received a hero's welcome.[93] West Bank Palestinian peace leaders began to reach out to more mainstream and even right-wing Israelis. However, when members of Sari Nusseibeh's own faction discovered that he had conducted talks with the Israeli Likud party, they beat him up. When he signed an agreement with Moshe Amirav, Likud expelled Amirav.[94] But negotiations persisted.

Until Madrid, Israeli-Palestinian dialogue was a grassroots and unofficial "track two." After Madrid the grassroots and the diplomatic tracks cross-fertilized. Some diplomats in Madrid had taken part in unofficial dialogues, and some continued to do so.[95] The breakthrough of Madrid was in form not content: it shattered taboos of public contact. Shafi, the official Palestinian spokesperson, opened the conference with the acknowledgment that Israeli-Palestinian dialogue "opened the hearts and minds of many Palestinian leaders to the possibility, indeed the advisability of a compromise solution."[96]

* *

The intifada sent shock waves of recognition of Palestinians' plight throughout Israel and the world. It sparked new joint nonviolent activism, with cross-border and intra-Israel alliances to raise awareness, address inequality, and protest an occupation entering its third decade. Palestinians gained moral ground with a wide range of nonviolent protests and new civic organizations. New Israeli groups witnessed, protested, monitored, and made public the realities of occupation. New programs, hotlines, and organizations provided some relief, material aid, and voice to Palestinians. Israelis and Palestinians partnered to do the dangerous dirty work of serving workers, women, children, victims of violence, and those whose human rights were being violated with advocacy for political, economic, environmental, and feminist justice. Women's involvement was especially notable both as individuals and as separate and joint women's groups that deepened connections between women's and national liberation.

More people than ever before were convinced that there was no military solution. Instead, Jewish Israelis, Palestinian Arab Muslims and Christians, men and women, old people and young people, religious people and secularists, Zionists and anti-Zionists challenged oppressive policies in vigils and mass demonstrations, living rooms and jails, and high courts and small villages, where they educated, negotiated, advocated, prayed, and jogged new possibilities into being. This growth of joint nonviolence bred grassroots constituencies that urged leaders into unprecedented diplomacy.

Yet most people on both sides continued to believe that armed struggle and military might were the only means by which to achieve justice and security. Nonviolent activists could not prevent the escalating violence and divisive sectarian backlash that marked the end of the intifada. They could not stop militant Islamic Hamas's first suicide bombing after the intifada or right-wing militant Jewish settler attacks on Palestinians or continued settlement expansion in the West Bank. But they did create vital ways for people to work together for alternatives to daily degradation and danger. When they took a stand together against inequality and occupation, and for the security and dignity of both peoples, they lifted for a moment the veil of hatred and fear that obscured their interconnected needs, rights, and humanity.

## CHAPTER 7

# In the Wake of Oslo: 1992–1999

*It is time to put an end to decades of confrontation and conflict, recognize
mutual legitimate and political rights, and strive to live in peaceful coexistence,
dignity, and security to achieve a just, lasting and comprehensive peace
settlement and historic reconciliation through the agreed political process.*
THE DECLARATION OF PRINCIPLES, OSLO ACCORDS, 1993, YASSER ARAFAT,
CHAIR OF THE PLO, AND YITZHAK RABIN, PRIME MINISTER OF ISRAEL[1]

"I don't refuse the existence of Israel! But I also don't accept Israel without a Palestinian state!" Fadi is a fourteen-year-old Palestinian, one of
fifty-four teenagers at the first Seeds of Peace summer camp in Maine for
conflict resolution, in the summer of 1993. Teens from Gaza, the West
Bank, Israel, Egypt, and Jordan won competitions to attend. A surprise
diplomatic breakthrough brought the campers to the White House lawn
to witness Arafat's recognition of Israel's right to security and Rabin's
agreement to Palestinian self-rule. Fadi's new thirteen-year-old Israeli
friend Haran hopes the agreement will mean he will not have to face his
friends in battle: "Now there will be no more dead Palestinians, no more
dead Israeli soldiers."[2]

The Oslo Accords elicited reactions from deep skepticism to daring
hope. But thousands of Israelis and Palestinians on the front lines of joint
nonviolence gave in to momentary elation. The proliferation of their
work, despite rejection by their own people, nurtured a demand for a historic compromise. No one knew at that moment how far the leaders would
get in implementing the protocols of peace. No one knew what would
happen to joint nonviolent initiatives with a peace process in motion. But
no one who had stood face-to-face with the enemy in peace marches, pris-

ons, playgrounds, or acrid dialogues of tough truth doubted their own role in bringing the two antagonists together.

* *

### From "Traitors and Whores" to Knesset Reps

Before 1992, Israeli liberals criticized women who worked on joint nonviolence as "bleeding hearts," and Likud conservatives called them "traitors and whores." The Israeli election of 1992 was a *mahpach* (Heb. revolution, reverse). As the first challenge to Likud since 1977, it shifted the modus operandi from life on the sword to land for peace, and made Yitzhak Rabin prime minister. Three Israeli parties joined to form the Meretz coalition, which urged Arabs to vote rather than to boycott elections. They won twelve seats, joining Labor and Arab parties in the government to pursue peace.[3] Two winners had perticipated in joint nonviolent initiatives: Meretz's Naomi Chazan and Labor's Yael Dayan. Chazan and Dayan flew to Europe for talks with PLO leader Nabil Shaat in the Netherlands. Their action was public and illegal, and it caused the repeal of the law against contact with the PLO.[4] Grassroots activists trusted Chazan and Dayan to bring nonviolent, nonmilitary solutions into the diplomatic realm.

While Labor's victory gave both Arabs and Jews a sense of potential change, daily life said otherwise. The Israeli government refused to hold direct talks with the PLO.[5] Hamas launched the era of suicide bombers, stepping up attacks on soldiers and civilians. Prime Minister Rabin responded by deporting four hundred Hamas activists, imposing closures and curfews in the occupied territories, and continuing settlement expansion.[6]

Peace Now demonstrated under the slogan "Fight Hamas with peace! Deportations—no! Peace—yes!" In December, activists protested deportations outside the High Court by erecting a peace tent in front of the prime minister's home in Jerusalem.[7] The Committee of Arab Mayors approved the action, turning the tent into a gathering place for Palestinians and Israelis to engage in intense discussion. Classes from Arab schools met with Jewish youth. Orthodox Hasidim argued theology with Muslim sheikhs. Hundreds of deportees' wives, including devout Muslims, joined demonstrations with Israelis. Over a hundred lawyers from Gaza attended Supreme Court proceedings. It was the first time the Israeli Islamic Movement participated in joint action with Jews.[8] Together they demanded negotiations.

As violence continued, Bishop Riah Abu el-Assal implemented his own vision of nonviolence. He gathered Jews, Muslims, and Christians to renovate the Anglican Church in Jerusalem. The Christians did the stonework and woodwork; Muslims created crimson crosses and stained glass windows; Jews installed air-conditioning and created a stained glass window above the altar depicting Jesus as Teacher.[9]

The year 1993 became a milestone in the history of Palestinian-Israeli joint activism. Labor's victory ended neither the killing of Palestinians and Israelis nor the destruction of Palestinian homes. In January, the Women and Peace Coalition held a conference in Jerusalem to address these matters with Women in Black, Women against the Occupation, Women for Women Political Prisoners, Peace Quilt, Bridge for Peace, Haifa Women's Group, and Women's International League for Peace and Freedom. They protested deportations and struggled with how to deal with a "progressive" government that continued occupation. Palestinians braved danger to attend the conference to let Israeli women know of continuing restrictions on their lives. One woman explained:

> I decided to come because I believe in people and I believe that people are the ones who make the change. The conditions that are imposed on us as Palestinians are such that we are forced to enter negotiations whatever the conditions. We believe negotiations themselves will change the conditions.[10]

Shukri B. Abed, a Palestinian-American from the West Bank, and Edy Kaufman, a Jewish Israeli, published *Democracy, Peace, and the Israeli-Palestinian Conflict*, the culmination of a five-year joint project that asked: "Can Israel stay democratic while facing recurrent wars and exercising military rule over a disenfranchised population?" And "Can Palestinians become a democratic polity, given the historical, religious, and cultural obstacles?"[11] The volume exemplified what Bassam Abu-Sharif called "the urgency of moving from points of conflict to points of convergence." Other studies asked, Do "tensions between rule of law and security considerations," and the denial of rights to Palestinians, imperil democracy?[12]

Both sides responded to political urgency with a steady drumbeat of joint work. Jewish and Palestinian Israelis founded the Arab-Jewish Community Center of Jaffa as part of a "paradigm shift" in the way local authorities approached "shared civic participation." Arabs and Jews of all ages met informally, in facilitated encounters, and in a day care center that reached children at risk with meals, therapy, academic tutoring, and the arts. Through Women's Voices, Israeli Arab women mentored others, and in Youth Leadership Development Jews and Arabs lived together after high school to work for social change.[13]

In New York City in February 1993, Palestinian and other Arab militants attacked the World Trade Center. John Wallach, an award-winning American foreign correspondent, responded by creating the Seeds of Peace summer camp in Maine. Teens attended two–hour coexistence sessions each day to process "messy emotional experiences," "angry tirades," difficulties with an enemy flag being raised each morning, and singing the Palestinian anthem only to find out it was anti-Israel. They listened to stories that contradicted what they thought they knew and prepared counterattacks. They called friends traitors, claimed to suffer more than the other, denied the other's pain, and despaired of peace.[14]

The second week of the camp, sick of fighting but unable to find their way out, they cried over death and horror. "The story of their pain was the most important thing they had to say," said Wallach. "Below the surface lie incredible hatreds. To build an honest peace, the youngsters have to deal with them." Tears were a turning point; the others listened in silence instead of demanding to be heard. Arabs learned that the Israeli flag doesn't symbolize rule from the Nile to the Euphrates and that far more than 20,000 Jews died in the Holocaust. They read Elie Wiesel's *Night* and visited a Holocaust museum. Palestinians said, "It should never happen again." Israelis heard about terrorist bombs back home. They withdrew, cried, and then heard Palestinians say: "We share your sorrow; we oppose terror." When the enemy paid attention to you, had fun with you, comforted you, anything seemed possible. The participants returned home to rejection and a barrage of messages from media, family, and school that reinforced hatred. Israelis felt newly responsible for Palestinians who felt newly committed to nonviolence. They remained in contact online.[15]

## The Oslo Accords

Six weeks after their first summer camp, the Seeds sat in dazzling sunshine on the emerald green lawn of the White House. On September 13, 1993, under the attentive eye of President Bill Clinton, two bloodstained leaders of enemy peoples, Rabin and Arafat, signed the Declaration of Principles (DOP). Unofficial meetings between PLO and Israeli representatives had opened the secret "Oslo Channel."[16] Clinton asserted that this was an example of "the leaders leading the people" when, in fact, Palestinian and Israeli activists had piloted these possibilities for change for decades.

The DOP was not a peace treaty but a timetable for deciding key issues. It gave "limited authority and autonomy" to Palestinians in the West Bank and Gaza, and outlined a sequence of Israeli military withdrawals based on an Israeli-PLO agreement:

> it is time to put an end to decades of confrontation and conflict, recognize their mutual legitimate and political rights, and strive to live in peaceful coexistence, dignity, and security to achieve a just, lasting and comprehensive peace, . . . [and] to establish a Palestinian Interim Self-Government Authority . . . in the West Bank and Gaza, for a transitional period not exceeding five years, leading to permanent settlement based on UN Res 242.[17]

An emotional process cracked the customary cynicism of the leaders. Breakthroughs were often awash with the tears born of the possibility for an end to a long struggle. When Abu Alaa, a Palestinian representative in Oslo, stood before two enemy governments,

> in one hand he held prepared text and in the other a large handkerchief. He waged an unequal struggle with his tears. No sooner had he begun speaking than he began crying, and so he continued, speaking and crying, crying and speaking. . . . The intensity of his emotion affected everyone in the room.[18]

Skepticism jockeyed with hope, dry-eyed realism with desperate dreams of ending occupation and terror. Palestinians predictably diverged between supporters of Fatah, who represented them in negotiation, and supporters of Hamas, who sought to "liberate" Greater Palestine from the Jordan River to the Mediterranean. Israelis predictably diverged between the right-wing demand for more settlements in a Greater Israel from the Jordan River to the Mediterranean, and left-wing support of giving up land for peace.

Everyone's worst fears were immediately confirmed. Israelis feared that Palestinians sought a tactical peace in order to continue attacks, and Palestinians worried that Israel would continue to build settlements and never withdraw from the occupied territories. In 1994 and 1995, Hamas and Islamic Jihad, two military arms of Palestinian militant Islam, began suicide-bombing Israelis in an attempt to derail the peace process. A Jewish right-wing fundamentalist massacred twenty-nine worshipers at the Ibrahimi mosque. Scores of Palestinians were being killed, one or two at a time, by settler vigilantes.

## Grassroots Responses, 1993–1995

At first the joint nonviolent activists held their collective breath. Would the initiatives need to continue at all? Was work for peace and against occupation complete? What needs would emerge as the DOP timetable progressed? Women in Black disbanded for several months, only to renew their vigil, recommitting to weekly demonstrations until occupation ended.[19] The Palestinian canon of St. George's Cathedral in Jerusalem, Naim Ateek, corroborated the necessity of continuing to work together:

> When peace is finally achieved and peace treaties are signed between Israel and its surrounding neighbors, there will still be a lot of work to be done in order to effect reconciliation between the two nations which have only known violence, injustice, and bloodshed.[20]

Tensions mounted as the image of two old warriors shaking hands clashed with deportations, settlement expansion, suicide bombings, and retaliatory massacres. This tension unleashed a flurry of joint initiatives that were breathtaking in scope and pace. For the next two years, projects emerged in media, politics, business, environment, music, education, and women's activism. If sworn enemies could sign the DOP, then Bassam Abu-Sharif and Uzi Mahnaimi could finally publish *Best of Enemies*. The book revealed their secret, illicit ten-year relationship to further Israeli-PLO recognition. It was a joint venture possible only in a post-Oslo environment.[21]

After thirty-six years, *New Outlook Magazine*, a cross-border venture between Israelis, Palestinians, and Arab intellectuals across the Middle East, published its last issue. The next winter Victor Cygielman and Ziad AbuZayyad, journalists who had worked for decades on mutual recognition of national rights, created the *Palestine-Israel Journal*. Arabs and Jews, as contributors, editors, and the board, strove to:

> promote rapprochement . . . [and] foster a climate of constructive criticism and mutual respect, active dialogue and exchanges within and

between the two civil societies, . . . and broaden the base of support for the peace process.[22]

In the glaring, sun-parched desert of the Arava Valley, a second diplomatic turning point gave a third dimension to cross-border work. Thirteen months after Oslo, King Hussein of Jordan and President Ezer Weizman of Israel signed a second peace treaty. Border crossings opened for tourists, workers, and merchants. Hezbollah protested this termination of belligerency with rocket attacks on Israel from Lebanon.

Now Israeli, Palestinian, and Jordanian environmentalists convened a historic tripartite meeting at Taba in the Sinai desert to form the Middle East chapter of Friends of the Earth, an international advocacy organization that focused on "justice and the planet." Together they worked to protect the environment from the consequences of overdevelopment and conflict. When Oslo stalled, both sides attacked Friends of the Earth and the peace process as a conspiracy to maintain an oppressive status quo. But the environmentalists continued to work together to face the crisis of unsustainable water practices.[23]

The Israel Palestine Center for Research and Information's Center for the Environment fostered peace by working together to resolve mutual ecological degradation. Researchers from Israel and the Palestinian Authority met in conferences and mediation. For years they combated deterioration of the mountain aquifer under the West Bank, built environmentally sound sewer systems, and worked on desalination.[24]

Musicians crafted a new sound in the collaborative ventures opened by Oslo. Some Arab and Jewish artists presented their musical collaborations as peacemaking. Others took a stridently antipolitical stance, claiming that the best musicians to play the most cutting edge music just happened to be Arabs and Jews. They did not have to be explicitly political to have a political impact. Ethnomusicologist Ben Brinner, in *Playing across a Divide*, traced Arab and Jewish musicians' personal artistic journeys to break free from the narrow confines of their respective musical communities, "the relative stagnation of the local Arab music scene and . . . the imitative nature of much other Israeli music which took . . . its cues from American and European trends."[25] The band Bustan Abraham sought an original synthesis of East and West while avoiding the domination of one type of music over the other in order to:

> pioneer a unique form of instrumental music which combines elements of both Eastern and Western forms without sacrificing the musical

integrity of either. . . . The combination of these instruments has never before been presented on the concert stage. . . . Bustan Abraham aspires . . . to pave the way for other creative joint efforts between Arabs and Jews.[26]

When Palestinian oud and violin player Taiseer Elias and Israeli guitar and banjo player Miguel Herstein formed White Bird, they were explicit about modeling the creative benefits of peaceful coexistence through music. But later, in Bustan Abraham, they lamented that this interpretation was "forced on them by reporters" and that "musical motivations" trumped "socio-political ones." Yet Brinner argues that "whatever their intentions . . . on stage, without saying a word, [they] embodied the principles . . . of future peaceful coexistence."[27]

Fifteen months after the Oslo Accords, the Nobel Peace Prize was awarded to Israeli and Palestinian leaders in Oslo. Yair Dalal organized a Peace Concert extravaganza. The peace activist was a relatively unknown musician whose parents were Iraqi exiles expelled during the destruction of that country's 2,500-year-old Jewish community in the 1950s. He brought together Palestinian and Israeli musicians and children choirs singing in Hebrew and Arabic, accompanied by the Norwegian Philharmonic and conducted by Zubin Mehta, to perform Mehta's *Zaman al-Salam* (Ar. Time of Peace). Later, at the height of violence of the second intifada, the film of the concert was cheered in Palestine. Dalal toured with Palestinians and the Bedouin, becoming a champion of music rooted in Middle Eastern traditions.[28]

The Oslo concert inspired George Sama'an, a Palestinian from Israel, to create a cross-border musical collaboration in the last years of Israel's security zone in southern Lebanon, with children from southern Lebanon and northern Israel. He hoped the Syrian-Israeli peace talks would result in a peace treaty at whose signing these children would perform. But Israel's unilateral withdrawal from Lebanon made it impossible for the children to meet, and the Syrian-Israeli negotiations collapsed.[29]

The Oslo Accords generated a new wave of youth initiatives to build a different future. Windows: Channels for Communication was formed in 1991 to publish a magazine in Hebrew and Arabic for children, inspired by the South African children's magazine *Molo Songololo*. They could not find support for their "Magazine for All Children" until after Oslo. Now they formed a junior editorial board of fifty young Palestinian and Jewish Israelis, as well as Palestinians from the West Bank and Gaza. They created a bimonthly publication in Arabic and Hebrew to dispel stereotypes and end occupation. *Windows* distributed to 20,000 high schools, youth centers, and libraries in Israel, Jordan, and Palestine, with a message that reconciliation depends on mutual knowledge. Their Friendship Center in Tel Aviv provided "a long-term intensive process of dialogue and empowerment" dealing with "human rights, life in mixed cities, [and] tough historical events."[30]

Religious schools were not usually cites of cross-border encounter. Now the Jewish Pelech Religious Experimental High School for Girls met with Palestinian twelfth-grade girls from Abu Ghosh High School to study the peace process, Palestinian autonomy, human rights, and challenges to hatred and fear. The girls learned about each other's culture and developed friendships.

At one college a lecture on medical ethics turned into a rousing student debate on Islamic and Jewish approaches to abortion by students of each faith. Seven Palestinian students had invited Ben Mollov, a Jewish political science professor, to this meeting that turned into the Project for Arab-Jewish Dialogue at Bar-Ilan University, a research university founded on Jewish values. They teamed up with the University of Hebron under the leadership of Musa Barhoun, professor of educational psychology and technology at Al-Quds Open University.[31] The project catalyzed careers in conflict resolution when, for example, Ayman Ismail graduated from Hebron, led an interfaith group, then attended the University of Notre Dame for a Master's in Peace Studies.[32]

Women activists complained that they were marginalized in the post-Oslo funding frenzy. Yet their initiatives proliferated separately and together. The Palestinian Civic Forum Institute supported women to hold local government council seats. Civic sessions taught about democratic processes, the values of equality, and human rights. Women sought active engagement in society as participants in governance by local authorities.[33]

Women were essential to nation building. The Palestinian Center for Women claimed that no peace process could succeed without "the involvement of women in all aspects of Palestinian civil society . . . [and] in final status negotiations."[34] Since the 1989 Brussels women's peace conference, Palestinian and Israeli women had continued to engage in joint actions. Now the European Union funded the Jerusalem Link to coordinate activities between two independent women's groups: Marcaz al-Quds la-Nissah (Ar. Jerusalem Center for Women) and Bat Shalom (Heb. Daughter of Peace). Separately and together they ran programs on "peace, democracy, human rights, and women's leadership." Each side wrote a column in the other's newsletter on being a woman in her own war-torn patriarchal society. The Jewish and Palestinian Israeli feminists of Bat Shalom worked for an end to occupation and "an equal voice" in Israel.[35] For fifteen years the Jerusalem Link ping-ponged between horror and hope. Emblematic of this was their opening day celebration on International Women's Day in the afterglow of Oslo, which was precipitously canceled due to the Hebron Mosque massacre.[36]

Nisan was the first organization led by and for young Israeli Arab and Jewish women. They longed to mutually support each other on the basis of shared struggles against patriarchy. But when the Arab Israeli women asked the Jewish Israelis to call them Palestinian, Israelis thought they were identifying with terrorists. They realized they had to work on inequalities based not only on gender but also on nationalism. They learned to work on stereotypes in separate groups in order to return to dialogue together.[37] Arab and Jewish high school girls learned leadership development skills that fostered relationships and empowerment in the Young Women's Resource Center.[38]

Social scientists and health professionals founded the Israel Association for the Advancement of Women's Health to improve the quality of life for Israeli Jewish, Muslim, and Christian women. The women were urban, rural, religious, and secular, of all classes, ages, and sexual orientations. The association taught women to make informed health decisions, educated practitioners about women's needs, and influenced policy makers on women's health.[39]

Regarding women's activism after the 1993 signing of the DOP and the 1994 peace treaty with Jordan, scholar-activist Ayala Emmett observed that the "peace politics of the margins have become the legitimate politics of the state." She wrote that after 1994 it was hard to remember that just a few years earlier the words *peace, coexistence*, and *Palestinian* were "silenced in official [Israeli] public discourse," while advocates were called traitors.[40]

## Derailment

In September 1995, Rabin and Arafat reiterated their commitment to a nonviolent negotiated peace by signing "Oslo II," as President Clinton, Egyptian president Hosni Mubarak, and King Hussein of Jordan stood witness. In this second phase, Palestinian self-rule would be expanded, Israeli forces would withdraw from six large West Bank cities, Palestinian police forces would replace the Israeli army in particular Palestinian areas, and Palestinian Authority elections would be held. In October, Rabin articulated his vision of a permanent peace to the Knesset, where legislators approved Oslo II by a single vote. At a huge Likud rally, Benjamin Netanyahu accused Rabin of "causing national humiliation by accepting the dictates of the terrorist Arafat."

The Oslo Accords had survived suicide bombings and rejectionists. But one month after Netanyahu declared war on peace, a right-wing religious Jew gunned down Rabin at a peace rally in Tel Aviv. His death dealt a major blow to the peace accords. Hamas further pummeled the peace process by killing fifty-seven Israelis with suicide bombs that gave the next election to the hawkish Likud. As expected, Israelis reacted to rising fear by moving right. The new prime minister, Netanyahu, paid lip service to Oslo while doing everything to "arrest, freeze, and subvert" it by waging a war of attrition with Palestinians.[41]

Arab neighbors tried to keep the peace process alive. Egypt convened an Arab summit to reverse the "no peace, no recognition, no negotiation" stance of 1967. Twenty-one Arab states warned Israel's new government not to change the terms of peace negotiations. The Arab leaders committed to peace with Israel, calling "for the resumption of Arab-Israeli negotiations on all tracks . . . [and] upon the new Israeli Government, without equivocation, to continue to abide by the letter and spirit of the principles agreed upon."[42]

Netanyahu bowed to international pressure to sign the Hebron Protocol in 1997, dividing the city into Palestinian and Jewish sectors, and the Wye River Memorandum in 1998, withdrawing Israeli control from 13 percent more of the West Bank. His right wing bolted and brought down the government. Labor won a landslide victory in 1999, signaling the people's will to revive the peace process. Prime Minister Ehud Barak, a disciple of Rabin, nevertheless undermined the peace process when he accelerated settlement building and turned away from Palestinians to make a bid for peace with Syria that ultimately failed.[43] By 1999 the deadline for the final status talks passed, the peace process languished, and King Hussein of Jordan was dead from cancer after his forty-six–year reign.

## Grassroots Responses, 1996–1999

Palestinians and Israelis refused to bow to the inevitable siege against peace by rejectionist sectors on both sides. A teetering peace process released a wellspring of energy for cross-border work through political activism, legal advocacy, economic development, dialogue, the arts, education, environmental efforts, medicine, and telecommunications. In the next three years, ordinary Palestinians and Israelis implemented actions that responded to writer David Grossman's plea:

> The best thing for the two peoples is to maintain as many connections of different kinds as possible. Economic, commercial, cultural, touristic, and athletic ties . . . [will] peg the new tent [of Oslo] we've erected to a ground of reality with thousands of ropes and tent pins. . . . If we do not live side by side we will perish together.[44]

Oslo II called for economic support from various funding sources, including the European Union, for an NGO cooperation effort called People-to-People (P2P). This gave official sanction and funding to joint nonviolent projects but signified a problematic shift. Instead of being alternative grassroots ventures, they became linked to changing governments, funders' savvy or lack of savvy, and the vicissitudes of the official peace process. P2P funding gave rise to a cottage industry of joint nonviolent nonprofit groups, some of which did real work and others of which were sinecures. Funders could not always discern groups' conflicting agendas, unrealistic expectations, and the strains of inequality.[45]

Arab organizations inside Israel mobilized for equality and those outside Israel mobilized for independence. Palestinian Israeli lawyer Hassan Jabareen and his Jewish wife, lawyer Rina Rosenberg, both Yale fellows, founded Adalah (Ar. Justice), the Legal Center for Arab Minority Rights in Israel, for the defense of Palestinian rights in Israel, the West Bank, and Gaza. He was legal director; she headed the international advocacy division. The staff was Palestinian, Israeli, and international. He had "extensive experience in litigating landmark constitutional law cases before the Israeli Supreme Court [and] . . . deal[ing] with . . . rights of Palestinian citizens of Israel . . . [and those] living under Occupation."[46] Award-winning Palestinian lawyers in Israel canceled demolition orders on Bedouin homes, overturned a ban on Arabs living in Jewish communities, and opened doors for Arabs to run for office.

In Gaza, the Palestinian Center for Democracy and Conflict Resolution focused on children with disabilities, child abuse, violence against women, and education for building civil society. They eventually expanded to the West Bank.[47] Also in Gaza, Palestinian lawyers and activists founded the Palestinian Centre for Human Rights to "promote the rule of law, . . . develop democratic institutions, . . . and support self-determination."[48]

Hanan Ashrawi created the Peace and Democracy Forum in East Jerusalem to mobilize support for the negotiations. It sought to advance "legal, economic, and social means" of democratic behavior; to "promote openness, transparency, [and] accountability"; and to show how peace is "a necessary element" of Palestinian statehood.[49] Lucy Nusseibeh founded Middle East Nonviolence and Democracy (MEND). Its "Pledge of Nonviolence" was a commitment to respect self, others, and nature; to find safe ways to express anger; to listen to those who disagree; to consider others' needs; to apologize and forgive; to avoid violent entertainment; and to stand up for others.[50] MEND worked through schools, film, the internet, radio, bumper stickers, and other media to change "the local attitude to nonviolence" from skepticism to appreciation. She noted that "now even the Palestinian President talks about nonviolence."[51]

Palestinian academics at Al-Quds Open University honored the neurosurgeon who died waging peace by founding the Issam Sartawi Center for the Advancement of Peace and Democracy.[52] Wi'am (Ar. cordial relationships), a Palestinian Conflict Resolution and Transformation Center, dealt with disputes within the Palestinian community through the traditional Arab means of *sulha*, as well as Western approaches. Although the Palestinian Authority officially ruled towns in the West Bank, in reality there was an authority gap that Wi'am attempted to fill with its interventions.[53]

Two new Israeli organizations addressed Palestinian hardships by focusing on housing demolitions and forced evictions. Arabiya Shawamreh, her husband, and her seven children lived in a house that was destroyed and rebuilt many times. The Israeli Committee against Housing Demolitions eventually turned the Shawamrehs' home into the Beit Arabiya Peace Center.[54] Bimkom (Heb. in place) was an organization of professional planners and architects who advanced human rights through "spatial planning." They challenged housing policies in Israel and fought discrimination against the Bedouin in recognized and unrecognized villages and against Palestinians in northern Israel, East Jerusalem, and the West Bank. They worked with hundreds of communities on home demolitions, inadequate infrastructure, and affordable housing.[55]

In Jerusalem, "on the seam lines between [its] major identities," Hisham Najjar and Aharon Ben-Nun helped found the Jerusalem Intercultural Center. They gathered a psychologist, a feminist author, a priest, a rabbi, a lawyer specializing in Islamic law, a community dialogue expert, the founder of a soup kitchen network, and an advisor to the Foreign Ministry to help diverse residents to become "responsible active partners" in developing their communities.[56] Professionals created dialogue; educated government officials; and convened neighborhood, religious, and business leaders for conflict resolution.

The Arabic-Hebrew Studies Center in Jerusalem enabled students to study each other's languages "in constant dialogue." Many of the participants were Arab and Jewish leaders of joint initiatives.[57] Deliberative Democracy worked with impoverished Arabs, new immigrants, and ultra-Orthodox Jews on democratic processes that made deliberation central to decision-making. One study found that the process of deliberative democracy could help Palestinians and Israelis find a shared set of goals and come to agreements on actions to attain them.[58]

Leah Green, an American Jew, took nine delegations of tourists to meet Palestinian and Israeli peacemakers through MidEast Citizen Diplomacy. These tours evolved into the Compassionate Listening Project in Israel and Palestine when Green teamed with Gene Knudsen Hoffman.[59] Their work was based on the teachings of Vietnamese Zen master Thich Nhat Hanh, Martin Luther King's nominee for the Nobel Peace Prize, who taught the practice of compassion for enemies. His protégé Hoffman stated that "an enemy is one whose story we have not heard."[60] Professor Frida Kerner Furman's research argued that reconciliation based on compassion was a necessary step toward a just resolution of conflict.[61] In Israel, Jordan, and the territories governed by the Palestinian Authority, listeners sought the truth of the person being questioned, seeing through "masks of hostility and fear to the sacredness of the individual."[62]

Noah Salameh's doctoral training in conflict analysis and resolution at Cairo University and his master's degree in international peace studies from the University of Notre Dame served him well as director of the Palestine Center for Conflict Resolution and Reconciliation. The center stressed "human need, not simply political agreements between powers," as well as "social and moral value, which spreads love, respect and acceptance based on justice and equality." Salameh combined his state-of-the-art training with traditional Palestinian *sulha* to deal with the "lawlessness of the occupation" and support young negotiators, interfaith encounters, and Islamic approaches to peace.[63]

When Orthodox Jew Yitzak Frankenthal's son Arik was kidnapped and killed by Hamas militants, he was surprised to discover that as a teenager, his son had spoken out for peace. So he foreswore the government's promise of retaliation. Instead he tracked down Israeli and Palestinian families whose children had been killed by the other side. The Parents Circle Family Forum brought bereaved Palestinian and Israeli parents together to speak about their losses. They held meetings in Gaza until the second intifada. Israeli and West Bank families continued to meet until six hundred families were working for reconciliation with their enemy. The unbearable feelings they harbored toward those whose beliefs and actions had killed their children were the same feelings that perpetuated the killing of children. Instead they spoke truth, wept, and supported nonviolent means to end occupation and conflict.[64]

Shimon Peres, Noble Peace Prize recipient because of Oslo and future president of Israel, opened the Peres Center for Peace in the Arab-Jewish city of Jaffa. Joint nonviolent initiatives brought professionals together in medicine, sports, business, education, technology, civic leadership, media, and art. Cross-border initiatives included joint olive oil production, regional water research, high-tech business partnerships, a community leaders network, photojournalism, medical cooperation, and virtual dialogue. The Center spearheaded environmental projects for integrated crop management, advanced water treatment, and nanotechnology.[65]

On a kibbutz in the southern desert, near the Jordanian border, the Arava Institute for Environmental Studies gathered Palestinian, Jordanian, Israeli, and international graduate students. Together they immersed themselves in environmental science, law, management, policy, and ethics. When the second intifada closed borders to Arab students, the Institute focused on Palestinians and Jews in Israel. Eventually Palestinians from the West Bank, Gaza, and Israel joined Egyptians, Jordanians, and Israeli Jews to study coral reef management, sustainable agriculture, desert ecology, and cross-border dialogue.[66]

The Palestine Council on Health joined with the Israel Economic Cooperation Forum and the Society for the Protection of Nature in Israel to form the Palestinian-Israeli Environmental Secretariat and to tackle problems by nonviolent means. Codirector Imad Khatib lamented that "politics interfere with every aspect of our lives." Binational NGOs were vulnerable to political winds even when their honorary copresidents were Rabin's widow, Leah, and Arafat's brother, Fathi.[67]

Scientists and doctors set up several cross-border projects to help children with heart conditions. Save a Child's Heart expanded for the next fifteen years and saved hundreds of lives. More than three thousand children from forty-two countries, including Palestine, Jordan, Iraq, and Morocco, benefited. Over 1,200 children from the territories governed by the Palestinian Authority had open-heart surgery. Palestinian and Israeli doctors trained other doctors in the surgical procedures so they could save even more children.[68]

The Heart of the Matter Project brought Palestinian and Israeli physicians together for postgraduate training in pediatric cardiology, anesthesiology, prenatal diagnosis, and critical care, while fostering cross-border communication between doctors. Two Jewish scientists founded The NIR School of the Heart, where Arab and Jewish young people studied medical sciences with a focus on cardiology. Students from Jordan, Palestine, Israel, Egypt, and Morocco studied in Jerusalem, Amman, Nazareth, and Acre, delivered social services, and met with social psychologists to identify and deal with political inequality. NIR students received diplomas jointly issued by the Harvard-MIT Biomedical Engineering Center.[69]

Artists came together to explore living visions of a nonviolent society. Israeli Adi Yekutieli and Palestinian Suhair Fritach codirected Pieces for Peace, bringing 150 Palestinian and Israeli artists to work with children on a three-year project to create three thousand feet of mosaics, painstakingly assembled from thousands of tiles, to place in a park on the border of Palestine-Israel. They wrote to Ehud Barak, Yasser Arafat, and Bill Clinton in the midst of what would be the leaders' last negotiation:

> We believe that true peace is possible only through direct human interaction. . . . When we began to paint together, . . . Israelis and Palestinians knew . . . only images of war and fear. . . . As we worked together as artists, children, and families, the possibility of life without fear evolved. . . . [We are] an old mosaic excavated underneath many layers. . . . Please remember us, the young generation whose will is to live together in peace.[70]

### Defiant Alliances

A defiant alliance of grassroots activists formed as the peace process deteriorated. Arabs and Jews in Israel reasserted their determination to face and repair inequalities within their own country. Jewish and Bedouin civil engineers, educators, and health care workers formed the Negev Coexistence Forum for Civil Equality to organize services, rebuild demolished houses, and address injustice to the Bedouin, who lived in the formidable, sparsely populated southern desert. Their displacement had begun with the Ottoman Land Law in 1858 and accelerated after 1948 when the Bedouin became refugees relocated to seven townships built by the government. Dislocation, sedentarization, and reduction of grazing area made traditional livelihoods unsustainable. Small family clusters formed un-official shantytowns and lived off the grid without electricity or access to municipal water systems as they had always done.[71]

Devorah Brous founded Bustan (Ar. garden) by organizing a two-day festival in an unrecognized village of Driejatt in the Negev. Hundreds of Bedouin and Jewish Israelis discussed Bedouin history and environ-mental issues, and collected signatures for official recognition. They won the battle. For the next decade Bustan worked in Bedouin communities doing "hard physical work . . . to clean up the nightmare conditions." With Rabbis for Human Rights, the Palestine Medical Relief Society, the Israeli Committee against Housing Demolitions, and Physicians for Human Rights, they opened a school, refurbished a clinic, brought sup-plies, and publicized the Bedouin plight.[72]

Arab and Jewish actors and artists used the arts to help their commu-nities. Arches graced an old stone building in the ancient city of Jaffa that was home to the Local Theater. Arab and Jewish actors performed plays focused on sociopolitical issues. The company coproduced plays with Al-Saraya Theater. The Arab Hebrew Theater in Jaffa used both languages in their productions. In contrast, the Galilee Multicultural Theater played "with objects, puppets, and their bodies with almost no words." Language was not an obstacle when expression was nonverbal. Some of the per-formers "had lived in the area for generations; others immigrated from all corners of the world. . . . [Together they] developed a very personal stage language." They met "on equal terms and worked together toward a common goal."[73]

High on a hill overlooking Wadi Ara, amid a constellation of Pales-tinian villages near Haifa, the Umm el-Fahem Art Gallery became a cul-tural center for the Arab population in Israel. Palestinians created and ran the gallery, which exhibited contemporary works by Arab and Jewish Israelis portraying aspects of Arab life and history in the area. A decade after the gallery's inception, ambitious plans formed to build the first con-temporary Arab art museum in the world. To support the project, Arab and Jewish artists formed the Middle East Center for the Arts, led by Palestinian artist and activist Said Abu-Shakra and Eugene Lamay, son of an Arab Catholic family who had converted to Judaism and whose work intertwined abstraction with indigenous imagery.[74]

Arab feminists founded Kayan (Ar. being) to raise the status of Pales-tinian women in Israel and defend their social, economic, and civil rights. They addressed violations of female childcare workers' rights and reached

1,300 women who had not previously been organized. Women Demand Mobility brought public transportation to Arab villages in need. They wrote the first Arabic version of a leaflet on the Law against Domestic Violence.[75] A women's crisis shelter in Haifa was a short-term emergency shelter for victims of domestic abuse, sexual assault, rape, and incest. Jewish, Arab, and new immigrant women staffed the only facility of its kind that provided services in Hebrew, Arabic, Russian, Amharic (Ethiopian), and English. Hundreds of women and children found safety there.[76]

Young people organized educational programs to reach Arab and Jewish children living in poverty. Inspired by the power of the largest student strike in Israel's history, Palestinian and Jewish students formed Mahapach-Taghir (Heb./Ar. turning the tables), as a "grassroots, feminist, Jewish-Arab organization for social change through education and community empowerment." Directed by one Jewish and one Palestinian Israeli woman, Mahapach-Taghir reached hundreds of Arab and Jewish children and their parents. They organized learning communities in seven towns, including the Druze Maghar and Muslim, Christian, and Bedouin neighborhoods in Tamra, Yafat el-Nassera, and Tira.[77]

In another case Palestinian and Jewish parents drove their children past police barricades and neighbors' warnings to a school they created together. After living for years in neighboring towns without contact across cultural, historical, and power divides, Hand in Hand opened two little schools in 1998: a makeshift classroom in Jerusalem with twenty students, and a small school between Kibbutz Eshbal and Arab Sakhnin in the north:

> A critical mass of courageous parents pioneered the risky project. . . .
> Late night planning sessions in Sakhnin . . . [and] so many meetings . . .
> [helped] prepare us for what might happen on the first day of school. . . .
> But the children blended so naturally we realized we were the problem,
> not them.[78]

This was the first time Jewish parents bused their children to school with Arab children. Surrounding violence constantly tested the schools, like at the start of the second intifada, when Palestinians in the area were killed in clashes with the police. Despite the barricades, counselors helped the staff "work through their raw feelings, questions, and sorrow." Both schools survived and became models for new schools in the next decade.

Arabs and Jews in mixed cities like Jaffa, Ramla, and Lod, and in neighboring towns like Nazareth, Afula, Ramat Hasharon, and Kafr Qasim, remained mostly segregated. A New Way brought people together in one of the many educational initiatives to show how art, music, and drama could teach tolerance and address inequality. Arab and Jewish mayors, parents, and teachers focused on the other's culture in multiyear programs in schools.[79] When the Ministry of Education became involved, it enabled the program to reach more students but shifted the emphasis away from equality and toward intercultural exchange.

The ALON Social Involvement Organization brought Arab and Jewish teen volunteers who were just out of high school to live with college-graduate supervisors and work with three hundred students each year in academic and social milieu. Sixty percent of Israelis couldn't pass Israel's matriculation exam. So students from Kfar Saba formed ALON to change "the harsh social reality . . . of widening social gaps that threaten . . . a healthy society." They targeted the twin pillars of poverty and lack of education with interventions for Palestinian Arabs, Arab Jews, the Bedouin, and immigrants from Ethiopia and the former Soviet Union. Over a thousand volunteers served more than 30,000 children in over a hundred projects. Those eligible for the army lived together and worked in disadvantaged communities for part of their national service.[80]

Young People against Racism challenged "entrenched habits" and antidemocratic trends buoyed by racism. It was part of Friendship Village, an international education center supporting a multicultural society and reconciliation because "change is vital for the survival of both people." They saw education as a key to tolerance, human rights, and justice. Through Friendship Village, women, young people, political leaders, and schoolteachers engaged in international summer training programs in partnership with Palestinian organizations.[81]

For eighteen months, Arab Jews and Arab Palestinians, men and women, secular and religious people, able-bodied and disabled people, Mizrahis and Ashkenazis met to tackle pain, difference, identity, and inequality in a diverse and divided Israel. They hammered out a vision together that became the foundation for Merchavim (Heb. Chariots): Institute for the Advancement of Shared Citizenship in Israel. Supported by the Ministry of Education, they worked with students in kindergarten through twelfth grade on "five core concepts: identity, access, fairness, limits of agreement, and active shared citizenship." Headquartered in Ramla because of its microcosmic Israeli demographic, Merchavim eventually reached five hundred schools in three Israeli educational streams:

Jewish-secular, Jewish-religious, and Arab-Israeli. Its programs allowed students to wrestle with the underpinnings and complexities of its contested motto, "7.7 Million Israelis, One Shared Citizenship."[82]

* *

Meanwhile, at Sharm el-Sheikh, between the jagged pink-gold peaks of Sinai and the jewel-blue Red Sea, Prime Minister Ehud Barak and President Yasser Arafat signed an interim agreement in 1999, with a new timetable for final status talks to begin in 2000 and for the peace treaty signing on the seventh anniversary of the Oslo Accords in September.[83] Elements of the five-year transition plan to Palestinian self-determination and peace for Israel had been implemented: the PLO and Israel had recognized each other; the Palestinian Authority had gained limited powers of self-government, with control over 40 percent of the West Bank and 65 percent of Gaza; the PLO had renounced violence; the Israeli military had withdrawn from Gaza, Jericho, and areas of the West Bank; and Palestinians had voted for their first Palestinian Legislative Council. The toughest issues, like the border between Palestine and Israel, settlements, the status of Jerusalem, Israel's military presence, and the Palestinian right of return, were all left to these final status talks.

Rejectionists on both sides failed to derail the peace process with suicide bombings, the assassination of Rabin, and the rise and fall of Israeli governments. Yet so much wind had been knocked out of the sails of peace that skeptics doubted the boat had ever existed. Israelis despaired of Palestinian ability to be a real partner in negotiations if they couldn't stop Hamas's terror. Palestinians doubted Israel's will for peace with a sovereign Palestine in the context of land confiscation, settlement expansion, and new bypass roads that chopped the West Bank into disconnected enclaves and strengthened Israeli control. Rabin's assassination and the subsequent election of Likud was a declaration of war on peace. Even when Labor won a landslide mandate to complete the peace treaty, settlement activity accelerated, undermining the territorial integrity of Palestine. What began as a historic compromise to end occupation, give Israel a secure peace, and launch Palestinian political independence became a vanishing chimera.

The diplomatic aims of the Oslo Accords were not fulfilled. But due to and despite the vicissitudes of the negotiations, joint nonviolence escalated not just in the number of participants or projects, but in sophistication in confronting occupation, the imbalance of power, and dangers to Palestinian and Jewish lives. Labor's electoral victory gave more Knesset seats to women, Palestinians in Israel, and joint activists. More Palestinians in Israel participated in grassroots engagement to transform their political situation. Scientists, doctors, artists, engineers, academics, lawyers, and parents of children who had died by enemy fire all formulated unique and powerful responses to persistent hardships. Arab and Jewish musicians' cutting-edge sounds translated new encounters of mutual respect into expressions of joy.

New international funding paid activists to work full time on joint projects. Many joint groups that did not receive funding nevertheless persisted, and those that received grants learned that funding did not guarantee success. Subsidies introduced competition and conflict among groups who were striving for a piece of the peace pie. Financial incentives attracted people who were more interested in funds than function. But with or without funding, joint nonviolent activists wove a multidimensional web of initiatives for equality and security that brought them closer than ever to living as two independent nations in mutual support.

## CHAPTER 8

# Suicide Bombs and Circuses: 2000–2005

*In the middle of the intifada . . . people said it was unrealistic for us to continue
with an Israeli-Palestinian circus. There were attacks happening all over
Jerusalem, and . . . both Arabs and Jews had been killed. Yet not one of the kids
missed a single rehearsal. And when we performed, the audience was full—half
with Arabs, half with Jews. I can't describe the feeling of hope I got from that
performance, the feeling of poetry. The feeling that everything is possible.*

ANNIE, MOTHER OF YOUNGEST (FIVE YEARS OLD)
MEMBER OF THE JERUSALEM CIRCUS[1]

*We, the members of . . . the Israeli-Palestinian expedition to Antarctica,
. . . [journeying] by land and sea from our homes in the Middle East to the
southernmost reaches of the Earth, now stand atop this unnamed mountain. By
reaching its summit we have proven that Palestinians and Israelis can cooperate
with one another with mutual respect and trust. Despite deep differences . . . we
carry on a sincere and meaningful dialogue, . . . rejecting the use of violence in
the solution of our problems.*[2]

SUMMIT STATEMENT FROM BREAKING THE ICE, AN
ISRAELI-PALESTINIAN EXPEDITION TO ANTARCTICA

A fourteen-year-old Orthodox Jewish boy from West Jerusalem and a
Muslim Palestinian boy from East Jerusalem perform gravity-defying
stunts. One leaps trustingly into the arms of the other. Young Israeli and
Palestinian girls barrel down mats, jumping through hoops and somer-
saulting. Young people are literally cartwheeling across the divide during
the bloody second intifada, overcoming fear and relying on nonverbal
communication to challenge limits, language barriers, stereotypes, and
relentless bloodshed. A Tunisian Arab-Jewish Israeli art teacher started

the Jerusalem Circus as a place where kids physically support each other to express themselves. The Arab kids don't show up after someone in their village is killed, and Jewish kids stay away after a terrorist attack.[3] But they find their way back to each other amid a mounting death toll.

Another Israeli watches the forest burn across from his village and hears an Arab mob chanting in rage. He gathers Jewish immigrant kids from Karmiel and Palestinian kids from nearby Majd al-Krum, Bi'ina, and Deir al-Asad to form the Galilee Circus.[4] They help each other overcome fear to enact acrobatic feats, swing from a trapeze, leap on a trampoline, and juggle swords before an audience of religious and secular Arabs and Jews, Bedouin children and battered wives, disabled people and the terminally ill.

The wake of Oslo—as in the aftereffects—turned into the wake of Oslo—as in vigil over a corpse. The Accords died in the summer of 2000 at a meeting between Yasser Arafat and Ehud Barak, with US president Bill Clinton at Camp David and were buried at Taba, Egypt in 2001. Detailed accusations blamed Israel or the Palestinians for the failure. Frustration ran high when Likud leader Ariel Sharon took an incendiary walk, accompanied by a thousand security guards, above the Western Wall to the *Har Habayit* (Heb. Temple Mount) or *Haram al-Sharif* (Ar. Noble Sanctuary), the holiest site in Judaism, with three thousand years of tradition, over which seventh-century Arab conquerors built the Dome of the Rock and Al-Aqsa mosques to mark the third holiest site in Islam. Palestinian riots spread from Jerusalem to other cities in the Occupied Territories, sparking the second, or Al-Aqsa, intifada.

Prior to the uprising, in the seven years of the Oslo peace process, Palestinians had killed more Israelis than in the previous fifteen years combined, and Israelis had killed hundreds of Palestinians. In the next four years of war, deaths skyrocketed, claiming over three thousand Palestinian and one thousand Israeli lives, the vast majority those of noncombatants. Palestinians continued to employ nonviolent tactics like mass protests, daily demonstrations, and general strikes, but also turned to heavy use of force: suicide bombings, the launching of Qassam rockets and mortars, kidnappings of Israeli adults and children, shootings, stabbings, assassinations, and lynching.

Israelis responded with force that some judged excessive. They curbed Palestinians' movement with new checkpoints and curfews, attacked police and prisons, and used riot control, tear gas, rubber-coated bullets, live bullets, and "targeted killings." Israel built a massive concrete wall that it called the security fence or antiterrorist fence, and that the Palestinians called a segregation or apartheid wall. By any name, the gray winding scar seemed as much about annexing illegal settlements as about protecting Israeli citizens. The wall diminished attacks in Israel while trespassing over the Green Line and dividing Palestinian villages.

These first years of the new millennium should have been a death knell to joint nonviolence. Participants were repetitively chastened by the other's capacity for cruelty, which made encounters repulsive. It is not surprising that during the gory years of the second intifada, many joint initiatives went on hold or sank under fear and fury, overwhelmed by grassroots cries for violence. A sense of betrayal overwhelmed those who had risked their lives for peace. But it is surprising to find that Palestinians and Israelis expanded old initiatives and launched dozens of new ones separately and together.[5]

* *

## Building Civil Society

With the peace process moribund, occupation in its fourth decade, and violence increasing, joint activists moved to buttress two civil societies that they still hoped would someday live side by side in mutual respect. Nonviolent activists burrowed in for the long haul to address deeper obstacles to peace and to work out details of a negotiated settlement. New organizations focused on strengthening democratic process, leadership, law, and citizenship. Ta'ayush (Ar. living together) was a "grassroots movement of Arabs and Jews working to break down the walls of racism and segregation." They took action daily in solidarity to end the occupation and achieve "full civil equality." They demonstrated against the separation barrier, stood side-by-side in the Occupied Territories, and faced military tactics employed to disperse them. Their activism spanned agriculture, business, civil society, information technology, medicine, media, arts, and sports.[6]

Civil society activists in the areas governed by the Palestinian Authority created Tawasul (Ar. linkage) to pursue peace, democracy, and the two-state solution. They aspired to be "a catalyst of nonviolent communication between all levels of Palestinian society" and encouraged "women and youth in decision-making processes in society."[7] Other Palestinian Authority conflict resolution groups included the Palestinian Center for Alternative Solutions, the People's Campaign for Peace and Democracy, and Children of Abraham.

The Palestinian Center for Policy and Survey Research was a think tank that analyzed Palestinian-Israeli relations. It examined security issues, psychological impediments to peace, implementation of peace agreements, and mutual challenges facing both societies.[8] Palestinian academics established the Palestinian Center for Research and Cultural Dialogue to promote dialogue between cultures and to foster mutual recognition. They trained Palestinian youth to be leaders in peace building and democratic processes in a future Palestinian state.[9] The twenty-year-old Palestinian Academic Society for the Study of International Affairs, headquartered in East Jerusalem and Ramallah, and the forty-year-old Van Leer Institute in West Jerusalem asked Palestinian and Israeli scholars to compare the conflict with that in Northern Ireland.[10]

Ir-Amim (Heb. City of Peoples/Nations) was an Israeli organization that worked with Palestinian groups to strengthen civil society in East Jerusalem. It reached out to the Israeli public to promote an "equitable and stable Jerusalem," in an effort to turn the city from "a volatile flash point" to a "sustainable city whose future is determined by a negotiated process." Together they opposed the destruction of Arab homes and expansion of Israeli building, reported arrests and expulsions of Arab leaders, protested racism, and filed petitions on behalf of Palestinian children denied access to schools. Young Palestinian and Israeli filmmakers produced "Jerusalem Moments," about the complexity of daily life.[11]

A sense of emergency propelled the Palestinian and Jewish Israeli Coalition of Women for Peace to join forces with Women in Black, the TANDI Movement of Democratic Women, Women's International League for Peace and Freedom, Women for Coexistence, Noga Feminist Journal, the newer Mothers for Peace, New Profile, and Machsom Watch. At the kick-off conference in Nazareth they agreed on two states for two peoples and a just solution to the refugee problem based on UN resolutions.[12]

Palestinian lesbians in Israel formed Aswat (Ar. voices) as a safe place for lesbian, bisexual, transgender, queer, and intersex people who face triple inequalities as women, Arabs, and LBTQI people.[13] Israeli anarchists with the double-entendre name Anarchists against the Wall stood with Palestinians to face the Israeli army in efforts to block the building of the separation wall on Palestinian lands. They did not endorse a two-state solution because for anarchists two states were "two states too many."[14]

University president Sari Nusseibeh and former Shin Bet head Ami Ayalon founded the People's Voice. The Israeli-Palestinian civil initiative urged the creation of two states for two peoples, with Jerusalem as the capital of both states, and recognition of Palestinian refugees' right of return to a state of Palestine.

The Geneva Accord was a joint initiative that detailed a peace treaty based on previous negotiations, UN resolutions, the Quartet Roadmap, the Clinton Parameters, and the Arab Peace Initiative. Its media campaigns argued for the sustainability of two states.[15] Peace Now helped to create the Israeli-Palestinian Peace Coalition, which was composed of public figures who pushed for an end to occupation and the right of each people to a state with secure borders.[16]

From refugee camps to kibbutzim, the One Voice Movement sought to give expression to the "moderate majority" willing to recognize both sides' right to "independence and justice." Joint research by Palestinians and Israelis produced the Citizens Negotiation Platform, in which 180,000 people voted on ten issues of the conflict, exposing surprising areas of consensus and disparity. "Outreach programs, person-to-person recruitment, internet campaigns, and mobile voting kiosks" reached Palestinians and Israelis over the age of fifteen. Over three thousand Israelis and Palestinians went through young leadership training and, by video, urged their heads of state and two thousand dignitaries at the World Economic Forum at Davos, Switzerland, to keep the two-state solution alive.[17]

To address the gap between consensus on the details of a two-state solution and the inadequacy of the negotiating process itself, Israelis and Palestinians enlisted two internationally accomplished negotiators, Roger Fisher and Landrum Bolling, to analyze the issues that contributed to the breakdown. The Harvard Negotiation Project helped establish the Israeli Palestinian Negotiating Partners to hone skills and interest-based best practices to upgrade the process of working toward a peaceful resolution.[18]

Joint initiatives addressed the problems of segregation and inequality in the Galilee. Professional Arab and Jewish planners and architects sought to change the mainstream model of segregated areas in the Galilee to one that gave "expression to the common interests" of the two populations and remedied the need for housing in Arab communities. There were 210,000 Arabs in the region, including Muslims, Christians, Druze, and the Bedouin, in towns formed before the State of Israel. Fifty thousand Jews lived in places created in the previous forty years. Neighbors for Joint Development in the Galilee addressed inequities in land allocation for construction while working on "preserving a maximum area of green open space."[19] Mifgashim-Likaʿat (Heb./Ar. Encounters): Alternative Voice in the Galilee was an intercultural meeting place between neighboring Arab and Jewish towns. Located in the Arab village of Kaukab Abu al-Hija, the joint steering committee hosted debates, documentaries, and dialogue.[20]

At one point when tensions among Palestinians in the Galilee exploded during the intifada, Israeli police responded by killing thirteen people, including six youths. A massive outcry made the government order an investigation. In its report, the Orr Commission blamed the violence on escalating police aggression and Arab anger at discrimination. The Abraham Fund constructed a Police Relations Initiative, with cross-cultural officer training, police trainings in cooperation with Arab community leaders, Arab-Jewish problem-solving partnerships, Arabic language instruction for police, and improved protection for Arab citizens supervised by an Arab-Jewish steering committee. Next the Abraham Fund asked: Is it "possible to transform a system that estranges its Arab citizens . . . into one that promotes shared citizenship," with equal services to minority populations? Government advocacy programs educated employees and administrators about inequality and interventions.[21]

In the Negev region, Bedouin and Jewish youth lived together for one year of full-time community service in AJEEC, Arabic for "I am coming toward you" and an acronym for the Arab-Jewish Center for Equality, Empowerment, and Cooperation. It addressed the dire needs of the Negev Bedouin, the most dependent group in Israel. Interventions such as an early childhood education program empowered people and addressed violence.[22] The Citizens Accord Forum for Arabs and Jews, formed by former Knesset member Rabbi Michael Melchior, confronted inequity by gender, religion, political party, and language.[23]

## The New Media

Faced with suicide bombs and a barrier wall, people employed new digital technologies to make contact in ways previously impossible during wartime. Innovative initiatives seized new media to challenge the invisibility of joint nonviolence. Just Vision came into existence to spotlight activists on the internet and create films to increase "the power and legitimacy of Palestinians and Israelis working to end the occupation and resolve the conflict nonviolently."[24] Its commanding web presence and award-winning documentaries showcased peace builders.

The Traubman family, founders of the Jewish-Palestinian Living Room Dialogue in San Francisco in the 1990s, launched a website compiling joint nonviolent initiatives in Israel, Palestine, and beyond. Their web pages overflowed with links to organizations and resources, such as films, interviews, and activities.[25] Encounter, or Mustadafa/Mifgash in Arabic and Hebrew, was an international email list and website for networking about binational peace activities — not theoretical discussions, but actions. People around the world registered, and during the intifada the message boards sizzled with joint actions.[26]

Language Connections gathered specialists in new media to build an intercultural web-based community of learners, with dialogue between Jewish, Christian, and Muslim educators; Jews and Muslims in Tel Aviv, Jaffa, Jabal Mukkabir, and West Jerusalem; and teachers in East Jerusalem.[27] Makom Bagalil (Heb. a place in the Galilee) created a bilingual online newspaper called *Dugrinet* (*dugri* means "straight" in Arabic) to bring people in the region together around shared interests.[28]

The online journal *Bitterlemons* facilitated the civil exchange of diverse views by a broad range of participants. The cofounders were Birzeit University professor Ghassan Khatib, who directed the Palestinian Authority Government Media Center, and senior Mossad official Yossi Alper, who was former director of the Jaffee Center for Strategic Studies. They focused each issue of the journal on a different aspect of the conflict. They opened five websites in ten years, each with a different focus, such as in-depth discussion by prominent people and an international site for world perspectives.[29]

Hello Peace! was a free phone service for Palestinians and Israelis to "call over the wall" at a time when physical travel was a death-defying act. In the first month, a young Israeli woman reached Jihad, a Palestinian in Gaza. Each was surprised to find comfort amid hardships of war and challenges to their assumptions. His friends called her, and she put them in touch with her friends. Some screamed, some befriended the other, and many did both. The phone line was a response to the intifada by the bereaved parents of Parents Circle. It handled over a million calls in the next seven years.[30] One Israeli family met their Palestinian phone partners regularly at a checkpoint to bring insulin for their son.[31]

The Peace We Can website stressed the urgency of facing the psychological barriers of fear and mistrust for both peoples. Yitzhak Frankenthal, who had founded Parents Circle for bereaved parents in the 1990s, now started the Arik Institute for Reconciliation, Tolerance, and Peace, which used the internet to bring Palestinian advocates of reconciliation into the

> limelight of Israeli society (and possibly the global society), . . . to arouse Israeli and global awareness of the tragic consequences of occupation, [and for] the people to create massive pressure on leadership to make . . . peace.[32]

Community Histories by Youth in the Middle East was a digital story-telling project, brainchild of Brandeis University in Massachusetts and the Center for Digital Storytelling in California. The project's schedule inadvertently coincided with the second intifada. Jews and Arabs from Givat Haviva in Israel, Masar in Jordan, and the Palestinian House of Friendship in the areas governed by the Palestinian Authority learned to create personal narratives with story, music, and images on user-friendly technology. They met together in fall 2001, but the deteriorating conditions of the uprising limited recruitment. With Nablus under curfew and partially destroyed by a military siege, Palestinians could not travel, so they participated through the internet. Youth created videos for a collection called "Our Community: How We Live Today," in which they spoke of aspirations and problems and used children's books to deepen their conversation together.[33]

Palestinian and Israeli high school students competed for acceptance into the Middle East Education through Technology summer program supported by the Massachusetts Institute of Technology. The students acquired advanced leadership and technological skills to work for social change in their communities. Jews and Arabs who grew up a few miles from each other without the possibility of contact now entered a rigorous three-year curriculum in computer science and entrepreneurship, with active alumni networking. Hebrew University and Al-Quds Open University donated lab space.[34]

All for Peace Radio was the "longest-running independent joint Israeli-Palestinian media outlet in the Middle East," broadcasting round-the-clock to Israel and the areas governed by the Palestinian Authority. Young Palestinians and Israelis streamed programs live on the web and through Facebook, but they insisted on also broadcasting over FM radio for those without digital access. The Israeli Givat Haviva Jewish-Arab Center for Peace, the Palestinian NGO Biladi, and the *Jerusalem Times* were its joint sponsors. The station was willing to talk to everyone, even Palestinian militants and right-wing Israelis, with "cutting-edge talk shows and diverse music selection."[35]

The Israeli-Palestinian Media Forum dealt with journalists' bias in covering the crisis. Ninety editors, columnists, and reporters gathered under the joint auspices of the Palestinian International Peace and Cooperation Center and the Peres Center for Peace. Journalists established ongoing professional connections in meetings during the intifada, focusing on misperceptions and stereotypes, narrowing the information gaps on both sides, increasing objectivity in reports, and discussing coverage of issues like the separation barrier, political rumors, and the Geneva Accord.[36]

## Spiritual Seekers and Scientists

The carnage continued as spiritual seekers and scientists from opposite sides of an epistemological divide mobilized, each in their own way. Each Friday afternoon in Jerusalem, as Jews hurried to pray at the Kotel (Heb. Western Wall) and the imam preached in a mosque above it, a small group of Jews, Muslims, and Christians sat on the ground in a silent circle. Sometimes a Japanese Buddhist priest or a Sufi sheikh joined the circle, which was gathered by Eliyahu McLean, son of a Jewish mother and Christian father, grandson of a Baptist minister, who was raised in a mystical branch of Sikhism in Hawaii and reclaimed his Jewish roots at age twelve. McLean founded Jerusalem Peacemakers with Sheikh Abdul Aziz Bukhari, whose family headed the Naqshabandi Sufi order in Jerusalem for four hundred years, and Haj Ibrahim Abu El Hawa, whose family had lived on the Mount of Olives since the Umayyad Caliphate 1,300 years before. They formed a "network of independent peace-builders dedicated to reconciliation in the Holy Land."[37]

The Peacemakers joined with others to form the Sulha Project for "reconciliation of the Children of Abraham." Although *sulha* is a traditional Arab means to resolve conflict, the Sulha Project was more a product of postmodern festival culture in Israel. Over the next decade it brought together tens of thousands of Israelis, Palestinians, and Jordanians for a three-day festival of all-night music, dance, listening circles, interfaith rituals, multicultural workshops, and communal meals from Muslim, Christian, Jewish, Druze, and Bedouin traditions. If anyone slept, it was on the ground under the stars.[38]

Hundreds of Israelis and Palestinians joined an eight-day silent peace walk from Jaffa to Jerusalem. Based on Buddhist teachings, the new joint initiative, Middle Way: Compassionate Engagement in Society, tapped into the "longing felt by thousands of Jewish and Arab Israelis to find novel ways to end to the cycle of violence, hatred and fear." The silent peace walks flourished, each one ending with dialogue circles. Participants walked the West Bank, blessed by a sheikh, a rabbi, and a mayor. Middle Way fostered spiritual activism based on "love, interconnection and . . . common humanity."[39]

Violent clashes in the West Bank and Gaza made encounters dangerous or impossible. For one encounter, over half the Palestinians from Nablus, Ramallah, Hebron, and Bethlehem were denied travel permits. Others traveled through mud on foot, evading curfews and checkpoints, to reach the Nablus Youth Federation to meet Israelis from the Interfaith Encounter Association. The interreligious focus did not prevent participants from arguing about questions like, Which came first, occupation or terrorism? One Israeli woman walked out, insisting that a Palestinian video was propaganda. Two youths had just been killed in Nablus, and a Palestinian woman wanted to leave. But a Jewish woman embraced her while she mourned and raged. Palestinians watched Jews celebrate the Sabbath with song and dance. At the last session, people hugged and cried. Some had never met the enemy and were surprised at their delight once they did so. One Palestinian said that she expected people to mock and curse her, "but I don't care, I need to tell everyone I know that every Jew is not the same." Others said, "We want Israelis to know that there are lots of Palestinians who support peace, . . . [and] we want to know Jewish people."[40]

Religious activists formed the Interfaith Encounter Association with the conviction that religion could be a source of reconciliation. The core ideas of all religions could nurture a society of tolerance, understanding, and respect. Six joint study groups formed, with six hundred people engaged in interfaith dialogues. Over the decade they grew to include eight thousand Muslims, Christians, Jews, Druze, and Baha'is in Israel, with seven Palestinian organizations in the territories governed by the Palestinian Authority. They helped form the Middle East Abrahamic Forum with Egyptian, Iranian, Jordanian, Lebanese, Palestinian, Tunisian, and Turkish organizations. Weekend retreats for women and youth showed "how multiple faiths can live side by side."[41]

Israel's Christian communities included the Greek, Russian, Armenian, and Romanian Orthodox; the Maronites; Armenian and Syrian Catholics; Ethiopian Copts; the Protestant Church of Scotland; the Swedish Theological Institute; and Western Roman Catholic congregations. The Jerusalem Center for Jewish-Christian Relations engaged Israeli Jews with indigenous Christians who were not from abroad. These groups' complex relationship had been ignored. Jews had lived in the pre-seventh-century, Christian-ruled Middle East as a persecuted minority, but now Palestinian Christians were a persecuted minority under a Jewish majority. The Center combated "ignorance and prejudice" by inviting thirty Palestinian Christian and Jewish Israeli religious leaders from the Galilee to the Tantur Ecumenical Institute to probe divisive issues.[42]

On the other side of the epistemological fence, Israeli and Palestinian scientists, doctors, and health professionals took joint action. Despite war, supply shortages, restrictions on travel by Palestinian scientists, and the political polarization of researchers, the Alliance of Middle Eastern Scientists and Physicians circulated a petition by Palestinian and Israeli professionals asserting their "legitimate and reconcilable" claims to the common homeland in a peace plan to end occupation with a two-state solution.[43]

Scientists worked together across the divide. The Israeli-Palestinian Science Organization produced "high quality research in science and learning." Professors Sari Nusseibeh (Al-Quds Open University) and Menahem Yaari (Hebrew University) met at a UNESCO roundtable and mobilized the International Science Council of Nobel Laureates to fund eleven research projects by Israeli and Palestinian scientists. They eventually submitted sixty-two proposals in agriculture, medicine, biomedicine, medicinal chemistry, environment, and science education.[44]

*Bridges* was the first public health magazine produced by Israeli and Palestinian health professionals. Each issue explored adverse health repercussions of the conflict and how to address them. It highlighted the "human dimension . . . of the public health emergency" among Palestinians and sought to implement the World Health Organization's action protocols to share "health-related goals . . . among conflicting parties." This forum for research and cooperative ventures reached isolated communities and showed the impact of peace and equality on health.[45]

At the height of the violence, young Palestinians and Israelis established the first Jewish-Arab high-tech incubator in the Arab sector in Nazareth. After lobbying the Israeli government for two years for its creation, the Center for Jewish-Arab Economic Development opened New Generations Technologies as a joint venture to aid young companies. Investors, board members, and staff were Jews and Palestinians in Israel. Sobhi Saoub, a Bedouin, received a grant to research better medication for diabetes based on local plants and herbs in his laboratory in Nazareth.[46]

Water issues were core sources of cross-border tension that were often overlooked in official peace processes. Problems related to allocation, sustainable management, lack of sewage treatment, overpumping of aquifers, and excessive diversion of surface water imperiled health and peace. Environmental scientists at Friends of the Earth Middle East established Good Water Neighbors to bring Palestinians, Jordanians, and Israelis together to address these challenges. Eleven communities partnered in Israel, Palestine, and Jordan for improvements, and this number doubled after the intifada. When I visited the Friends of the Earth Palestinian office in 2005, it was a rare hub of activity in an otherwise eerily subdued Bethlehem. Scientists also built Sharhabil Bin Hassneh Eco Park just over the border in Jordan to plant indigenous flora and preserve biodiversity. They planned to eventually build cabins, picnic areas, and campsites for ecotourism.[47]

## Artists and Educators

The arts can provide a refuge from terror, a means to confront war, and a vision of a different future. Amid continual danger, artists found each other to work together. Both sides flocked to care for children in formal and informal educational programs that enabled encounter with the enemy. Martial arts, for example, empowered young people by teaching them to "fight" their enemy within a structured code of respect, humility, harmony, and self-control. Budo for Peace (Jap. stopping conflict), founded by an Australian Jewish Israeli, was a trilingual program that brought together educators, martial arts teachers, and young people from diverse socioeconomic backgrounds, including girls and youth at risk, to train the mind, body, and spirit. Sixteen martial arts clubs and instructor courses in the West Bank, Gaza, Jordan, and Israel fostered unity and shared values. Youth often trained separately, then met for matches and dialogue.[48]

Jewish and Arab young people learned to make music together, honing skills and opening hearts. The Jewish Arab Orchestra, playing since 1979, found it too dangerous to meet during the second intifada. The Jewish director and the Palestinian master conductor instead expanded work with an all-Arab youth orchestra while Israeli students studied elsewhere. Despite continual terrorist attacks, the Arab students doubled in number. Jews and Arabs reconvened in 2003, and by 2004, 120 students were playing *darbuka*, piano, oud, saxophone, *kanoun*, clarinet, violin, *bouzouki*, mandolin, accordion, and guitar. They performed throughout Jerusalem on Jewish, Muslim, and Christian holidays, directed by the prominent Palestinian Israeli director Taiseer Elias.[49] In Jaffa, the Voice of Peace Choir met in the Arab-Jewish Community Center, with Muslim, Jewish, and Christian youth. They performed diverse music in Arabic, Hebrew, and English to mixed audiences in Israel and performed for Pope Benedict during his 2009 visit to Jerusalem.[50]

In the draining final year of the intifada, the twenty-five-year-old School for Peace at Neve Shalom/Wahat al-Salam created over a hundred Arab-Jewish teacher and student encounters. Jewish and Palestinians teachers met at Bethlehem's Center for Conflict Resolution and Reconciliation; supervision was provided for senior facilitators of joint initiatives in Jordan; staff engaged in a session critiquing postmodern theories of conflict; a course was presented on "women in times of change"; Palestinian-Jewish elementary school staff received training; participants worked with Lucy Nusseibeh's Middle East Nonviolence and Democracy (MEND) in the West Bank; Arab and Jewish teachers received training for cooperation in the Negev/Naqab; solidarity tours exposed participants to the "security wall" in the West Bank towns of Jays and Azzun; youth received leadership training; women participated in a program with Nablus Youth Federation; and students from Ramla-Lod, Kfar Menachem, Tayibe, Givat Brenner, Nablus, and Birzeit, Tel Aviv, Haifa, and Hebrew universities encountered one another. Lectures were presented on "women against the wall," the role of language in conflict, the School for Peace's approach to conflict, and developmental theories of identity.[51]

Emotional devastation and tightening restrictions on Palestinian movement in the West Bank and Gaza limited most initiatives for Palestinians and Jews in Israel. Palestinian Amal Jamal, of the department of political science at Tel Aviv University, headed the new Walter Lebach Institute for Jewish-Arab Coexistence through Education. The Institute developed pedagogical methods to nurture a culture of coexistence and researched "inhibiting and facilitating factors." Palestinian social psychologist Nadim Rouhana teamed up with Jewish political scientist Yoav Peled to investigate diverse views in both communities on the right of return and irreconcilable historical narratives.[52]

The war spurred Arab and Jewish teachers to push Arabic studies. Arabic was an official language of Israel, the mother tongue of a million Palestinians in Israel, and part of the cultural roots of three million Jews of Middle Eastern descent, out of six million Jews in Israel. Arab schools mandated Arabic, English, and Hebrew study. But Jewish schools either did not offer Arabic or limited it to electives. Due to the disparity between written and spoken dialect Arabic, the Abraham Fund did extensive research to create a new curriculum for teaching "Communicative Arabic" that included spoken and literary elements.[53] The Ya Salam program began in Haifa and Karmiel and by the next decade had reached over 23,000 children in two hundred schools per year. Studies showed that the fifth and sixth graders who studied Arabic in the Ya Salam program over the next decade did not react to the Arab violence with anti-Arab attitudes as did their peers.[54]

The slopes of the Wadi Ara valley close to the Green Line was a region Israelis stereotyped as unsafe, so people from its Arab towns and Jewish agricultural communities seldom met. In the midst of increasing danger, Palestinian and Jewish parents formed Bridge over the Wadi in Palestinian Kafr Qara. They partnered with Hand in Hand, whose Galilee school remained a haven of contact amid explosive tensions. They began their new school with over a hundred students in kindergarten through third grade and added one grade per year. By the end of the decade, they had five locations with over a thousand students and three thousand community members.[55]

In a Galilean forest between the Bedouin village Ka'abiyya and the Jewish kibbutz Harduf, a small center emerged organically from encounters between young Arabs and Jews. They called the place Sha'ar La-Adam/Bab lil-Insan (Heb./Ar. gate to humanity), and they used arts and ecology to address inequality and the alienation of young people. They met for Harduf-Shefaram Theater Track for tenth and eleventh graders, Crafts Caravan, toy building, tutoring, the Forest Center, Muslim-Jewish women's events, and an annual multicultural three-day religious "Fire for Peace" festival.[56] Makom Bagalil created Neighbors to bring Jewish and Arab high school and college students into dialogue for yearlong programs on history, democracy, equality, social change, and friendship.[57]

A rich collection of archeological artifacts from ancient settlements at the Ein Dor Museum of Archaeology in northern Israel provided educational experiences for Arab, Jewish, Bedouin, and Druze youth and their teachers. The relics taught the diversity of early cultures in their land in a school-twinning three-year program for fifty Arab and Jewish elementary schools. Arab, Bedouin, Muslim, Christian, Jewish, and Cherkassy residents of the Lower Galilee participated in interactive, multilingual video-based exhibits that helped them face prejudice.[58]

Artists "who felt alienated by political activism and who sought to 'speak another language'" founded Artists without Walls. Dozens of Palestinian and Jewish Israeli artists participated in projects in the visual arts, theater, film, video, sculpture, performance art, and architecture to seek "a more human understanding of each other's societies."[59] For the first time, large groups of Israeli artists visited Ramallah on the West Bank, and Palestinian artists visited Israelis in Tel Aviv and Jerusalem. In an April 1 event they created a virtual window on both sides of the separation barrier in Abu Dis, with two closed-circuit video cameras connected to projectors to allow people on both sides to see each other. The window turned "surveillance and control technology into a spectacle," and separation into connection. During the regular protests against the separation barrier in the West Bank village of Bilin, Artists without Walls wrote anti-occupation slogans on a large mirror to hold in front of the approaching soldiers, who thus saw themselves facing an army while demonstrators saw the soldiers with anti-occupation slogans appearing to be their freedom fighters.[60]

Jewish filmmakers shot two documentaries during the second intifada that focused on joint work. *Promises* (2001) received international acclaim. It was nominated for an Oscar for Best Documentary, and won two Emmy Awards for Best Documentary and Outstanding Background Analysis. *Promises* focuses on seven Palestinian and Israeli children living twenty minutes from each other in two unequal and disconnected worlds who crossed the line to meet.[61] *Crossing the Lines* follows fifteen diverse Palestinians and Israelis, including a Palestinian legislator, a journalist, a conflict resolution center director, an Israeli city planner, a soldier and peace activist, and a rabbi.[62]

Four weeks after a major restaurant bombing in 2003 in Haifa, the Clore Neighborhood Center opened in the Ein Hayam Arab-Jewish working-class neighborhood on the shores of the Mediterranean. The Center offered opportunities that had never before been available to a population that was made up of 60 percent Muslim and Christian Arabs and 40 percent immigrants from the former Soviet Union and Mizrahi Jews who had settled in the 1950s. Services included community-powered urban renewal, leadership training for youth and adults, hip hop and oriental dance classes, football, exercise class, birthday parties for Arab and Jewish seniors, and the Arab-Jewish Walk for Fitness.[63]

On the road between Bethlehem and Jerusalem, a small abandoned house in the buffer zone became All Nations Café. Between Israeli checkpoints and areas governed by the Palestinian Authority, a Palestinian Muslim, Israeli Jew, and two internationals, one Christian and the other born to a Jewish mother and Christian father but recently converted to Islam, built a safe space that was geographically accessible to both sides. A Palestinian-Jewish-German band performed on opening night. In the following months people taught classes in *dabka*, Arabic, and cooking. Over the next decade, they created joint summer camps with bilingual theater workshops, mural painting, music, and costume parties, and they expanded to include disabled children and adults. All Nations Café toured Jordan, performing with Palestinians, Israelis, Egyptians, Syrians, and Iraqis. They held a kids camp in Sinai, joined the Arab-Hebrew theater NANA to "practice a Middle East version of Brecht's *Caucasian Chalk Circle* with Circassian dance," held a mass cleaning of the Ein Haniya nature area, and ran Arab-Jewish fairs for farmers, shepherds, and craftspeople.[64]

Jerusalem-born Armenian Kevork Alemian founded Chefs for Peace after he "watched three cooks—one Christian, one Muslim, and one Jew—work in perfect harmony in the kitchen where cooperation was essential." He saw that "the kitchen can be a dangerous place. There are all kinds of sharp knives, . . . and flames are everywhere. You work for twelve to fourteen hours straight without even a fight!" The organization modeled "cultural identity, diversity, and coexistence" through the culinary arts. The chefs agreed not to discuss politics, so they talked instead about sex and pleasure but demanded that leaders negotiate for peace. Over the next decade they grew to include thirteen chefs who cooked all over the world. Event rules required that there be a Muslim, Christian, and Jew cooking, that there be no alcohol in any dish, and that everything be kosher and halal.[65]

Palestinian and Jewish women used holistic modalities to build relationships in which they could heal from trauma caused by violence. They created safe spaces to speak out, reclaim their own and the other's humanity, and turn anger into compassion and callousness into a heart-wrenching sense of wanting to protect the other from harm. Beyond Words began with nine Arab and Jewish women working to reduce prejudice through bodywork, holistic touch, deep listening, and attention to pain. They grew in awareness of similarities, respect for differences, and a sense of strength in building a common future.[66] Circlework in Israel and Palestine sponsored encounters for women that awakened "interconnectedness and unity."[67] They worked with Creativity for Peace, where young Israeli and Palestinian women trained for "collaborative leadership and peacemaking."[68]

Experienced and newly minted social workers in Israel and Palestine were professionally committed to work with respect for all humans, but protracted violence left them reeling with fear, feelings of disgrace, and negative stereotypes of the other. To help incorporate their professional values into the harsh reality, Al-Quds and Hebrew Universities created a seminar titled Social Working Together that prepared social workers from East and West Jerusalem to approach problems with a deeper understanding of the other's suffering and aspirations.[69]

## Allies

When cross-border alliances became physically and emotionally impossible during the height of violence, there was a surge of activity by allies, individuals and groups whose work in separate societies supported the other side. Israeli women from all segments of Israeli society formed Machsom Watch to "oppose occupation and denial of rights of Palestinians to move freely in their land" (*Machsom* means "checkpoint" in Hebrew). Every day they observed, recorded, and published what happened at checkpoints in the West Bank, along the separation barrier, in "the seam line zone," on "out-of-the-way dirt roads," and in military courts. They sent reports to elected officials and the media to expose "the everyday nature of reality" under occupation.[70]

Israeli combat officers and soldiers formed Seruv (Heb. refuse). "Raised upon the principles of Zionism, sacrifice, and giving to the people . . . of Israel," they had "always served in the front lines, . . . were first to carry out any mission . . . to protect and strengthen the state."[71] Their prolonged experience in the West Bank and Gaza taught them that military action there "had nothing to do with the security of our country." Instead it "destroyed all values we absorbed growing up in this country":

> We know the Territories are not Israel. . . . We shall not continue to fight beyond the 1967 borders in order to dominate, expel, starve, and humiliate an entire people [but will] continue . . . [to] serve Israel's defense. Missions of occupation and oppression do not serve this purpose and we shall take no part in them.[72]

Jewish Israeli Eitan Bronstein took Jewish high school students on tours to Arab villages. During one such tour, a Jewish teacher talked about his part in the demolition of Arab villages during the 1948 war. Arabs living nearby told about the destruction of their villages. Bronstein founded Zochrot to teach Jews about the *Nakba*. The Hebrew word *zochrot* means "remembering," but its feminine form connotes an aspect of memory that includes the other. The group contrasted the many signposts commemorating three thousand years of Jewish history with the lack of such markings for Palestinian memory.[73]

Yafit Gamila Biso was a Jewish woman who grew up in Syria with friends from Palestinian refugee camps. She fled to Israel with her children to escape an abusive marriage. Her experience as "a second-class citizen" with restricted movement in Syria made her want to ease constrictions for Palestinians in Israel.[74] When two children from Gaza received treatment at an Israeli hospital and the family couldn't afford food or transportation, Biso brought them food and drove them home after the children's release. Humans without Borders grew out of these efforts and eventually had 250 volunteers to drive and support Palestinian families needing Israeli hospitals for treatments like dialysis. Long-term caring relationships connected humanitarian aid with peace.[75]

Palestinian allies pursued political independence in ways that publicly stood up against threats to Jewish Israeli lives. Some expressed public outrage at the brutality of anti-Semitic persecution and understood that its persistence necessitated a safe haven for Jews. Some intuited that at the heart of anti-Semitism was demonization and isolation of Jews, with the killing of Israelis as its twentieth- and twenty-first-century incarnation. Others saw that anti-Semitism targeted Jews first but hurt Palestinians as well. Palestinian allies cultivated friendship, stood up for Jewish Israelis' humanity, and denounced endangering them.

Khaled Kasab Mahameed established the first Arab holocaust museum in the world, the Institute for Holocaust Research and Education in Nazareth. The 43-year-old lawyer, husband, and father had learned of the Holocaust while studying at Hebrew University, and he realized that Arab history books omitted the Nazi genocide of six million Jews. Mahameed argued that understanding the atrocity was key to attaining Palestinian goals. The shock he experienced when he took his two children to see the twenty-foot-high concrete barrier wall compelled him to drive them to the Yad Vashem Holocaust museum. "It was very moving. I couldn't breathe." It occurred to him that "we Palestinians are victims of the terrible things that were inflicted on the Jews."[76]

Mahameed set up a one-room museum and discovered that even the militants said, "You're bringing us an atomic bomb. We need to think about this." Other times the reaction was hostile, even from his family and from Jews. Mahameed followed Gandhi's teaching that truth leads to nonviolence.[77] He made visible the invisible bludgeon of anti-Semitism that spurred Israel's militarism. "It is the obligation of all Arabs and all Muslims to understand the significance of the Holocaust, . . . [which] made its terrors a burden on the Palestinian people."[78]

Released after eighteen years in an Israeli prison, Mahmoud Al-Safadi, a former Palestinian militant in the Popular Front for the Liberation of Palestine and a combatant in the first intifada, wrote a letter to the president of Iran to express fury at his denial of the Holocaust. Not knowing about "the Nazi industry of death," he warned, was "an enormous error" that would hurt him and the Iranian people. "Millions of people in the world—among whom, alas, are innumerable Palestinians and Arabs"—also deny the Holocaust. [In prison he read books with ideas] "that our ideology . . . made inaccessible to us," including those written by Palestinian intellectuals Edward Said and Azmi Bishara, and books about racist aims to eradicate the impure races. He wrote:

> The crime is monumental. Any attempt to deny it deprives the denier of his own humanity and sends him to the side of torturers . . . [To] divide the world into two camps: imperialist-Zionists and the adversaries of imperialism who know the truth and uncover the plot . . . [is] a great disservice to popular struggles the world over. . . . Negation of the Holocaust as an expression of support for Palestinians . . . [is] a mistake. . . . [There can be] neither victory nor independence without knowledge of the genocide perpetrated against the Jewish people.[79]

At the height of violence, Father Emil Shufani, the archimandrite of the Greek Catholic Church in Nazareth said, "There is no chance for true dialogue and reconciliation unless we [Arabs] have an in-depth understanding of . . . the Holocaust, unless we touch the suffering, the memory, the terminology."[80] He organized seminars for Palestinians and Jews from Israel to study the Holocaust and to visit the Auschwitz-Birkenau death camp in Poland. Nazir Majli, a journalist and Shufani's colleague in the project, was asked "Why are you going to Auschwitz when the Israelis are killing our children in Jenin?" He replied, "I'm out to cleanse myself and my people of the hatred that exists today." He traveled to Cairo to gain the support of intellectuals and the foreign minister.[81]

Some Palestinian allies understood that if you isolated the Israeli people, if you didn't reach for those that could be allies, then the suffering of both peoples would intensify. The British higher education union barred Israeli faculty from academic conferences and joint research in response to Palestinian complaints about Israeli government actions during the intifada. Sari Nusseibeh opposed the U.K.-led boycott against Israeli academics. He urged "cooperation based on mutual respect rather than boycotts or discrimination." Nusseibeh argued that boycotts could not work because "peace must be built on the bridge between two civil societies."[82] He argued that "If we are to look at Israeli society, it is within the academic community that we've had the most progressive pro-peace views and . . . [people] seeing us as equals." Nusseibeh told the U.K. to protest occupation's effects on Palestinian academia by supporting the joint research of the Israeli-Palestinian Science Organization.[83]

George Sa'adeh, a high school principal in Bethlehem, was driving home from the supermarket with his wife and daughters when Israeli soldiers opened fire on their car and killed his twelve-year-old daughter. The next year, he joined hundreds of Israeli and Palestinians families in the bereaved Parents Circle Families Forum. He reflected:

> The hardest part was to meet with people from the other side despite all the pain they caused us. It was difficult to clear our hearts of hatred, have a clear conscience and face the other side with forgiveness. It isn't easy to control ourselves; this requires strong determination, deep belief and a high level of forgiveness.[84]

Feminist peace leader Gila Swirsky attended an antiwar demonstration with ten thousand Jews and Arabs in Tel Aviv. Signs there read: "There is a limit," "Soldiers who refuse to serve the occupation," "The occupation is killing all of us," "Dismantle Settlements," and "Share Jerusalem." She described a poignant moment of

> transformation of a beloved Zionist song, *Ein li eretz aheret*. Reciting this song in two languages, Hebrew and Arabic, suddenly infused it with new meaning: "I have no other country to go to. And even if the land is burning under my feet, this is my home."[85]

As the second intifada drew to a close, four Palestinians and four Israelis flew to the tip of Latin America. They set sail through the Straits of Magellan, across six hundred miles of "the wildest sea on Earth," to trek the perilous glaciers of Antarctica. "Breaking the Ice" took them eight thousand miles from their homeland to scale an icy mountain peak 9,090 feet above sea level. Some of the Israelis had served in elite commando units, one was a right-wing lawyer, and one was a former cow herder who had trekked from her tiny village in Ethiopia to Israel via Sudan when she was an illiterate fourteen-year-old. Some of the Palestinians had spent years in Israeli prison, some were from Fatah, one had lost a brother to a killing by the Israel Defense Forces; and one was the only Palestinian woman on the Israeli national volleyball team. They received death threats before they left home, and they fought over politics as they ascended the mountain. Roped together on sheer ice cliffs, they took responsibility for each other's survival in near-zero visibility. Tense political interactions cleared at the summit as the climbers won new understanding of "what we as Israelis and Palestinians are capable of doing when we set our minds to it."[86]

* *

When Yasser Arafat died in November 2004 after leading his people for almost four decades, the second intifada had largely collapsed. Two months later, Mahmoud Abbas won an election that was boycotted by Hamas and Islamic Jihad. President Abbas and Prime Minister Sharon signed a cease-fire that was honored by the rejectionists. In August 2005, the Sharon Plan ordered Israel's unilateral withdrawal from Gaza. The Israel Defense Forces removed the settlers and remaining occupation forces from there and from four settlements in the West Bank.

Gaza was finally free of Israeli occupation. The United States, the European Union, and the United Nations lauded Sharon's bold move. But Israelis feared it would intensify terrorism. The Palestinian Authority welcomed the withdrawal of Israeli troops and settlers from its territories. But Palestinians saw unilateral action as a way to sidestep negotiations for an independent Palestinian state. Previous peace accords with Egypt and Jordan had been bilateral. Unilateral disengagement could not move a peace process forward. Some Israelis and Palestinians and their supporters criticized the withdrawal as a flagrant repudiation of Oslo, Geneva, and Roadmap proposals.

The Israeli media portrayed the peace movement as dead and its supporters as murderers. It was inconceivable that joint nonviolent initiatives continued amid the bloody siege of the second intifada and the fourth decade of occupation. It was always hardest to maintain contact when one's own people were dying from the other people's fire. Tightening repression in the West Bank and Gaza made Palestinian border crossings and internal travel for joint work almost impossible.

Palestinians and Israelis did turn inward to focus energy on building the pluralistic, egalitarian foundations of their own separate civil societies. But they also used new online social media to leap tall physical, political, and psychological barriers with virtual contact. Countless old and new joint initiatives combated militarism, racism, sexism, anti-Semitism, and poverty. Children and young women, artists and anarchists, lesbians and chefs, educators and psychologists, spiritual seekers and scientists, Bedouin and Druze, and neighbors from forbidden villages built up schools, technologies, the arts, medical care, democracy, and detailed peace treaties. Their actions touched every facet of life.

More Israelis than ever before understood that occupation strangled Palestinians, guaranteed no peace for Israel, and corrupted their country's ideals. More Palestinians than ever before understood that violence could not deliver statehood. Together they renewed their commitment daily to tackle what was unacceptable and to create a different life together.

I visited Israel and Palestine in the summer of 2005, two weeks before Israel withdrew from Gaza, to interview Palestinians and Israelis about their joint initiatives dating back before the second intifada. But all they wanted to talk about was their meeting yesterday and the one planned for tomorrow. They were brimming with anticipation for beginning anew. They were alive with the tough work of constructing a world for two peoples to live in dignity, equality, and security, with no more children sacrificed.

## CHAPTER 9

# Co-Resistance: 2005–2008

*As a child I fought the occupation. . . . At age twelve . . . a boy was shot by a soldier. . . . From that moment I developed a deep need for revenge. . . . We threw stones and . . . [then] hand-grenades. . . . In prison, . . . as we were beaten, . . . I decided to try and understand who the Jews were. This led to conversation with a prison guard, . . . dialogue and friendship. . . . He even became a supporter of the Palestinian struggle. . . . This transformation . . . made me realize the only way to peace was through nonviolence.*

BASSAM ARAMIN, FORMER TERRORIST, COMBATANTS FOR PEACE, 2010[1]

*I was brought up . . . to defend our country [against] another Holocaust. . . . I took part in hundreds of military operations. . . . The turning point for me came . . . at three in the morning . . . [when we went] to arrest a suspected suicide bomber. Everyone was forced out, . . . a young woman carrying a baby followed by her 7-year-old daughter. Suddenly this young girl started running towards me. I had seconds to decide whether she was about to blow herself up or . . . was just a terrified child.*

ZOHAR SHAPIRA, FORMER COMMANDO, COMBATANTS FOR PEACE, 2010[2]

These stories were the weapons wielded by Combatants for Peace. When former Palestinian terrorists began meeting in secret with former Israeli soldiers, they felt that they were meetings between "true enemies." The men described their violent actions and the turning points that made them realize the futility of force to end their peoples' suffering. They declared: "We refuse to take part any more in the mutual bloodletting. We will act only by nonviolent means so that each side will come to understand the national aspirations of the other." Then in 2007, Aramin's ten-year-old daughter, Abir, was shot by an Israeli soldier while standing with classmates outside her school. He could have turned back to "hatred and ven-geance" but discovered that there was "no return from dialogue." He af-firmed, "One Israeli soldier shot my daughter, but one hundred former Israeli soldiers built a garden in her name."[3]

Exhaustion and depression permeated both sides after the more than four taut years of danger and death of the second intifada. An indepen-dent Palestinian state and security for Israel seemed more elusive than ever. The cease-fire signed by Ariel Sharon and Mahmoud Abbas led to a decrease in but not a cessation of violence. Israel's unilateral withdrawal from Gaza undermined the Palestinian Authority's power by increasing Hamas's authority. The George W. Bush administration pressured Israeli prime minister Ehud Olmert to go against the advice of his generals and enter into a second war with Lebanon to cripple Hezbollah. It was a clas-sic case of the United States setting up Israel to do its dirty work against Israel's own interests.[4] Hamas won the 2006 Palestinian Authority par-liamentary elections, and Fatah maintained controlled of the executive branch. Fighting between Hamas and Fatah led to the takeover of Gaza by the former and consolidation of control over the West Bank by the latter. Hamas launched rocket attacks on Israel, and Israel bombed Gaza, killed Hamas leaders, set up a blockade, built more settlements in the West Bank, and lengthened the separation barrier.

Battered by terrorism and military force, shattered by the loss of loved ones, captive to the Israeli mantra that there was no one to talk to on the other side, and targeted by Palestinian antinormalization messages that joint work meant capitulation, diplomatic peace processes evaporated. Hamas's commitment to armed struggle against Israel as an illegitimate state led to a decrease in foreign aid to Palestinians. A worldwide eco-nomic downturn attenuated the European Union's fiscal support for joint initiatives.

Yet commitment to nonviolence continued to spread in both societies. Palestinians developed civil society organizations to undergird an inde-pendent state, sometimes with their Israeli supporters. Israelis worked in their country to confront racism and inequality and to end occupation and settlement expansion, in cooperation with Palestinians. Together they practiced co-resistance to the political, economic, and social status quo in joint businesses, schools, medical clinics, and activism; they painted, composed, performed stand-up comedy, made films, and uttered painful truth to power. The persistence of these subversive encounters collec-tively rejected failed diplomacy, militant religious ultranationalism, anti-democratic forces on both sides, and pursuit of independence that disregarded interdependence. One young Palestinian activist observed onstage, amid a rousing performance by a Palestinian-Israeli rock band, "What you see here on stage is not the reality back home. . . . We need to co-resist before we co-exist."[5]

* *

### Repairing Rights, Restoring Lives

During the second intifada Israel reoccupied parts of the West Bank that had gained autonomy under the Oslo Accords. Joint organizations addressed the war's legacy of shredded human rights. Israeli activists worked to protect Palestinian rights under occupation. Yesh Din (Heb. there is law) aimed for "long-term structural improvement" by pressuring authorities to remedy violations and by reporting them in the media to encourage debate. They appealed to Hamas to end the inhuman, illegal treatment of the kidnapped Israeli soldier Gilad Shalit, who had been held in isolated captivity for over five years.[6] Jews and Arabs formed Gisha ("access" or "approach") as the legal center for freedom of movement, with a focus on Gaza. After Israel's unilateral disengagement from Gaza, Israeli authorities held onto control in ways that Gisha monitored as violations of the rights to life, medical care, education, livelihood, family unity, and freedom of religion. Jews and Arabs worked together to insist that Israel abide by human rights laws.[7]

Local leaders of the Palestinian peace camp taught democracy, fought corruption, and demanded adherence to human rights in their own society. Al-Tariq (Ar. the way) was a grassroots institute for development and democracy that educated Palestinians about nonviolence. Their motto came from Martin Luther King: "Returning violence for violence multiplies violence, adding deeper darkness to a night already devoid of stars." They conducted a Young Leaders' Summer Academy program, nonviolence workshops, and joint youth leadership training for reconciliation, with trauma education.[8]

The Peres Center for Peace organized medical initiatives to meet the increasing demands of a growing population on the Palestinian health care system. To address the lack of residency opportunities for Palestinian doctors, the center created fellowships and trainings in Israeli hospitals for a range of specialties and subspecialties. A pediatric hematology-oncology unit supported an independent Palestinian center for the diagnosis and treatment of Palestinian children with cancer, particularly blood and lymph cancer, in cooperation with an Israeli hospital. Israeli and Palestinian youth learned first aid and the seven principles of international humanitarian law together.[9]

Arabs and Jews donated bone marrow to save each other's lives. Amal Bishara, a Palestinian woman from Israel with a doctorate in microbiology and immunology, established the only registry in the world for Arab bone marrow donors in Jerusalem's Hadassah Medical Center. After founding the project in 2008, Bishara visited over sixty Arab towns to further her research, educate others, and network to gather nine thousand Arab donors, enabling six transplants. Her work addressed the high percentage of Arab children with hereditary diseases due to consanguineous marriages.[10]

Midwives for Peace sought to ensure a "joyous and safe" childbirth "despite the armed conflict raging around" the mothers giving birth, and to "save lives by providing critical pre-natal care and childbirth support."[11] Jewish Israeli and West Bank Palestinian certified birth professionals worked together for four years before they began talking to each other and the birthing mothers about their own lives, living under occupation or with terrorist attacks. They incorporated international best practices into a dual commitment to their profession and to peace. Israeli midwives also worked with Sudanese and Eritrean women refugees.[12] Madre and Circle of Health provided training and links to a global network of midwives working in war-torn regions.

When Hezbollah bombs fell on Nazareth, very few people had access to bomb shelters. Palestinian activist Nabila Espanioly called an emergency meeting at her Al-Tafula Childhood Center to launch an education campaign for a public alarm system with an Arab-language radio station. In conjunction with Shatil, Al-Tafula produced over six thousand stress-relief kits that sixty volunteers distributed in fifty-four towns, with ten thousand packs of school supplies and trauma manuals.[13]

Wounded Crossing Borders brought together angry hardcore nationalists. When the Palestinians finally arrived at one meeting, their leader, Sulaiman Khatib, bitterly ranted about the humiliation and endless waiting at multiple army checkpoints. "What is this f***ing Russian . . . doing here? We were born here but we have no freedom."[14] His Israeli co-leader mirrored Khatib's words about the Russian immigrant soldier at the checkpoint, repeating them to the larger group, and asked Khatib if he had captured his meaning correctly. Khatib said yes. Then Arabs and Jews paired off to speak and mirror. Like the Israeli founder, David Shilo, each one had perpetrated violence. For Khatib, Israeli prison was his "university," where he read King, Gandhi, and Jewish history, but he didn't really know any Israelis until the Palestinian-Israeli trip to Antarctica. Since then he had worked ceaselessly for reconciliation. Palestinian Carol Daniel Kasbari, a professional facilitator for dialogue groups, listened to hundreds of stories of loss and despair, and she saw change happen when people crossed emotional and physical borders to listen to the unconvinced.[15]

Aziz Abu Sarah's brother died after being imprisoned and tortured. Abu Sarah grew up angry, refusing to learn Hebrew until he had to for the sake of a job. In his Hebrew classes, the stories of survival of his Jewish classmates challenged everything he believed. Dedicated to using personal stories to help people gain new understanding, he founded Mejdi, a tour company for social change that presented dual narratives, allowing people to hear the other's story, and promoted Palestinian business and reconciliation. The travelers stayed in Palestinian homes, even in refugee camps, but also went clubbing in Ramallah and Tel Aviv.[16]

## Economies for Equality

Cross-border business initiatives addressed the devastating effects on the Palestinian economy of occupation, the second intifada, and the worldwide recession. Political analyst Muhammad Daraghmeh reported that 90 percent of Gazan strawberry and cherry tomato growers began to meet European agricultural production standards when the Palestine Trade Center (Paltrade) teamed up with the Israeli-Palestinian Center for Research and Information (IPCRI). Coordinator Muhammad Hamlawi remarked:

> Politics aside, Israeli agricultural expertise is an important source
> for developing agriculture in Palestine. In addition to being the most
> advanced, it is the closest. If IPCRI . . . provide[s] permits for our teams
> to enter Israel . . . [for] research and training, this will be very important
> for us.[17]

Paltrade also worked with the Peres Center on business-to-business events and private sector plans, publishing joint papers on obstacles to and avenues for trade.[18]

Green Action was an Israeli environmental and social change organization that worked with Palestinian farmers on the West Bank to set up agricultural cooperatives and help them to achieve organic, fair-trade certification. Products packaged under the SAHA label (Heb. acronym for fair trade and Ar. for good health) included olive oil, za'atar, *dibbes*, jam, and herbal teas. To help meet the threat to Palestinian farmers' livelihood created by the separation barrier, farmers created the Zaytun Cooperative and worked with Green Action to produce fair-trade organic olive oil.[19] Green Action also worked with the Jerusalem Community Kitchen to help low-income women run food businesses, and with the Women's Association of Wadi Fukin to plant gardens for making pickles.[20]

Sindyanna means "Palestine Oak," a symbol of the endurance, stability, and rootedness of Palestinian citizens of Israel who did not leave in 1948. Sindyanna of the Galilee was a women-led agricultural association committed to social change. Founded in 1996, it moved from a tiny room in the village of Majd al-Krum, to a bigger and more modern warehouse located in Kafr Kanna. It expanded its support for olive industry growers and producers from the Galilee and the territories governed by the Palestinian Authority on the basis of the principles of land preservation, environmentalism, and fair trade. Its olive oil, za'atar, soaps, carob, honey, almonds, and baskets were part of the Fair Trade Fair Peace project, with partners such as the Bethlehem Fair Trade Artisans.[21] Peace Oil was an extra virgin olive oil produced by Jews, Druze, Arabs, and the Bedouin in conjunction with the London-based company Radius Works.[22]

The Center for Jewish-Arab Economic Development still thrived after twenty-five years, engaging in field activity from the Negev to the Galilee to help Palestinian women establish over 1,800 small businesses employing over four thousand women. The Jasmine Project provided women-owned businesses from all ethnic communities in Israel with access to finance. Across the border they joined with the Palestinian Media and Development Institute and the Jerusalem Women's Association to expand women's employment opportunities. Arab businesspeople benefitted from Arab investors and scientists participating in joint businesses, and Naqab Bedouin benefited from a Regional Council for Unrecognized Villages.[23]

The Negev Institute for Strategies of Peace and Development (NISPED), in association with the Arab-Jewish Center for Equality, Empowerment, and Cooperation (AJEEC), facilitated joint initiatives. The Bedouin partnered with Shorouq (Ar. dawn), a Palestinian society for women in the territories governed by the Palestinian Authority, to promote rural development in Palestine by helping women start businesses. Young and old, married and single women studied goat-raising, cattle-raising, greenhouse vegetable production, hairdressing, and photography. NISPED and the Young Entrepreneurs of Palestine partnered to train over eighty women in product development, handicrafts, marketing, and management in the West Bank and Israel. Entrepreneurs founded the

Negev Arab Businessmen's Forum to represent the region to the government, receive funds from Israeli banks, and implement projects.[24]

Unemployment rates were 19 percent for Israeli Jewish women ages twenty-five to thirty-four and 73 percent for Israeli Arab women of the same age. To combat the double discrimination against Arab women in Israel, who earned less than their peers both as Arabs and as women, the Abraham Fund launched an economic development venture, the Sharikat Haya (Ar. partnership for life) Arab Women's Employment Initiative, to provide training and job placement. It advocated policies that fostered greater integration and equal employment opportunities for women ages 20 to 50 without university degrees.[25] Over the next decade the initiative combated poverty, raised the status of Arab women in their families and in the country, and provided business and government with "replicable social change models that holistically address" socioeconomic inequalities.[26] Arabs and Jews managed another initiative, the Kav Mashve (Heb. equator), an Israeli Equal Opportunity Initiative, which raised employment among Arab university graduates, whose numbers had recently grown tenfold.[27]

## Communities across the Divide

In the small rural region of Gilboa, Israel, 40 percent of the thirty thousand inhabitants were Arab, and 60 percent were Jewish. The head of Gilboa's Regional Council was a Jew, and the deputy was an Arab. They could have split the regional governing body into two councils like other towns had done. Instead, they asked themselves, "If we can't live together in a regional council, how will we live together in a country?"[28] They initiated an annual Bible-Quran contest for teens. Twelve teams each had a Jew and an Arab contestant answer questions in Hebrew and Arabic about their holy books, and they were judged by a mixed team of teachers.

Across the border, the town of Jenin in the northern West Bank suffered intense violence. During the second intifada, the Israel Defense Forces responded to a slew of suicide bombings in Israel by leveling part of the town in a massacre. Then, in 2005, the army evacuated four Jewish settlements near Jenin to reduce friction. Armed militants used Jenin's hospital as a dorm until 2007. The governor, Musa Qadoura, had spent time in Israeli prison and was a recognized Fatah leader. Now he built relationships with Israeli Daniel Atar and Palestinian Eid Salem of Gilboa.

The three met frequently to plan economic cooperation projects. This opened the way for Israeli authorities to give daily permits to some Israeli Arabs to bring supplies from Israel to be made into clothing in Jenin. Israeli Palestinians began attending university in Jenin. The government removed key checkpoints to allow for more natural movement and issued new visas and building permits. By the end of the decade the three leaders had launched joint tourism projects, and the checkpoint turned into an ordinary border crossing.[29] They planned joint health care projects and an industrial center, but in 2012 when Palestinian assailants opened fire on Qadoura's house, Qadoura died of a heart attack.

The village of Barta'a straddled the border created in 1948, the western half in Israel and the eastern half in the West Bank. The new separation barrier cut the residents of East Barta'a off from their lands, families, medical care, schools, livelihoods, and services. With the support of the Jewish-Arab Middle Way, the Palestinian Authority allocated a building in East Barta'a to house a holistic family medical clinic that held classes and Arab-Jewish meetings. Middle Way also arranged for access to an Israeli hospital. Free weekly treatments in the clinic included homeopathy, reflexology, chiropractic care, and reiki. Palestinians from Israel taught Hebrew and Jews listened to Arabs' trauma.[30]

In Northern Israel, the mixed city of Acre erupted in violence on Yom Kippur, the Jewish holy day focused on forgiveness and compassion. Palestinian resident and media personality Zouheir Bahloul attributed the violence to the powerlessness of segregation. In response, he founded the Acre Group for Joint Living. Israelis, Palestinians, and immigrants from Ethiopia and Russia hammered out their vision for a truly shared city with the mayor, municipal departments, and schools.[31]

Far to the south, the 24,000 residents of Sederot lived within a mile of the Gaza border. It had been built in the 1950s as a temporary refugee camp for Jews from Kurdistan and Iran, and later from Morocco and Romania. Since the intifada, Gazans had targeted them with Qassam rockets. As attacks intensified, residents from Israeli border communities formed Other Voice, a grassroots citizen initiative for a "civilian solution to the conflict." They contacted Gazans to call for an end to the siege on noncombatants from both sides. Thousands of Israelis, Palestinians, and internationals met in weekend gatherings, held a peace conference, and participated in Israeli-Gazan youth seminars. Media campaigns pushed for a long-term cease-fire, opposed the blockade on Gaza, and donated medical and humanitarian aid.[32]

## Antiwar Arts

The Museum on the Seam stood between East and West Jerusalem in what had been an army outpost when the city was divided. In 2005 it was turned into a "socio-political contemporary art museum" with exhibits on human rights, like "Dead End," dealing with violence in the social fabric; "Equal and Less Equal," on work, slavery, globalization, and migration; and "Bare Life," on disintegration of the boundary between the normal and abnormal when temporary emergency turns into the status quo. "HeartQuake" exposed the anxieties of injurers and the injured; "HomeLessHome" explored the relationship between the private home and the state; and "Right to Protest" looked at ideology and creativity.[33]

Palestinian and Israeli photojournalists met at the Peres Center for Peace to learn how their work perpetuated stereotypes and exacerbated hostility. "Frames of Reality" was an exhibit of photographs that a pair of Arab and Jewish photographers took of each other's worlds and grew out of their ongoing dialogue. Seventy photojournalists worked together for several years, producing three books that sold thousands of copies around the world.[34]

Thirty Palestinian Arab and thirty Jewish Israeli women from all walks of life told about their "practical approaches" to peacemaking in Arabic, Hebrew, and English. Sixty lifetimes of "struggle, spirit, and sheer leaps of faith" wove a tapestry of "mutual destiny" in a luminous photo essay and video about women activists. Patricia Smith Melton, founder of Peace X Peace women's organization, created the book *Sixty Years, Sixty Voices* to honor their achievements on the sixtieth anniversary of Israel and the *Nakba*.[35]

The Jewish Arab Ensemble at the Safed College Ethnic Music Academy performed *Maqam Dulab Hijaz*, directed by Jewish Israeli Eliana Gilad. Palestinian Muslims, Christians, Druze, and Jews played classical Arabic music together. Palestinian Israeli Taseer Elias was head of Arabic music at the Jerusalem Academy for Music and Dance. As founder of the Jewish Arab Ensemble, he conducted ten Palestinians and Jews performing classical Arabic and Middle Eastern music.[36]

Wassim Bashara, born in the Arab village Tarshiha in Israel, played in classical Arab and Israeli music and theater productions. He founded the band Sahana with Arabs and Jews to perform throughout Israel, as well as at the Ramallah Summer Festival, which hosted ethnic bands from around the world. With Argentinian Israeli artist Pablo Ariel they created and performed the play *Neighbours* at the Galilee Multicultural Theater.[37]

Tamer Nafer was a nationally celebrated Palestinian hip hop artist who grew up in the mixed Arab-Jewish city of Lod surrounded by poverty. His first album, *Stop Using Drugs*, opened dialogue about problems in his community. Shatil backed his production of "Born Here," about civil rights. His band, DAM (Heb./Ar. blood), went on a mixed-cities concert tour with Jewish and Arab musicians.[38]

"Your ribs didn't hurt when he was beating you from inside," said the biological mother. The older adoptive mother broke down, "I taught him to eat, to walk, to speak, and to love." One of the most challenging events to mark Israel's sixtieth anniversary was Cameri Theater of Tel Aviv's production in Hebrew of the play *Return to Haifa*, adapted from the novella *Returning to Haifa*, by the prominent twentieth-century Palestinian writer Ghassan Kanafani. The mixed Arab and Jewish cast portrayed the wrenching struggle between a Holocaust-survivor adoptive mother of a young soldier and his Palestinian refugee biological mother, who arrives with her husband to reclaim the son they abandoned in 1948. The actor playing the biological father was from a Palestinian refugee family.[39]

Tensions between Arab and Jewish actors reached a boiling point in rehearsals for Mohammad el-Thaher's bilingual play *Six Actors in Search of a Plot*, inspired by Luigi Pirandello's play *Six Characters in Search of an Author*. The director, Billy Yalowitz, called in an Arab and a Jewish midwife to help them with the play's theme of childbirth. Thaher's script took lines written by Arab and Jewish teens of Peace Child Israel, a joint initiative that used theater to cultivate tolerance, to explore how we distort truth. Almost every line sparked real arguments between the actors. Both sides felt attacked, "unwilling to give up their . . . [version of] history. It's their weapon," said Thaher. They performed in Qalansua, Umm al-Fahm, and various kibbutzim.[40]

"A Palestinian flew from Chicago back to Jerusalem on El Al, Israel's airline. The bathroom door didn't say 'occupied' but 'disputed territories.'" That's a line from Palestinian Ray Hanania's comedy routine. Hanania continues, "Alan Dershowitz escorted him back to his seat explaining why it had to be given away to someone else." Hanania cofounded the Israeli-Palestinian Comedy Tour with Israeli comedian Charley Warady. Both of them are from Chicago's South Side. They were joined by Aaron Freeman, an African-American convert to Judaism, and Yisrael Campbell, a Catholic convert to a Hasidic Jewish sect on stages across Israel and Palestine, making people laugh about racism, anti-Semitism, terror, and occupation.[41]

Arabs and Jews made documentaries and feature films about cross-border contact. The 2005 award-winning documentary *Knowledge Is the Beginning*, directed by Paul Smaczny of Germany, details the artistic collaboration between Palestinian-American Columbia University professor Edward Said and Argentinian-Israeli conductor Daniel Barenboim that birthed the West-Eastern Divan Orchestra. Young Arabs and Jews from Palestine, Israel, Syria, Lebanon, Jordan, and Egypt rehearsed and performed Western classical music in Weimar, Seville, Jerusalem, and Ramallah. The film exposes the prejudices of the young musicians and the power of music making to help confront and transcend them. Said and Barenboim believed that the orchestra was a metaphor for what could be achieved in the Middle East.

*Paradise Now*, directed by Hany Abu-Assad and released in 2005, focuses on two West Bank friends on a suicide-bombing mission to Tel Aviv. It won a Golden Globe Award and was nominated for an Academy Award. The film crew faced a land mine explosion in the West Bank, an Israeli helicopter missile attack, and the kidnapping of their location manager by a Palestinian faction. In a *Tikkun Magazine* interview, Abu-Assad said that if he'd grown up in the West Bank he might have been a suicide bomber. What gave him hope was

> the conscience of the Jewish people. The Jews have been the conscience of humanity, always, wherever they go. Not all Jews, but part of them. Ethics. Morality. They invented it! I think Hitler wanted to kill the conscience of the Jews, the conscience of humanity. But this conscience is still alive.[42]

*West Bank Story*, directed by Ari Sandel and also released in 2005, is a twenty-minute musical comedy that won the Academy Award for the best live-action short film in 2006. It is a *West Side Story* parody with campy slapstick about two lovers from rival Palestinian and Israeli fast-food falafel joints. *The Haifa War Diary—Eli and Nasser*, directed by Gili Shapira and Avishai Kfir and released in 2006, is a thirty-five–minute documentary about the summer of 2006, when Hezbollah rained missiles on Haifa and residents were holed up in "safe rooms." Eli Levy, a Jewish radio journalist, and Nasser Nasser, a Palestinian photojournalist, raced through the streets of Haifa, making the trauma visible.

A former Israeli settler, a Palestinian ex-prisoner, a bereaved Israeli mother, and a wounded and bereaved Palestinian brother are the focus of *Encounter Point*, directed by Ronit Avni and Julia Bacha and released in 2006. It documents how they confront and transcend anger and grief within themselves and surrounding them in their respective societies, with commitments to nonviolence as a means of redressing grievances. It is one of several powerful films produced by Just Vision.

*Refusing to Be Enemies: The Zeitouna Story*, directed by Laurie White and released in 2007, documents twenty-four months of dialogue among twelve ordinary American-based Arab and Jewish women, including survivors of the Holocaust and the *Nakba*, who spoke of the "devastating complexities" of their histories. They slowly came "to be able to hear the voice of the 'other'—her pain and her joy" as it mirrored their own. The Zeitouna sisters, as the participants called themselves, then went to Israel and Palestine, where they became "living proof of how the journey of personal transformation may pave the way to socio-political transformation."[43]

*Waltz with Bashir* is an animated full-length feature film directed by Ari Folman and released in 2008 about Folman's experience as a soldier during Israel's 1982 Lebanon War and the massacre of Palestinians in the Sabra and Shatila refugee camps by Christian militias as Israelis looked away. The animation mixes dreams with distorted memories in a nightmare of war that explores Folman's subjective truth in an outcry against violence. The *New York Times* called the film a "unique, exemplary work of astonishing aesthetic integrity and searing power."[44]

*Lemon Tree*, directed by Eran Riklis and released in 2008, is a feature film based on the true story of a Palestinian widow's legal efforts to stop her new next-door neighbor, the Israeli defense minister, from destroying her family's lemon grove. The defense minister's wife had a complex relationship with the Palestinian widow, who took her grievance to the Israeli Supreme Court. The movie was filmed in West Bank villages and refugee camps with Israeli and Palestinian actors.

## For Young People: Long-Term Initiatives

The lion's share of nonviolent joint initiatives primarily reached children. The bottom line of grown-up risk-taking for peace was an urgency to save the next generation from trauma, loss, violent threat, and statelessness. There was hope that early relationships with people from the other side would nurture a generation for whom mutual recognition was natural. Building skills and befriending the enemy enabled the development of perspectives otherwise unimaginable under daily segregation, humiliation, and danger. Decades-old joint organizations expanded their reach to connect children with the enemy through study, sports, community service, and the arts from kindergarten through college.

By 2005, the twenty-year-old Neve Shalom/Wahat al-Salam had grown to fifty-four Arab and Jewish families who could equally express their national and religious identities. Its bilingual primary and junior high school had grown to an enrollment of three hundred students in kindergarten through eighth grade and had added an adult women's department. Youth encounter workshops reached thirteen thousand teenagers and adults to address difficult social and political realities on the basis of personal experience. Using Hebrew and Arabic in all workshops slowed the pace of discussion but raised awareness of the potency and provocative nature of word choices.[45]

Seeds of Peace had reached over four thousand young people in its fifteen-plus years of summer programs in Maine. It held year-round regional activities, and alumni worked to train leaders in Amman, Cairo, Gaza, Jerusalem, Ramallah, Tel Aviv, and beyond. The Seeds engaged in ongoing dialogues, conferences, and professional opportunities. They honed communication and negotiation skills and worked in international affairs, politics, business, medicine, nonprofits, and media.[46]

For over twenty years Sadaka-Reut's Building a Culture of Peace project coupled Palestinian and Israeli teenagers in two-year programs to address fear, racism, and segregation. In 2006 they founded Markaz (Ar. center) in Jaffa for political education and activism toward "a joint struggle to build a different future." Community in Action was a yearlong leadership project to develop a binational community of young activist high school graduates and university students working on social justice. They worked with over five thousand students to challenge behavior regarding inequality.[47]

After ten years, Yad be'Yad (Heb. hand in hand) schools thrived in the Galilee, Wadi Ara, and Kafr Qara. They opened a new permanent campus in Jerusalem, located between Arab and Jewish neighborhoods and serving 530 students. Muslims, Arab and Armenian Christians, and secular and religious Jews studied together. Their families were socioeconomically diverse, with parents ranging from doctors to cab drivers.[48]

Jewish, Muslim, and Christian children sang "Jingle Bells" in Arabic and Hanukkah songs in Hebrew, and they ate a potluck meal for Iftar at the end of a Ramadan fast organized at the Jerusalem International YMCA "peace kindergarten." Words and numbers in Hebrew and Arabic mixed with Russian and Amharic for refugee children from Sudan and Eretria.

The preschool, established in 1981, was part of the YMCA's commitment to interfaith and interracial support. They rejected the melting-pot model to create "a coexistence of diversities."[49]

Students exploded in violence in "Roadblock," a play written and performed by teens from the Arabic Qalansua High School and the Hebrew Maʿayan-Shacher School. For eighteen years, Peace Child Israel helped Palestinian and Jewish Israeli teens delve into the challenges of coexistence through theater arts, role-playing, reverse role-playing, collage, movement, and improvisation. They learned "compassionate listening, critical thinking and nonviolent communication," and seven troupes from paired schools performed in Arab and Jewish towns in Israel, as well as abroad.[50]

"I know you are an informer for Israel," an angry brother yelled at an older brother, who could not meet his eyes. This West Bank scene was being rehearsed at Nemashim (Heb. acronym, Youth Play Peace), a theater "commune" between two tough neighborhoods in Haifa where Jewish and Arab teens hardly ever met. The first year participants came monthly for two-day bilingual workshops. The second year they lived together and performed community service and plays. Swiss-born Israeli Uri Shani and Palestinian actor Shadi Fakhr al-Din guided them to express the complex difficulties of their lives and to confront racism against Arabs and Jewish Ethiopians.[51]

Palestinian kids warmly greeted nervous Israelis at the Center for Creativity in Education and Cultural Heritage, founded in 1991. As they mingled happily despite language barriers, they watched their parents talk and laugh together as adults' fears diminished. The Center used folklore to bring students into communication. Jewish fifth-grade children from the TALI School in West Jerusalem were guests of the Bet Hanina School for Boys and the Shuʿafat School for Girls in East Jerusalem, who had been their guests in West Jerusalem five times a year for two years.[52]

Building Bridges for Peace was an "intergroup intervention for Israeli, Palestinian and American teens." Their best practices report detailed the long-term impact of intergroup interventions regarding identity, integration, and gender with near-peer mentoring. It was a project of Seeking Common Ground based in Colorado and Israel that graduated almost two thousand participants from Israel and Palestine, as well as from Northern Ireland, South Africa, and the United States over two decades. Students were trained in empathy, compassionate listening, and leadership and learned to see the conflict from differing points of view without simplifying what was complicated.[53]

An alternative-media Hebrew-Arabic magazine by and for youth had a unique triangle framework that gave equal representation to Palestinians from the West Bank, Jewish Israelis, and Palestinian citizens of Israel. For over twenty-five years, Windows: Channels for Communication imparted new "meaning to the idea of a joint struggle" in service to "human rights, liberty, dignity, equality and democracy." It helped youth to survive wars, intifadas, and political crises through "critical discourse" and friendship.[54]

The Adam Institute taught that "competing tendencies exist within each of us, both for and against democratic principles, so that an external conflict becomes an internal dilemma." For over twenty years the Institute educated young Arab and Jewish residents of Jerusalem on equality and tolerance. Annually over sixteen thousand Palestinian, Jewish, and international school-age children, new immigrants, women's groups, soldiers, and police officers attended games and workshops ranging in duration from one day to three years. Regional partnerships used democratic principles to solve conflict.[55]

Secular and religious Arab and Jewish high school students studied for three years in integrated classrooms with Jewish and Arab teachers for civics lessons. Living in Jerusalem: Citizenship and Multiculturalism was a new program of the Jerusalem Foundation, a Jewish Israeli organization that had partnered with Palestinian and international organizations for two decades. Arab and Jewish youth came together for education, arts, music, sports, and equal access to resources across political, economic, and cultural divides. The Foundation supported the Alpert Music Center's youth orchestra; a science club at the Bloomfield Science Museum; the I Am You Are film workshop at the Jerusalem Cinemateque, an art film theater, which explored identity and filmmaking; special needs students at the Naggar School of Photography; and arts programs at the Djanogly Visual Arts Center, which was a "haven of creativity."[56]

In twinned Israeli and West Bank basketball clubs, Arabs and Jews ages six to fifteen played on mixed teams in Peace Players International. They studied "peace education and life skills . . . in year-round, frequent, and structured integration" so that "children who would otherwise rarely interact formed lasting friendships." Youth were trained as assistant coaches, as conflict managers, and in neighborhood service. Peace Players teams were the first integrated teams to enter the prestigious Israeli National Basketball League.[57] Al-Quds Association for Democracy and Dialogue, headquartered in Ramallah, partnered with the Peres Center for a joint peace sports school program, in which Palestinian and Israeli youth learned individual and team skills while challenging negative stereotypes to "broaden circles of supporters" for nonviolent resolution to national conflict.

The IPCRI Education for Peace and Democracy conference in Turkey brought together ninety Israelis, eighty-five Palestinians, and internationals from twenty countries. In 150 workshops over four days, educators, facilitators, leaders of young people's joint nonviolent initiatives, academics, and activists tackled theory, practice, and criticism and evaluation of "peace and democracy educational developments in Israel and Palestine." Participants urged IPCRI to create an international network for peace educators who use citizen action to address conflict through nonviolence, human rights, and socioeconomic and ecological justice.[58]

At university, an Arab woman in a long *jalabiyya* (Ar. full-length traditional dress) and headscarf held her newborn baby as she stood next to an Orthodox woman clothed from head to toe and trailed by two toddlers. They were receiving diplomas from Beit Berl University in Kfar Saba between the Green Line and the Mediterranean Sea. They traveled far distances each day to study at the largest multidisciplinary academic institution in Israel, where Arab and Jewish students studied side by side as a medium for social change. Learning together was fraught with difficulties and required constant effort, sacrifice, and commitment. World-renowned scholars were among 150 faculty who taught in Arabic. One professor had been a student there twenty years before when the school operated under a ruler-ruled paradigm. Now she was UNESCO Chair for Multicultural Education and promoted Arab trips to Auschwitz and Jewish study of the *Nakba*.[59]

Haifa University appointed the first Arab dean in the history of the State of Israel, Majid al-Haj, to be dean of research. Al-Haj acknowledged that the appointment was "historic" but noted, "if it took the state and its academic institutions 57 years to appoint the first Arab as dean, then it shows the depth of discrimination."[60] Al-Haj became the first Arab member of the Council of Higher Education.[61] The Jewish-Arab Center, an interdisciplinary institute founded in the 1970s, conducted research, offered courses, and held conferences on Arab-Jewish challenges. One three-year project developed a bicultural syllabus integrating Jews and Arabs at all levels of schooling "to end segregation, inequality and lack of common ground."[62]

## For Young People: New Initiatives

Besides the work of long-standing organizations that served Arab and Jewish youth, many new organizations emerged after the second intifada. Young volunteers founded the Future Generation Hands Association to help youth in the northern West Bank, particularly Nablus, heal from trauma, and to provide medical care, nutrition, and creative projects. They also sought ways to participate in the social and economic development of Palestine.[63] The Palestinian Youth Forum for Cooperation responded to the urgent needs of West Bank residents by organizing nonviolent actions with the Young Israel Forum for Cooperation. Their award-winning joint initiative, Fresh Start, developed leadership abilities of young Palestinian and Israeli professionals so they could take collective action.[64]

In Beersheba, the largest city in the Negev, Arab and Jewish parents created the Hagar Association: Jewish Arab Education for Equality. To help build an egalitarian society, they developed an educational space for Arab and Jewish children, parents, and educators to have daily contact. Over the next decade, they opened the first bilingual, multicultural day care center, and the Hagar Kindergarten grew to three kindergarten classes. The school added first through fourth grades, and eventually all of the grades up to twelfth. Families celebrated holidays together and worked on their relationships in Arab-Jewish workshops.[65]

Ein Bustan (Ar. garden spring) was the first Jewish/Arab Waldorf kindergarten in the small Arab village of Hilf in the lower Galilee. Jewish children came from Kiryat Tivon and Bedouin children came from Zubaydat, Zarzir, and Basmat Tab'un. Teachers, parents, and locals plastered and painted to prepare a rented space for the children. Bilingual Arab and Jewish teachers used both languages in storytelling, conversation, gardening, music, and games inspired by the Waldorf humanistic values, which are based on social responsibility, nature, imagination, and the arts.[66] *El Zeitoun* (Ar. the olive tree) was the first Arab Waldorf School. It developed a friendship bridge program with the nearby Jewish Waldorf school in Harduf to share cultural days, day trips, and values for conflict resolution. Waldorf teacher Amina Sawaed, daughter of a sheikh who led forty thousand Bedouin in the Galilee, and Stefanie Allon, who helped found the first Jewish and Arab Waldorf schools, traveled together each week to the West Bank to mentor kindergarten teachers at the Jenin Charitable Society who taught 150 kindergarteners.[67]

Soccer for Peace, a New York–based organization, aimed to unite children from war-torn nations through a shared love for soccer. Their first overnight camp combined intensive soccer training and dialogue work-shops for twenty-five Arab and twenty-five Jewish children. In subsequent summers, they worked with the community services arm of the Maccabi soccer team in Tel Aviv to launch an after-school program.[68]

Arab and Jewish teens exuberantly performed their original song "Bukra fil mish mish" on YouTube and for audiences in Israel and Pales-tine and around the world. The title is an Arabic play on words meaning "when the impossible becomes possible." They were part of Heartbeat, a program that brought Palestinian and Israeli young musicians together to make music and build trust they had not believed possible.[69] It enabled them "to build critical understanding, develop creative nonviolent tools for social change, and amplify their voices to influence the world around them."[70] Twelve Israeli and Palestinian teenagers met weekly in musical dialogue, listening, playing, composing, and learning about "each other's communities, histories, political views, identities, and hopes."[71] They de-buted at the UN International Day of Peace concert before an audience of three hundred Israelis, Palestinians, and internationals at the Jerusa-lem YMCA. In the next decade, Heartbeat trained over a hundred young musicians, who toured their countries and the world, inspiring thousands of people.

At the northernmost tip of the Red Sea, Palestinian and Israeli stu-dents breeched the divide between two cities, Israeli Eilat and Jordanian Aqaba, to perform "Beresheet" (Heb. in the beginning,) in mime, music, and dance.[72] With decades of experience in arts education, Angelica and Yehuda Calo Livne created Beresheet LaShalom (Heb. a beginning for peace) as an Israeli foundation for religious and secular children from Arab, Jewish, Druze, and Circassian cultures to confront their problems. They created the Arcobaleno-Rainbow dance/music theater, and the Masks Off Project, and they performed *Pinocchio* in Hebrew and Arabic in Jaffa and collaborated with Italian cultural institutions from Angelica's roots.[73] They performed nationally and internationally to audiences of tens of thousands.

### The Net of Nonviolence

Activists used the Internet and new media to broadcast their existence, find funding, mobilize adherents, and discover who worked to end con-flict and occupation from every conceivable angle. "No effort is redun-dant. . . . Everybody has a role and all activities should be supported," proclaimed the Palestinian-Israeli Peace NGO Forum, which gathered a hundred joint nonviolent organizations on a website divided into three categories.[74] One focused on work "on the ground against the wrongs of the occupation" and in human rights, legal aid, and advocacy on urgent problems. A second "promoted a political solution to the conflict." The third included "more long-term, people-to-people activities, education for peace" for people of all ages, locales, religions, and professions.[75]

Mepeace.org was a "network for peace" in which "thousands of peace activists made millions of page visits" to "realize peace online and on the ground."[76] By 2008, they had over one thousand members, according to the online *Palestine-Israel Journal*, which supported the iPeace web initiatives in Israel-Palestine.[77] The Peres Peace Center ran peace computer centers linking Palestinian and Israeli youth in social networks.[78]

The Alliance for Middle East Peace hosted the first annual Middle East coexistence conference in Washington, D.C., with fourteen organizations in 2004, then grew to almost a hundred coalition members by 2006. Each year Israeli and Palestinian delegates met with Middle East ambassadors, Jewish and Muslim religious leaders, members of Congress, State Department officials, Middle East scholars, and activists. The Alliance's website showcased Palestinian NGOs that supported nonviolence. Al-Manarah (Ar. the Lighthouse) advocated for persons with disabilities. Women and children benefited from the Arafat Society for Culture and Human Care, the AREEN/Future Vision social justice initiative, and Shorouq. The Center for Democracy and Community Development supported community-based participatory equality. The Palestinian Agency for Food and Agriculture ran agricultural programs in Ramallah and Bethlehem and cabinetry programs in Gaza that targeted rural women. The Palestinian Peace Society spread the "ideology" of nonviolence, and Young Entrepreneurs of Palestine launched businesses.[79]

* *

Despite pundits' assessment that peace was dead and joint work buried, nonviolent initiatives formed an intricate, extensive, and often invisible world. In the visible realm of media and everyday life in Palestine and Israel, peace appeared to have no traction. Palestinians and Israelis were understandably scarred, drained, and defensive in the years following the second intifada. Hamas deepened conservative Islamic control over Gaza and extended influence into the increasingly lawless West Bank under the Palestinian Authority. Militant Islamic groups in Gaza shot Qassam rockets into Israel, and Israel carried out deadly attacks on Gaza. One casualty of this situation was the restriction of Gazans' participation in joint ventures with Israelis. The separation barrier elongated its seal on the West Bank; settlements expanded into lands demarcated for a Palestinian state; occupation entered its fifth decade.

Yet more people than ever before sensed that they had nowhere to turn but toward each other. Political independence and security could not be gained by triumphalist rejection of the other's aspirations or by maintaining occupation. Palestinians from Israel, the West Bank, and East Jerusalem worked together with Jewish Israelis, from the Negev to the Galilee and the West Bank to Gaza, as midwives and tour guides, small farmers and big agricultural exporters, Bedouin small business owners and web designers, doctors and comedians, filmmakers and photographers, classical musicians and rappers. All co-resisted the status quo with creative responses to the failure of political resolution. Activists reached for the next generation. Boys and girls, teenagers and young adults studied and honed skills in sports, community service, the arts, communication, colleges, and political dialogue. They became part of a larger network of Palestinians and Israelis who were learning respect and building relationships with neighbors of different ages, ethnicities, nationalities, races, and religions.

Together they stood as vigilant sentinels in a stream of vitriol, incurring the wrath of their own families and friends to connect with the enemy. Together they advocated for human rights, equality, economic development, education, the environment, democratization, and an end to occupation; they argued, cried, laughed, danced, sang, and felt joy in the presence of the other. They were fragile counterweights to antidemocratic forces, corruption, and human rights violations under the Palestinian Authority, Hamas, and the Israeli government. They carved out spaces where people traumatized by war and burdened by unutterable loss found a temporary safe haven in each other.

## CHAPTER 10

# Missing Peace/Piece: 2009–2010

*An Orthodox Jewish supporter of the illegal extremist group Kach is now one of the most renowned Israeli feminist peace builders. A Palestinian imprisoned for a decade for building a bomb with friends to use against Israelis now works to bring Palestinian and Israeli youth together. A former West Bank settler who supported the ultra-ethno-nationalist Israeli Moldedet party now stands with the women of Machsom Watch to monitor soldier conduct at checkpoints. A wounded Palestinian spends four years in prison. He then forms an organization to promote nonviolence in Palestinian society.[1]*
RONIT AVNI, "JUST VISION"

*Inside the encounter, they are all human beings.*

*Outside the encounter, their freedoms, protections, and status—or lack thereof—are determined not by common humanity, but by the different identity cards they are issued by the authorities.*

*Inside the encounter, they face each other armed . . . with powers of communication.*

*Outside the encounter, lethal violence is an everyday expectation, with machine guns on ubiquitous display in public places.[2]*
MOHAMMED ABU-NIMER AND NED LAZARUS, "PEACEBUILDER'S PARADOX"

A Muslim imam and a Jewish rabbi pray on a hillside splattered with blood red poppy flowers. Arab and Jewish surgeons operate to save hundreds of children's hearts. Children of enemies run together in the grass playing soccer. Israelis and Palestinians stand side by side to protect a threatened olive grove. Young and old from Palestine, Israel, and Jordan gather in a eucalyptus grove for listening circles by day and in a meadow to make music all night under their one vast starry sky.

What difference does it make that thousands of Palestinians and Israelis engaged in hundreds of joint nonviolent initiatives over the course of a century? What does it matter that they met face to face in dialogue, social change projects, interfaith women's and advocacy groups, arts projects, political action, professional alliances, research, schools, and protest rallies, in acts of resistance or solidarity, learning or play? What does it signify that participants hailed from diverse points along political spectrums from religious to secular, anti- to ultra-Zionist, and radical to moderate Palestinian, to confront a perilous status quo side by side?

It seemed that the worse the ambient violence, the more audacious were the efforts. Why were they not more effective in bringing an end to conflict and occupation? Not only did they not bring peace, they failed to prevent conditions from getting worse. This chapter wrestles with these questions in three parts. The first part looks at effects of a changing political climate on joint work during and after the 2009 Gaza War, a time when the crescendo of violence again rendered encounter almost impossible. The second section presents critiques and appraisals of joint work by activists and scholars. The final portion offers conclusions.

## Joint Work in a Lethal Climate

By the end of 2008, Palestinians despaired as Fatah and Hamas jailed and suppressed the other's supporters in territories under their respective control. For three years they made and broke cease-fires, mediated agreements and betrayed them. In mid-December, a six-month truce between Hamas and Israel expired, and Hamas fired more than sixty rockets into Israel on Christmas Eve, wreaking havoc on Arab and Jewish lives. Three days later, Israel launched its three-week war against Hamas in Gaza. As inexcusable as the Hamas attacks were, there was a dramatic asymmetry of power. The international community accused Israel of excessive force and blamed both sides for human rights violations. Hamas denounced Palestinian Authority leadership for enforcing Israeli and Egyptian blockades of Gaza. Hamas was isolated, having lost support that at various times had come from Syria, the Muslim Brotherhood, Saudi Arabia, the Gulf states, and Iran.

As usual, rising fear gave the election to Israel's hawks. Analysts characterized Netanyahu's government as the most right-wing in Israel's history, while polls showed waning support for the peace movement.[3] For the first time, Prime Minister Netanyahu publicly endorsed creation of a

Palestinian state and declared a settlement freeze, but he kept tightening control over the West Bank and supporting settlement growth through "government-issued bids for building" mostly "on the Palestinian side of a line drawn by the Geneva Accord."[4] By the end of 2010, the first sparks of the Arab Spring kindled what looked like an Egyptian Revolution, followed by the rise to power and then removal of the country's Muslim Brotherhood, the beginning of the Syrian civil war in 2011, and sectarian crises throughout the region.

Activists hit a wall. The events felt like the final blow to a century of Palestinian-Israeli joint nonviolence. Women's cross-border groups, for example, had managed to meet during the second intifada. Even at the most unbearable points they met twenty times to present joint demands to diplomatic missions to end occupation and promote "women's participation in all peace-planning, peace-making and peace-keeping initiatives." After the intifada ended, they resumed joint action. But the 2009 Israel-Gaza war was too much. They pledged to work for peace separately in their own societies until they could again join forces in the future.

Other Israelis and Palestinians learned to operate "in a more openly tense environment."[5] Michelle Gawerc's research on twelve joint initiatives reveals the contortions necessary to keep initiatives alive. During the Gaza War, for safety's sake, the Seeds of Peace Palestinian staff worked from home, went to the office at irregular times, and told Israelis not to call them in case their lines were tapped. The Gaza War tipped a hard-won balance for Palestinian activists between their anger at Israelis and their commitment to shared humanity. Feeling powerless added to the sense of discouragement. The situation surrounding the encounters perpetually spun out of control. One Palestinian leader lamented,

> It's easy to get frustrated. It feels like we are going around in a circle. We are talking so much, and then we wonder why the people we are speaking to haven't changed. . . . Ninety percent of the Israeli public was in favor of what happened in Gaza . . . I need to reframe the message to not just talk about the occupation, but also . . . about the internal conflict. . . . We are not innocent and weak—we [Palestinians] are killing each other.[6]

A persistent problem that plagued joint work intensified in wartime: How could joint activists support the other's aspirations while staying credible in their own societies, which were prone to dismiss them as traitors? Palestinians couldn't bear Israeli partners' serving in the army. They asked them to publicly oppose the war. But when Israelis openly protested the war, they alienated the Israelis they needed to reach to bring about changes. They felt pressured by Palestinians to build a base for political change. But fellow Israelis perceived their protest of the Gaza War as one more existential threat in a decade of Hamas suicide bombers, Hezbollah rockets, and Gazan mortars. Israeli government hardliners attacked the strongest initiatives, like the School for Peace, Combatants for Peace, and other human rights groups, by auditing their funding.[7]

Frontline peace activists characterized these years as having less hope, commitment, and action. But this was not the whole truth. In the decade after the second intifada, "fewer Israelis were victims of terrorist attacks than in previous decades [and] fewer Palestinians lost their lives because of Israeli military activity."[8]

In the darkest months of 2009, Harvard-educated Gazan physician Izzeldin Abuelaish suffered the horrific deaths of his three daughters and a niece when Israeli tank shells shattered his house in Jabalya camp, an event broadcast live on Israeli TV. He created an international foundation for reconciliation and peace in Gaza to support Arab girls and to be a bridge between enemies. He made contact with Israelis and traveled the world to speak to Jews and others about this unspeakable disaster and to urge an end to war.[9] He founded Daughters for Life Foundation to aid Middle Eastern Muslims, Christians, and Jews of any nationality. Recipients of aid were "chosen not only for their academic achievements . . . in the face of socio-economic adversity, . . . but also for their character and commitment to improving the lives of girls and young women."[10]

In the midst of tragedy in Gaza, Palestinians and Jews reached for each other to listen, cry, and act. In the first months of 2009, hundreds of heart-stricken Palestinians and Israelis organized meetings that led to collective actions. The Israeli Sulha Peace Project and Palestinian Al-Tariq were in touch by Skype, holding high-emotion listening circles that included music and prayer. Israelis and Palestinians met at the Jerusalem YMCA for hours of sharing pain, finding compassion, and planning a citizens initiative to deliver blankets, food, diapers, and medicines to Gazans. Palestinians in Ramallah and Jericho gathered with Israelis around a fire at the Dead Sea to mourn and sing.[11]

Before the war, the Palestinian Peace Society had met for a week with almost fifty Israeli and Palestinian engineers in Aqaba, Jordan, to "plan for both new generations." When the war broke out, they collected aid for Gazan children and civilian victims. Palestinians, Israelis, and Jordanians met many times throughout the year, and at a Dead Sea beach they gathered to "refuse to continue living side by side as enemies."[12]

G.ho.s.t. was a brainchild of Israeli and Palestinian software developers. They met at a roadside café in the desert between Jericho and Jerusalem and by video conference to create a virtual computer with "a Web-based operating system that recreated the attributes of a personal computer's desktop" in any computer with an internet connection.[13] Businesspeople opened an Israeli-Palestinian Chamber of Commerce to "enhance bilateral trade and investments between Israel and the Palestinian Authority."[14] The Jewish-Arab town of Gilboa joined the West Bank city of Jenin on shared tourism projects.[15]

The arts expressed the heartbreak of living with war and repression. Seeds of Peace joined with Heartbeat in a musical dialogue between Israeli and Palestinian youth from Ramallah, Bethlehem, Hebron, Haifa, Ashqelon, and Beersheba. When war prevented them from meeting, they turned to social media to produce an album of their original music on war and freedom.[16] Seeds of Bliss was an Israeli artist's whimsical initiative to bring together Jews and Arabs from Israel, Palestine, and Jordan to shell sunflower seeds with the inimitable Middle Eastern maneuvers of teeth and tongue in order to produce a mass installation inspired by dissident Chinese artist Ai Weiwei's one hundred million porcelain sunflower seeds at London's Tate museum. Members of a team of seed shellers encountered people they would never otherwise meet because the teams paired Jewish and Arab neighborhoods and cross-border towns.[17] Seas of Peace taught the art of sailing to Palestinian and Israeli youth. They lived in tight quarters, and their survival literally depended on teamwork while they were in dialogue about conflict, occupation, and culture.[18]

Palestinians and Jews confronted inequalities and served communities' needs. Hand in Hand schools partnered with Hagar to open the first bilingual, multicultural center in the Negev for Arab and Jewish children from toddler age and up.[19] Project Harmony brought together Hebrew and Arabic speakers in Israel for a music and theater program at an English-speaking Jerusalem summer camp.[20] Shutafut-Sharakah provided a forum for training in democratic values and a shared society for all citizens in both national groups.[21] Nonviolent Communication, founded in Israel in 1992, now reached across borders to bring together hundreds of Israelis and Palestinians for training in compassion, authenticity, empathy, and listening to underlying needs in order to diminish mistrust and build alliances for social change.[22]

New women's joint initiatives emerged. Muslim, Jewish, Christian, and Druze women in Israel from the Trust-Emun interfaith organization visited the site of devastating fires in the north. They returned the following year to replant trees as a permanent memorial for the forty-four Prison Services Jews, Christians, Muslims, and Druze who died fighting the fire. A rainbow of faith communities attended the opening of the Garden of the Mothers for a silent meditation walk with the women of the fallen.[23] Shaʿar la-Adam/Bab lil-Insan founded an Arab-Jewish women's group to speak confidentially about their lives.[24] *My So-Called Enemy*, a film directed by American-Jewish filmmaker Lisa Gossels, documented the experiences of Palestinian and Israeli girls in a "painfully intimate portrait of . . . psychological complexities" of growing up amid protracted hostilities.[25]

Israeli women smuggled Palestinian women from the West Bank through the checkpoints so they could spend a day at the beach. Palestinian women removed their headscarves and traveled incognito in the back seats of cars with Israeli license plates driven by middle-aged Jewish women so the soldiers nonchalantly wave them through. Like most Palestinians in the West Bank, they had never seen the sea, even though they lived only an hour away from it. One of the Palestinian women was a pregnant thirty-six-year-old mother of three whose five brothers were in Israeli prisons and who had lost another brother when he was killed for entering a settler school with a knife. She proclaimed during her secret visit to Tel Aviv, "This is all ours." But she took surprising comfort in the Israeli women's company when they told her that it was their home too. Returning to her home in a refugee camp, another woman was confronted by family members who asked her if she was a collaborator. She responded with simple joy by describing her frolic with Jewish women at the sea. The smugglers formed We Will Not Obey to protest Israel's Law of Entry:

> We cannot assent to the legality of the Law of Entry into Israel, which allows every . . . Jew to move freely in all regions between the Jordan River and the Mediterranean while depriving Palestinians of this same right.[26]

The organizer of the day at the beach challenged her country's occupation of another country for forty-four of her fifty-three years. She worked with other Israelis to bring toys and supplies for Palestinian women in the West Bank to set up a kindergarten and to help them through medical and legal trouble. Other Israelis attacked the Jewish women for breaking laws intended to safeguard them, and a right-wing group reported them to the police. Risking arrest, the Jewish women stated,

> We were privileged to experience one of the most beautiful and exciting days of our lives, to meet and befriend our brave Palestinian neighbors, and together with them, to be free women, if only for one day.[27]

### Pitfalls and Paradoxes

Throughout this first century of joint nonviolence, Israelis and Palestinians critiqued the shortcomings of their joint work and raised salient questions about its significance. The failure of Oslo unleashed important debates about strategies and goals. Scholar Shany Payes frames them as questions: Do the groups enforce and perpetuate inequality rather than challenging the status quo? Do they weaken other modes of resistance, such as the development of political parties? Are they fertile ground for developing new leaders or do they divert leaders away from the political realm? For example, is the activism of Palestinian women in NGOs a breakthrough or a way of perpetuating their exclusion from the political milieu?[28]

Some critics felt that the groups unwittingly re-traumatized the participants and confirmed their worst fears. So-called understanding sometimes simply clarified of the other's apparent malevolence or the essential threat they presented to one's national existence. Others feared that the groups substituted grassroots work for necessary diplomatic action and dialogue for political activism. Some critiqued groups for avoiding political issues altogether or for privileging shared humanity over differences. Still others observed how vulnerable the groups were to political events. Violence compelled people on both sides to recoil in horror at the thought of sitting with those sympathetic to the perpetrators.

The most loaded issue was asymmetry of power. If Jews initiated and funded the majority of initiatives, then could the work actually challenge inequality, or did it mirror it?[29] The language of coexistence and peace could portray a false parity between the "two sides," erase the reality of one-way oppression, and mask Israel's domination. Mohammed Abu-Nimer examined how Israel's dominant discourse duplicated inequality within groups because of its power to frame issues and agendas.[30] It was important for Israeli Jews to face their role as the more powerful group and find ways to share leadership at all levels; for example, Hebrew could not be the main language of encounter because it turned Arabs into outsiders. Furthermore, Jews had an easier time exposing themselves with "techniques of emotional clarification" that were alien to Arab culture.[31]

Peace activist and scholar Nadia Nasser-Najjab further detailed the effects of asymmetry. Israelis had access to resources, wealth, knowledge, and professional training. They were better grant writers; donors felt more confident working with them; Israelis did more fundraising, evaluation, and recruiting; donors often gave Israelis more money. Palestinians lived in a devastated economy without freedom of movement to travel within their own lands, to Israel, or beyond. Military authorities refused them permission to attend joint meetings.[32]

Most confusing was how to take responsibility in the crunch between two one-way power imbalances. Rabbi Lynn Gottlieb stated that "dialogue which does not acknowledge the occupied-and-occupier relationship cannot succeed in undoing the system of structural violence which confines Palestinian life."[33] Israelis, as the more powerful group of the two, had to take responsibility for their role in perpetuating Palestinian suffering. Palestinians, as members of the powerful Arab and Muslim world, had to take responsibility for the safety of Jews in their midst. For Israelis, centuries of exiles and persecutions made it unbearable to face their own responsibility for the suffering of Palestinians. For Palestinians, Israel's occupation made it unbearable to face their role in endangering Jewish lives.

There were unacknowledged differences in each side's objectives. For example, Palestinians wanted occupation to end, with its abuses, imprisonments, and killings. They wanted political independence. They feared that working with Israelis indicated a level of normalization tantamount to accepting the status quo. Instead they argued for existence first and coexistence later. For their part, Israelis wanted the conflict to end, with its daily dangers and the horrors of war and constant military engagement. Peace meant being able to lead normal lives, not to have to send each of one's children on a different bus to school each morning, in case one of the buses blew up. It meant secure borders and neighboring countries' recognition of their legitimacy and integrity as a state.

Nasser-Najjab described Palestinians' perception of these discrepancies. Israelis seemed to want coexistence and mutual understanding; Palestinians wanted Israelis to know their suffering, to end occupation, and to recognize their state. Israelis seemed to want social and cultural interaction; Palestinians wanted a political platform. Joint work for Palestinians was a means to an end, not an end in itself. They wanted skills so they could compete with Israeli capabilities and achieve equality. Israelis seemed to think that Palestinians just wanted to show their misery, deny the Holocaust, have things one-sided. Israelis thought that Palestinians' suffering was a result of Palestinian rejectionist violence.[34]

Looking at joint nonviolence from a different angle, Palestinian ambassador and former minister Hind Khoury opined that in a time of "a deadlocked peace process," devastating poverty, targeted assassinations, and "bottomless injustice," ridiculously few resources went to "the great and courageous work" of Palestinian and Israeli "peace-oriented civil society" groups."[35] Others complained that the flow of funding during the Oslo years turned "rapprochement . . . into big business." They accused projects of operating under false assumptions that occupation and dispossession could be resolved in negotiation, so the remaining work was merely psychological.[36] Foreign funding for Palestinian human rights groups in the territories governed by the Palestinian Authority cast doubt on the sincerity of those on the payrolls.

Daniel Bar-Tal, former editor of the *Palestine-Israel Journal*, saw joint work saddled by "accumulated grievances," "deeply rooted" disagreements, and "mutual de-legitimization." The "ferocious, . . . destructive psychological repertoire" included Jews imprinted by continuous Palestinian violence that resembled their "long, collective traumatic history." Palestinians saw each new *dunam* of land and repressive measure of occupation as proof of unceasing Zionist expansion aims.[37]

Palestinians complained that Israelis merely wanted to show a compassionate, tolerant side of Israel, but did not want to take radical action to end occupation. Israelis felt Palestinians didn't care about Israel's existence or security but used Israelis to further their own goals. Israelis said the past couldn't be changed, so they should work together to build a different future. Nasser-Najjab said that for Palestinians, "their past was their future." If dialogue wasn't political, then it was just *kalam fadi* (Ar. empty talk). Yet crying *kalam fadi* was often a cover for fear of deep internal tensions caused by dialogue that catalyzed real change.

The absence of agreement on all these questions and issues was both a strength and a weakness. On one hand, it opened a wild frontier for anyone with vision to hitch his or her skills to the creation of nonviolent alternatives where people could learn, give, and take responsibility in ways otherwise impossible. On the other hand, differences bred division, judgment, and lack of cohesion. There was little contact between groups. Most participants had no idea of the range of nonviolent initiatives that existed. Most disagreed with, belittled, or felt directly threatened by other groups' ideological or tactical differences.

Paradoxically, these joint nonviolent initiatives were the only place to actually debate these problems and so many other questions: Could groups deal openly with inequalities rather than simply replicate Israeli control over Arabs? Did the groups challenge or benefit the status quo? Who defined the terms *extremist* and *terrorist*? Could Israel be a Jewish state as well as a state of all its citizens? Was the struggle for equality possible without Israel becoming a state of all its peoples? Was reform sufficient, or was radical restructuring necessary? Would Israelis share power through joint work or just participate to ease their guilty consciences? Were political groups more important than interfaith, social, and cultural groups? Did the latter merely avoid politics or did they build valuable trust? Was contact theory true or false in validating the importance of any kind of contact with the enemy? Could the groups overcome psychological, economic, and physical barriers? Did joint work threaten their nation's future as rejectionists claimed? Could it transform society or only individuals?

Abu-Nimer asserted that dialogue could be a vehicle for social change if it succeeded in inoculating participants against indoctrination with their own side's ideology. If dialogue remained only a chance to argue one side of the story and convince the other, then it failed. Dialogue worked when it helped participants to

> develop more self-critique, the kind that tortures you in a conflict situation. You want to believe that you are on the right side. . . . But through the work of peacebuilding, you come to see that you need and depend on the 'other' to get anywhere in resolving the conflict.[38]

Abu-Nimer wove religious elements, Arab conflict resolution traditions, and Islamic nonviolent teachings into these frameworks. He critiqued the dominant Israeli community for "cultural arrogance" and Palestinian secular leaders for privileging politics over culture. He stressed uninational preparation for binational work.[39] Abu-Nimer's and Ned Lazarus's "peacebuilder's paradox" conveyed the "dissonance between the epiphanies of genuine dialogue and the realities of intractable conflict":

> Inside the encounter, ground rules encourage empathy, openness, and respect to foster a "safe space" for all.

Outside the encounter, they are divided by barriers erected in the name of security for some.

Inside the encounter, discussion leaders mandate equality between participants.

Outside the encounter, power structures dictate that they live in separate unequal societies.

Inside the encounter, they may find hope in the discovery that in terms of emotion and psychology, they are mirror images of each other.

Yet outside the encounter, reality does not adapt itself to their new-found understanding.[40]

According to religious studies professor Frida Kerner Furman some skeptics of joint initiatives often privileged the "discourses advancing *realpolitik* for addressing conflict," a model that had "clearly failed to bring about peace." While it was impossible to know if initiatives brought peace closer, Furman suggested,

perhaps it is time to consider a paradigm shift, . . . one that recognizes that a model of engagement, reciprocity, and reflection, applied by the grassroots . . . could help show the way out of the trap of binary logic . . . of "winners and losers." . . . [These groups] clearly prioritize the shared humanity of people across political divides.[41]

Furman notes that the debate over political versus apolitical approaches ignore their interrelation. For example, a young woman was drawn to dialogue because of her Jewish Mizrahi minority status in Ashkenazi-dominant Israeli society. She identified with culturally marginalized Arabs. Yet she was afraid of Palestinians' claim to their own state. In "apolitical" interfaith dialogue she gained enough trust to reverse her political stand.

The political and the personal were, in fact, intimately intertwined. One young Palestinian man could not attend university due to the first intifada. So he worked as a waiter and bookkeeper in West Jerusalem. When he saw that the way he'd been raised to think of Jews was not reality, he read about Judaism and joined an interfaith dialogue group. He explains that his experiences with interfaith dialogue groups "fulfill my heart . . . [and] influence me in the way I raise my children. . . . I may not have influence on other people, but I have influence on my family."[42] The cost of this work for him was an "inner struggle": his children were hurt at seeing the comparative wealth and freedom of his Jewish friends, and his

Palestinian friends accused him of normalizing relations with Jews who engaged in dialogue but could not stop the occupation.

Joint nonviolent activists both overestimated and underestimated the significance of their work. On one hand, they had an inflated sense of ability. They "should" be able to bring peace, end occupation, and stop war. When faced with internal crisis at the *Palestine-Israel Journal*, for example, the editor thought, "We should [be able to] recreate an example of what should be good relations among people." On the other hand, a deflated sense of accomplishment obscured actual success. The joint work was a hothouse for facing difficulties together, not a refuge from the heat. Joint initiatives were the only places to directly communicate with the other about the injustices that plagued both peoples.

Joint activists experienced the hubris of high expectations that bred disillusionment, and cynicism that undermined real contact. They teetered between rising expectations and the devastating realities that made it easy to underestimate the power of nonviolent work. Yet their work remained a moral means to a just end and a catalyst for longer-term change. Like all activism, it was often impossible to fully comprehend the consequences of these actions. Nasser-Najjab observed that even in the midst of a second intifada, chances to meet in joint solidarity "transcended the turbulence."[43] Staff worked without salaries, proving their devotion to joint nonviolence, and participants kept connections alive. Julia Chaitin's study of civil society groups attributed their success to the fact that they met the requirements for resolving sociopolitical problems, including "complex thinking, multiple perspective-taking, and multiple solutions on . . . cognitive, affective, and behavioral [levels]."[44]

The most enduring initiatives were the ones that addressed long-term common interests — for example, when doctors were trained in a trauma center or educators wrote history textbooks with both sides' conflicting narratives. But one-year programs between teenagers were less able to change basic attitudes unless there were significant follow-ups. Long-lasting projects focused on participants fixing problems in their own societies.[45] Personal transformation by a religious Zionist, for example, led her to invite Palestinians to her home in the Ma'ale Adumim settlement in the West Bank near Jerusalem. Her neighbors complained that they used to feel safe, but no longer did when she brought in Palestinians. She responded,

> Every morning hundreds of laborers . . . come with permits . . . [as] garbage collectors . . . gardeners . . . stoneworkers, contractors, and you

still feel safe. But I bring in lawyers and doctors . . . who happen to be Palestinians with permits to talk about God, and all of a sudden you're terrified?[46]

Ziad AbuZayyad, a former Palestinian Authority minister, a member of the Palestinian legislature, and co-editor of the *Palestine-Israel Journal*, insisted that "people-to-people activities between Palestinian and Israeli civil society have become more important than ever." He saw no end of the need to "rebuild trust and open channels of communication." Despite Oslo's failure, a second intifada, and accusations of normalizing occupation, the joint work "deepen[ed] awareness of the benefits of peace" and highlighted shared interests.[47]

Payes's research showed that the joint work between Palestinian NGOs in Israel and Israeli Jewish groups raised awareness, challenged Arab "marginality," and shifted power relations. Their work "achieved considerable progress" in what she termed the "politics of allocation," redressing inequalities of state spending and infrastructure. It "enhanced the political participation of under-represented Palestinian citizens, and struggled to redefine . . . political discourse in Israel . . . [and] democratization processes." Activists expanded civil rights and political opportunity in ways that went "beyond equal citizenship to the protection of human rights" as a "national minority."[48]

The founder of the University of California at Berkeley's Peace and Conflict Studies program, Michael Nagler, wrote, "While nonviolent coexistence may be far off, there are a few beacons that illuminate what such a future could look like in a tangible form." He cited Neve Shalom/Wahat al-Salam and its School for Peace, which ran on an egalitarian basis. "The methods used to bring about the future will determine the shape of the future."[49]

## Missing Peace/Piece

The idea is alive today here and there among Jewish and Arab individuals frustrated with the evident insufficiencies and depredations of the present. The essence of that vision is coexistence and sharing in ways that require an innovative, daring and theoretical willingness to get beyond the arid stalemate of assertion and rejection. Once the initial acknowledgment of the other as an equal is made, I believe the way forward becomes not only possible but attractive.[50]

Edward Said's hope for "acknowledgment of the other as equal" occurred decade by decade, as joint work spread to more places and reached more people with more approaches in more fields of endeavor. It challenged leaders' policies and opened doors for people to stand together as allies in unprecedented ways. The work bolstered visibility and rights to Palestinians, Mizrahi Jews, women, children, gays and lesbians, and bereaved parents. Artists, educators, environmentalists, scientists, students, professors, businesspeople, athletes, architects and city planners, community organizers, and political activists took action on behalf of the humanity and needs of the other. The longer the conflict continued, the deeper the need for change became, the more persistently alliances arose.

Yet after over a century of joint nonviolent initiatives, Palestinians and Israelis were still missing peace. Other twentieth-century nonviolent movements contributed to concrete changes. They helped Indians stand up to the largest empire in the world, African-Americans to challenge white racism in the largest superpower, Poles to stand up to the Soviets, and Africans to end apartheid. In all these instances, the obstacles were deep and numerous, yet the initiatives achieved major breakthroughs in spite of ongoing struggles. The joint initiatives failed to implement the will of Palestinians to end occupation and of Israelis for secure borders. This section explores some of the conditions that contributed to this failure and some of the facets of their initiatives' success.

One fundamental reason for failure was that joint activists remained a minority during the century of the conflict's existence in societies that saw compelling arguments not to compromise. Most people on both sides saw peace as a luxury. Existence overwhelmed coexistence. Jews had been minorities under others' rule for almost 2000 years and had nowhere to go. They were determined to end the exile here and now. Palestinians had never ruled themselves but saw one group of Arabs after another gaining independent statehood. The threat that each nationalist movement posed to the other made connecting with the enemy seem like colluding with the enemy. Four other factors further undermined the impact of the joint initiatives.

First, overwhelming outside forces had always imposed their own will on the peoples who inhabited the tiny sliver of land between the Mediterranean and the Jordan River. A highway for conquerors and opportunists for millennia, it became in the past century a minefield of meddling international and regional interests that overshadowed any intention and ability of Jews and Arabs to make peace. The desire to survive as Arab and Jewish peoples, and later as Palestinian and Israeli nations, had been fodder for the machinations of Ottoman power (a six-hundred-year-old Turkish empire that ruled the Arab Middle East for four hundred years), British and French imperialists during World War I (with their contradictory secret promises for Jewish and Arab independence within unspecified borders), the British Empire—the largest empire in history (under the British Mandate), anti-Arab orientalists and anti-Semites (the latter of which committed the atrocities of the Holocaust; the former of which dispossessed 750,000 Arabs from Palestine a few years later), the Cold War superpowers—the Soviet Union and the United States (both of which cultivated dependency and division in the region), postcolonial Arab regimes (which attacked Israel and gave checkered support to Palestinians to bolster their own autocratic rule), and religious militant rejectionists on both sides.

Living in the interstices of these shifting domestic, regional, and international forces for so long produced impediments that should have rendered impossible not only peace, but also joint nonviolence. In my own work with Palestinians and Israelis decades ago, after each remarkable breakthrough participants would invariably conclude that if it were up to them alone, they could make peace. Yet external interventions kept both sides on the defensive and provided a never-ending supply of weapons.

Second, joint nonviolent initiatives never became a movement. The groups were scattered shards of light rather than a single focused beam. Despite intermittent and temporary coalitions, at no time did these hundreds of initiatives coalesce into something united. Payes warned that in order to have impact they would have to "go beyond independent activity and mobilize in the frame of a social movement—a loose alliance of organizations that act in concert with other social elements to promote political and social change."[51]

The very strength of the diversity that enabled the groups to create a broad cantankerous base of resistance to the status quo proved also to be a weakness. As a potential movement they were riven by opposing and contradictory ideologies, goals, and tactics. Most participants could not bear to join a group other than the one they were in. Others groups were too right-wing or left-wing, too angry or not angry enough, too passive or too misguided in their actions. Most participants were proud nationalists whose love for their own country was paramount. They saw alliances with the other side as requisite to freeing their own people from danger and oppression and as the best practice for bringing security to Israel and independence to Palestinians. Challenging nationalist narratives was central to transformation. Palestinian historian Rashid Khalidi argued, for example, that Palestinians had to see Zionism not only as a colonial venture but also as a national movement. The deconstruction of these ideas would be "crucially important to eventual reconciliation."[52]

A third factor limiting the success of joint initiatives was that most people on both sides still judged joint work as an existential threat. Many people regarded standing with the enemy as treachery. No matter how ostensibly apolitical an act might be—for example, Arab and Jewish children creating a mosaic portraying their lives—the very fact of meeting the enemy who was in that moment killing your people was anathema. Two seasoned activists, Zakaria Al-Qaq and Gershon Baskin, described how they were forced to spend an enormous amount of energy simply "advocating for the basic legitimacy and relevance of their positions" while their leaders and peers went to great lengths to discredit, dismiss, and dismantle their work.[53]

Daily life under occupation and terrorism seemed to confirm that the other's intent was not to help but to harm. This is what made the joint work so powerful for the participants and what confirmed for everyone else that the work was at best naive and, at worst, a nefarious plot to aid the enemy. It was seen not as a solution but as part of the problem, another strategy to betray and defeat the dream of living free, independent lives. These assumptions repeatedly occluded the reality of the interdependence of both peoples' struggle for dignity.

The fourth factor that prevented the initiatives from achieving their stated aims was the double helix of domination: orientalism and anti-Semitism. Elsewhere successful nonviolent activists had a single opponent, such as the British Empire in India or white apartheid in South Africa. Orientalist Israeli attitudes and actions promulgated one-way oppression of Palestinians, rejection of their political legitimacy, and threat to their existence on their land. Orientalism was manifest in Prime Minister Golda Meir's lament that Israelis didn't hate Arabs but hated that they forced Israelis to be soldiers. Orientalists blamed Palestinians for being victimized, saw their statelessness as proof of their illegitimacy, and unleashed an organized state military to violently suppress their opposition to Israel. The anti-Semitic aspects of Arab attitudes and actions promulgated one-way oppression of Jews. They accused Jews of being an insidious, offensive, foreign power and denied their legitimacy and roots in the land. Arabs blamed Jews for their having to attack them.

The hidden nature of this double one-way oppression undermined social activism. Critics of Israel were dismissed as anti-Semites or self-hating Jews, and these dismissals shut down dialogue about ending Palestinian oppression while leaving Israeli racism intact. Modern anti-Semitism was a powerful chameleon that confused the allies of both Israelis and Palestinians, convincing them that supporting one side meant attacking the other. Anti-Semitism gave big powers the appearance of defending the Jewish state when in fact it set up Jews as visible agents of the superpower. This was a traditional setup. As long as oppressed peoples' rage could be turned on Jews, then big powers maintained control and people's liberation failed.

Israel's aggression toward Palestinians had to be stopped. As long as Israelis conflated their Arab enemies with Nazis and others throughout history who had sought their destruction, they remained blind to their own responsibility for Palestinian suffering. And as long as Arab and Muslim peoples saw Israel as the main threat to Palestinians or to Arab and Muslim hegemony, they remained subjugated to the tyranny of their own leaders and blind to their part in perpetuating the threat to Jewish lives. It was not accidental that the emotional hatred directed at Israel for its oppressive policies was most intense among peoples who had ruled over Jews with institutionalized segregation and restrictions in Europe and the Middle East.

The factors that prevented the joint initiatives from becoming a movement were precisely what made them critically important. Only by standing together as allies could Jews and Palestinians expose and resist both orientalism and anti-Semitism. Many activists intuited this interdependence. A powerful way to stop Israeli aggression was for Palestinians, Arabs, Muslims, and Westerners to combat anti-Semitism. To stop Palestinian rejection of Israel's existence, Israelis had to stop endangering Palestinians' lives and stand up for their independence and equal rights. Palestinian nonviolent activist Ali Abu Awwad untangled the skein a bit by insisting that those who terrorized Jews hurt Palestinians:

> The Jews are not my enemy; their fear is my enemy. We must help them to stop being so afraid—their whole history has terrified them—but I refuse to be a victim of Jewish fear anymore.[54]

Tying his freedom to the healing of Jewish fear, Abu Awwad organized Roots, a nonviolent movement on the West Bank and a center for Palestinians and Jewish settlers to meet in the West Bank.[55] In many ways joint work unwittingly shook the roots of intractability of the conflict. Successful encounters made Israelis less afraid of Palestinians as they saw their willingness to work to stop threats against Jewish lives. Joint work gave

Palestinians confidence that there were Israeli allies who would stand up against threats to Palestinian lives and work to end occupation.

These crucial elements of the joint work were often intuitive rather than intentional, and this too undermined their clout. Most participants saw either the orientalist racism or the anti-Semitism, but not both. Lack of understanding of these intertwined racisms caused unconscionable suffering for Palestinians and Israelis over the past century. Palestinians and Israelis were both its victims and its perpetrators. Israel expanded control over Palestinians and resisted their cry for independence; Arabs and Palestinians conflated terrorizing Jews with progress toward liberation. Both strategies resulted in an ever-intensifying spiral of violence. The initiatives that worked best were the ones that turned this situation upside down with commitments to nonviolence and to hearing the pain of the other and taking responsibility to end it. The initiatives could take the contest over who suffered most and turn it into an opportunity to witness the other's trauma, to share compassion, and to promote policies to protect the other from harm.

Not all nonviolent efforts are created equal. For every insight into the humanity and needs of the other, there was confirmation of a participant's worst fears of the other's intent to harm. The outcome depended on how an initiative addressed or ignored power imbalances. Israelis with a nation faced Palestinians without one; a free people faced one under military occupation; four hundred million Arabs rejected the legitimacy of a nation of a few million Jews. The success or failure in addressing these imbalances determined whether joint initiatives lived or died, broke stereotypes or confirmed them, produced hope or reproduced despair.

Did joint initiatives effect social change while failing to produce political solutions? Did the work challenge or confirm demonization, advance or undermine connection, render peace more or less imaginable and desirable? Palestinians and Israelis risked working with the declared enemy out of a wide range of spoken and unspoken, conscious and unconscious, and often clashing motives. Was it enough that something powerful happened to the individuals involved? When they came together in prisons, schools, or refugee camps, mourning their children's deaths or celebrating religious festivals, was that enough to defy the dictates of protracted war?

Failing to produce an outcome of one state, two states, three states, or more, joint initiatives nevertheless provided chances to live the core values of each people's respective liberation movements. The Palestinian concept of *samud*, steadfastness, could be applied to the joint groups that succeeded in part simply by continuing to exist against the odds. In the midst of war and repression, joint activists created chances for people to at least momentarily live with dignity, security, and freedom. Together they opened arenas for democratic processes that transformed fear and hatred into respect and curiosity. They cultivated trust by facing tough truths and created alternatives to the failures of *realpolitik*. They altered the perception of what divided their peoples. Instead of Arab versus Jew, it was accommodationists versus rejectionists—those willing to live with the national aspirations of the other versus those who saw the other as an illegitimate, brutal obstacle.[56]

Participants in joint initiatives learned "response-ability," the ability to respond to the other. They showed that Palestinians and Israelis faced problems more productively together than separately. They lived out the dictum that in life there exist few cures but much healing. They experienced firsthand the philosophical assertion of Emmanuel Levinas that "the past of the other and, somehow, the history of humanity in which I have never participated, in which I have never been present, are my past."[57]

Joint initiatives were interventions with potential to heal trauma that perpetuated cyclical hostility. They revealed hidden connections between two peoples with deep roots in one land. They gave expression to ethical interconnections that arose out of three religious traditions that advocate justice, mercy, and compassion. Intimacy grew from asking the other to witness one's suffering, acknowledge complicity, and end it.

Their actions for the most part went unnoticed. But invisibility was a shelter from their own people's wrath when they broke taboos against contact. Beyond the glare of official diplomacy, without constituencies to appease, they had only their own determination and their desperation to face an overwhelming situation. They didn't wait until conditions were met, until the other recognized their political legitimacy, until bombs stopped falling, or until leaders found solutions. On the contrary, they brought their lack of readiness to face the other. They came without roadmaps and without knowing how to speak face-to-face, to risk meeting those who killed their loved ones.

Some activists went beyond tolerance to forgiveness and even love. Palestinians and Israelis spoke of lessons learned from Gandhi, King, Mandela, and those survivors of the Holocaust and the Rwandan massacres who forgave the perpetrators. Some heeded the story of a Tibetan monk, a friend of the Dalai Lama, who was imprisoned and tortured for eighteen years by the Chinese. When the monk was finally released, the Dalai Lama asked him, "Weren't you afraid?" "Yes," the monk said, "I was afraid I would not be able to forgive the Chinese."

When Sami Adwan was studying in the United States for his doctorate, he refused to take classes in which there were Jews. Many years later, in an Israeli prison, he discovered their humanity. Adwan became the co-founder of PRIME, a joint educational venture that he saw as an underpinning of social change. He had learned from Paulo Freire that "you can neither be free by taking away the freedom of another, nor be human by taking away the humanity of another." He had learned from Mandela and Gandhi that it is possible to transform an enemy into your friend. If you love your enemy, then you will cause him to hate himself for what he has done to you, and if he hates himself, then he will come to love you.[58]

This joint work by so many people in so many arduous or joyful encounters over so many years is a unique response to a century of conflict. In a worst-case scenario these subversive encounters could collapse tomorrow under the weight of repression and rejection. Or one side could achieve victory over the other and destroy the other's possibility for political independence or equality. Then the cost would be so high that both sides would have lost. In a best-case scenario, however, if negotiations manage to end occupation, then both sides will depend on the skills and relationships of joint activists to face problems, train leadership, and build partnerships between two free peoples.

To some degree the worst-case scenario has been in play for the past fifteen years. Oslo remains unimplemented, violence has escalated, the West Bank has been partially reoccupied, settlements have expanded, Hamas has consolidated power in ways that have further divided Palestine, the separation wall has grown, Israeli control over Palestinians lives has deepened, reactionary forces have harrassed their own people for meeting the other, and wars have persisted. Israel's right wing has delegitimized and attacked joint initiatives. Palestinian antinormalization forces have threatened and killed those who have partnered with Israelis.[59]

Yet nonviolent activists have continued their work. Second-track projects have occurred between unofficial but influential entities like the trilateral Palestinian-Israeli-international Aix Group, an economic study team which has pressed for official negotiations and influenced its various publics. Palestinian and Israeli change agents such as journalists and young leaders have continued to reach their peoples. Education programs have taught the values of peace and human rights. Joint meetings have built informal alliances through the arts, sports, dialogue, and religion. Professionals have coped with conflict-related issues such as water, the environment, and the economy. Midwives, doctors, agronomists, and chefs have found each other and reached thousands of people amid ongoing wars.[60]

These acts were some of the healthiest expressions of democracy and of peoples' will not only in Palestinian and Israeli societies, but in the region and around the world. They inspired many people who want to create a just world—with their activism, with the diversity of participants, and with the ways they learned about and stood against racism, sexism, anti-Semitism, poverty, inequality, occupation, and human rights abuses. They opened access to health care, protected women's and minorities' rights and the environment, and have created chances for children and adults to practice pluralism, tolerance, and respect for difference. They took on the Supreme Court, the military administration, and the army as they fought discrimination to safeguard the dignity of all.

When Arabs and Jews found ways to meet despite their own well-earned fears and fury, they were not wild idealists but sober prophets. They warned us time and again that if we didn't act differently, if we didn't take responsibility in difficult but necessary ways, if we didn't compromise, if we didn't overcome the compulsion to blame, rage, and take revenge for genuine injustice, then violence would escalate, more children would die, and security and freedom would elude their grasp. They were right every time.

When Arabs and Jews risked censure, discomfort, or death to connect with the enemy, they created a living peace. They breached walls, opened closed doors, and raised more questions than answers. Each moment of tentative, clumsy, uncomfortable exploration of the other's reality and each sharing of one's own reality with an enemy who seemed bent on one's destruction was a building block in an emerging foundation for nonviolent resistance. Each time Israelis took risks to advocate against injustices to Palestinians, and each time Palestinians defended Israelis' right to live in peace, they strengthened this foundation. Their history of joint action will remain a testament to an anomalous tale of two enemies who bucked the imperatives of their respective societies to risk becoming allies.

This peacemaking was not agreement or love, but a dynamic discipline of living with an other whose needs and hopes seemed an existential threat. It exposed the delusions that killing and humiliating the other were necessary for survival. Theirs was not a genteel peace, but a messy hash of pain, friendship, betrayal, commitment, disappointment, and inspiration. Arabs and Jews who found ways to work together bore witness to the tragedies of the past and took fresh action in the present because it was the only way to make a difference in the future. Like artists, nonviolent activists stood at the bloody seam of social, political, class, and national fissures. They entered the unknown, surrendering to and sundering limits.

As conflict continues to trump contact, students of history have observed that when a revolution happens on a certain date, the changes attributed to that revolution have been in the making for dozens if not hundreds of years. It is thus possible that these joint nonviolent initiatives throughout a century of the Palestinian-Israeli conflict were not in fact missing peace but were the missing piece of a revolution in the making. Perhaps our descendants will observe in retrospect that joint nonviolence hastened the cessation of hostilities, began to redress inequalities, and helped usher in a just peace. The Czech writer and former president Vaclav Havel wrote that "even a purely moral act that has no hope of any immediate and visible political effect can gradually and indirectly, over time, gain in political significance."[61] The words of American historian Howard Zinn may be an apt testament to these acts:

Human history is a history not only of cruelty, but also of compassion, sacrifice, courage, and kindness. What we choose to emphasize in this complex history will determine our lives. If we see only the worst, it destroys our capacity to do something. If we remember those times and places . . . where people have behaved magnificently, this gives us the energy to act. . . . And if we do act, in however small way, we don't have to wait for some grand utopian future. The future is an infinite succession of presents, and to live now as we think human beings should live, in defiance of all that is bad around us, is itself a marvelous victory.[61]

# Chronology

1875
First Muslim and Jewish neighborhoods outside Old City of Jerusalem

1876
Sultan AbdulHamid II rules the Ottoman Empire until 1909

1876
Arab and Jewish delegates attend first Ottoman Parliament

1878
First modern Zionist agricultural settlement Petah Tikva

1880s
Jews killed in pogroms in Russia; formation of Lovers of Zion for return to homeland
Almost 500,000 Arabs live in Ottoman Syria between the Mediterranean and the Jordan River

1882
Judah Pinsker writes in *Auto-Emancipation* that Jews will never be free except in their own nation
First *aliyah* (immigration wave) of Zionist settlers
Jews found Rishon Le-Tzion, Zichron Yaacov, and Rosh Pina

1885
Hebrew begins to transform into a modern spoken language

1887
Ottomans reorganize administration of Greater Syria, linking Jerusalem to Istanbul, and Nablus and Acre to Beirut

1890
Term *Zionism* coined for modern political Jewish nationalism

1894
Dreyfus Affair begins: French Jewish army officer falsely accused of treason

1896
Theodor Herzl, Austro-Hungarian Jewish journalist, writes *Der Judenstaat*, advocating Jewish state in the ancestral homeland under Ottoman rule

1897
First Zionist Congress in Basel, Switzerland, calls for establishment of home for Jewish people in Palestine; founds World Zionist Organization

1899
Yusif Khalidi, Arab mayor of Jerusalem, writes to chief rabbi of France to support Zionism but not sovereignty

1901
Fifth Zionist Congress creates Jewish National Fund to purchase land

1904–1914
Second *aliyah*; socialist labor Zionism: Jews reject colonialist model to redeem land with their manual labor

1908
First Palestinian Arab newspaper, *Al-Karmil*, fights Arab land transfer to Jews

1909
Degania, the first kibbutz, and Tel Aviv founded

1911
*Filastin*, large Palestinian newspaper, launched in Jaffa

1913
First Arab Congress, Paris

1914
World War I begins, Ottomans side with Germany and Austria against Britain, France, and Russia

1915
Hussein-McMahon Agreement: Great Britain promises Sharif Hussein of Mecca an Arab Kingdom if Arabs revolt against the Ottomans

1916
Arab Revolt against Ottomans led by Sharif Hussein

Sykes-Picot Agreement: Britain and France secretly promise to divide and rule Ottoman Arab lands

**1917**
Britain occupies Jerusalem
Balfour Declaration: Britain pledges support for a Jewish national home in Palestine, protecting rights of others
Russian Revolution

**1918**
World War I ends; Ottoman Empire destroyed
Sharif Hussein's son, Faisal Hussein, leads Arab delegation to Paris Peace Conference
Faisal proclaims independent Arab Kingdom in Damascus
Palestinian Arabs send delegates to form Damascus parliament
Nationalist Muslim-Christian Associations founded in Jaffa and Jerusalem

**1919**
Feisal-Weizmann Agreement supports Arab and Jewish nationalism
Palestinian National Congress in Jerusalem calls for Palestinian state, rejects Balfour Declaration, joins Arab Kingdom
Seven Palestinian National Congresses held in Jerusalem, Jaffa, Haifa, and Nablus, through 1928
Third *aliyah* of Jewish immigrants, through 1923

**1920**
League of Nations founded
British Mandate rules Palestine
France defeats Faisal's Arab Kingdom
Britain appoints Faisal king of Iraq
Jews create representative government with elected assembly
Jews establish Histadrut Labor Federation
Palestinian National Congress in Haifa forms Arab Executive Committee; Britain refuses formal recognition

**1921**
Britain prohibits Jewish settlement east of the Jordan River and in the Golan Heights
Arab anti-Jewish riots
British appoint Amin al-Husayni mufti of Jerusalem

**1922**
Modern Hebrew becomes official language with Arabic
Britain creates Transjordan by partitioning Palestine; appoints Faisal's brother, Abdullah, as king

1924
Fourth *aliyah* of Jewish settlers, through 1929

1925
Arabs establish Palestinian Workers Society trade union
Jews establish Hebrew University in Jerusalem

1929
Violent clashes over Western Wall in Jerusalem, Hebron, and Safed
Arab Women's Congress takes public nationalist stance
Fifth *aliyah*, increasing immigration due to rise of Hitler, through 1939

1930
British Passfield White Paper blames Jewish immigration and land purchases for
   Arab violence

1931
Pan-Islamic Congress in Jerusalem

1932
Istiqlal (Independence), first Palestinian political party

1935
New Palestinian political parties form, Al-Difa al-Watani (National Defense),
   Hizb al-'Arabi al-Filastin (Palestine Arab Party), Hizb al-Islah (Reform)

1936
Arab Higher Committee founded in all towns, some villages; outlawed by Britain
   the following year

1936–1939
Arab Revolt: Palestinian nationalist uprising, violent and nonviolent struggle
   against Jews and British

1937
British Peel Commission proposes partition of Palestine

1939
Britain defeats Arab Revolt
British White Paper stops Jewish immigration and land purchases over next ten
   years and calls for an Arab-ruled state repudiating the Balfour Declarations

1939–1945
World War II, Nazi genocide of six million Jews

1942
Zionist Biltmore Program calls for statehood in Palestine

1944
Arab National Fund revived

1945
United Nations formed
Arab League formed
Jewish refugees detained in displaced persons camps in Europe; British deny their
    entry to Palestine
Jews revolt against Britain; Haganah paramilitary forces and Jewish underground
    terrorists attack British targets

1946
Jewish Irgun blows up British headquarters in Jerusalem
Arab paramilitary groups form

1947
Britain submits Palestine Mandate to UN
UN General Assembly votes to partition Palestine into Jewish and Arab states;
    Arabs reject, Jews accept
Arab-Jewish civil war

1948
May 13, Britain evacuates Palestine
May 14, Israel declares independence
May 15, Egypt, Jordan, Syria, Lebanon, and Iraq invade Israel

1948–1949
Nakba; mass exodus of Palestinian Arabs from Israel

1949
Armistice Agreement cease-fire between Israel and Arab states; Jordan annexes
    West Bank; Egypt controls Gaza Strip; Jerusalem divided; Arabs don't recog-
    nize Israel
Jewish refugees from Europe, the Middle East, and North Africa immigrate to
    Israel through 1950s

1950s
Military rule imposed on most Arabs in Israel until 1966
Palestinian fedayeen attack Israel from Egypt, Syria, Jordan

1951
George Habash founds what will become the Popular Front for the Liberation
    of Palestine (PFLP)

1952
Arab League claims to represent Palestinian Arabs' cause

1956
Egypt nationalizes Suez Canal
Suez War: Britain, France, and Israel attack Egypt and *fedayeen*

1964
Palestine Liberation Organization (PLO) forms in Cairo

1966
Israel lifts martial law; Arabs gain legal citizenship

1967
Six-Day War: Israel gains Golan Heights, West Bank, Gaza Strip, Sinai
UN Security Council Resolution 242 calls for Israeli withdrawal from conquered
     areas in exchange for mutual recognition

1969
Yasser Arafat elected PLO chair by Palestinian National Council
Abdel Nasser of Egypt launches war of attrition against Israel

1970
Black September: Jordan defeats PLO; PLO moves to Lebanon

1972
Palestinians massacre eleven Israeli Olympic athletes in Munich

1973
October War: Arab countries attack Israel on Yom Kippur and Ramadan; US-
     Soviet–imposed cease-fire

1974
Arab states affirm PLO as sole representative of Palestinians
Arafat's first speech to UN calls for one democratic secular state

1975
UN resolution equates Zionism with racism

1976
First Land Day (March 30); Israeli Arabs protest
PFLP hijacks Air France to Entebbe, Uganda; Israel rescues 248 passengers

1977
Menachem Begin elected first Likud prime minister
Egyptian president Anwar Sadat flies to Jerusalem to offer peace

1978
Camp David I: Carter, Begin, Sadat

**1979**
Israel-Egypt peace treaty

**1982**
Israel withdraws from Sinai
Israel invades Lebanon; routs PLO, which moves to Tunisia
Sabra and Shatila massacres by Lebanese Christian Falange

**1985**
Palestinians hijack the MS *Achille Lauro*, kill wheelchair-bound Jewish American
    Leon Klinghoffer and travelers at airports

**1986**
Knesset law forbids Israeli citizens contact with the PLO

**1987**
First Palestinian intifada
Hamas founded

**1988**
Palestine National Council declares independence
Arafat renounces violence and recognizes Israel
US begins talks with PLO; Jordan relinquishes its claim over the West Bank

**1989-1991**
Soviet Union collapses; mass migration of Soviet Jews to Israel
Iraq invades Kuwait; launches Scud missiles against Haifa and Tel Aviv
Gulf War; US-led coalition defeats Iraq

**1991**
Madrid Peace Conference, US-Soviet–supported multilateral negotiations be-
    tween Israel, a Palestinian-Jordanian delegation, Syria, and Lebanon

**1992**
Yitzhak Rabin of Labor Party elected prime minister of Israel

**1993**
Attack on World Trade Center towers in New York City
Oslo Accords: Arafat and Rabin sign Declaration of Principles, a timetable for
    negotiating an end to conflict and occupation

**1994**
Peace Treaty between Jordan and Israel
Palestinian self-rule begins in Gaza and Jericho with Arafat as president of Pales-
    tinian Authority; Israel withdraws troops

1995
Oslo 2 signed by Yitzak Rabin and Yassir Arafat
Yitzhak Rabin assassinated by religious Jew at peace rally

1996
Palestinian Authority government elected
Netanyahu elected in Likud victory

1997
Hebron Agreement: Palestinian Authority expands control

1998
Wye Plantation talks; Israel releases prisoners and land
Palestinian Authority expands control
Arafat retracts official call to exterminate Israel

1999
King Hussein of Jordan dies; his son Abdullah assumes the throne
Ehud Barak elected prime minister of Israel in Labor victory; Syria peace talks fail
Israel and Palestinian Authority negotiate joint industrial area

2000
Camp David II; Barak and Arafat final status talks fail
Second intifada begins

2001
Ariel Sharon elected prime minister of Israel in Likud victory
Terror attack by Al-Qaeda destroys World Trade Center, New York City

2002
US president George W. Bush calls for independent Palestinian state in peace
    with Israel
First pan-Arab peace initiative supports two-state solution

2003
Bush announces Road Map for Peace
Israel begins building security barrier
Geneva Accord by Palestinians and Israelis details two-state solution

2004
Arafat dies in Paris hospital; intifada winds down

2005
Israel unilaterally withdraws troops and settlements from Gaza
Mahmoud Abbas elected president of the Palestinian Authority

2006
Hamas wins Palestinian Authority legislative elections and launches attacks on
    Israel
Hezbollah-Israel war in Lebanon

2007
Hamas takes over Gaza Strip, dividing Palestinian national movement

2009
Israel-Gaza war
US president Barack Obama supports two-state solution, opposes settlements

2010
Arab Spring democratic uprisings begin in Tunisia

# Initiatives by Category

Arranged into 14 categories, these 500 initiatives include most of the ones mentioned in the text. Many belong to multiple categories but are only mentioned once. Not all were "joint" but worked with or benefitted the other side. Beside each initiative are chapter numbers that reference their time period.

## The Arts: Visual, Theater, Film, Music, Culinary

Alei Hazayit (band) 6
All Nations Café 8
Arab Hebrew Theater: Jaffa 7
Artists Without Walls 8
Beersheba Municipal Theater 4
Beit Hagefen Arab Culture and Book Week 6
Beit Hagefen Folk Dance Troupe and Arab mobile theater 6
Beresheet LaShalom 9
Bustan Avraham (band) 7
Chefs for Peace 8
Committee of Creative Arts 6
Creativity for Peace 8
*Crossing the Line*, video (2002) 8
Dam Palestinian Hip Hop band Mixed Cities Tour 9
*Encounter Point*, film (2006) 9
Frames of Reality photojournalism, Peres Center 9
Galilee Multicultural Theater 7
Gypsies Street Theater Group (Tzoanim/Ghajar) 4
*The Haifa War Diary—Eli and Nasser*, film (2006) 9
Heartbeat 9
Israeli-Palestinian Comedy Tour 9
Jewish Arabic Ensemble: Safed College Ethnic Music Academy 9
*Knowledge is the Beginning*, film (2005) 9
*The Lemon Tree*, film (2008) 9

The Local Theater: Jaffa 7
Masks Off Project, Arcobaleno-Rainbow dance/music theater 9
Middle East Center for the Arts (MECA) 7
Museum on the Seam 9
*My So-Called Enemy*, film (2010) 10
Neve Shalom/Wahat al-Salam festival of the arts 6
Palestinian Artists Association 6
*Paradise Now*, film (2005) 9
Peace Child 6
Pieces for Peace 7
Project Encounter 6
Project Harmony 10
*Promises*, film (2001) 8
*Refusing to Be Enemies: the Zeituna Story*, film (2007) 9
*Return to Haifa*, play, Cameri Theater Tel Aviv 9
Sahana Music Band 9
Seeds of Bliss 10
*Six Actors in Search of a Plot*, play 9
Umm el-Fahem Art Gallery 7
*Waltz with Bashir*, film (2008) 9
*West Bank Story*, film (2005) 9
White Bird (band) 7
Yair Dalal, Nobel Peace Prize Concert, Oslo 7

## Civil Society, Human Rights, Democracy

The Abraham Fund (TAF) 6
Adalah: Legal Center for Minority Rights in Israel 7
Adam 5
Arab Association for Human Rights 6
Arab-Jewish Center for Equality, Empowerment and Cooperation (AJEEC) 8
Arafat Society for Culture and Human Care 9
Association for Civil Rights in Israel (ACRI) 4
Association for Peace and Equality, Abdul Aziz Zuabi 3
Bimkom 7
B'Tselem 6
Center for Democracy and Community Development 9
Citizens Accord Forum 8
Deliberative Democracy 7
Gisha 9
HaMoked hotline 6
Al-Haq 5
Israeli Committee Against Torture (I) 6
Issam Sartawi Center for Advancement of Peace and Democracy 7
Kav La-Oved "Workers' Hotline" 6
Al-Manarah 9

Merchavim: Institute for Advancement of Shared Citizenship
Middle East Nonviolence and Democracy (MEND) 7
Muwatin, Palestinian Institute for the Study of Democracy 6
Negev Coexistence Forum for Civil Equality 7
Neighbors for Joint Development in the Galilee 8
New Israel Fund 4
NGO Forum for Peace 8
Palestine Center for Conflict Resolution and Reconciliation 7
Palestinian Center for Alternative Solutions 8
Palestinian Center for Democracy and Conflict Resolution 7
Palestinian Center for Human Rights in Gaza 7
Palestinian Center for Peace and Democracy 6
Palestinian Center for Research and Cultural Dialogue 8
Palestinian Civic Forum Institute 7
Palestinian Human Rights Information Center 6
Palestinian Peace Society 10
Panorama: Palestinian Center for Dissemination of Democracy and Community 6
Peace and Democracy Forum in East Jerusalem 7
People's Campaign for Peace and Democracy 8
Shatil 5
Sikkuy 6
Ta'ayush 8
Al-Tariq: Institute for Development and Democracy 9
Tawasul 8
Wi'am: Palestinian Conflict Resolution Center 7
Yesh Din 9


**Communications: Print, Web, Technology, Radio, Journalism**

All for Peace Radio 8
Alliance for Middle East Peace (ALLMEP) 9
Arik Institute for Reconciliation, Tolerance, and Peace 8
*Best of Enemies*, Abu-Sharif and Mahnaimi 7
*Between Enemies*, Sana Hassan and Amos Elon 3
Bitterlemons.com 8
Community Histories by Youth in the Middle East (CHYME) 8
*Democracy, Peace, and the Israeli-Palestinian Conflict*, Abed and Kaufman 7
Dugrinet (Makom Bagalil) 8
Encounter, Mustadafa/Mifgash 8
Engineers' meetings in Aqaba 10
G.ho.s.t. Israeli-Palestinian software 10
Hello Peace! 8
Israel Palestine Forum 9
Israeli-Palestinian Media Forum 8
Just Vision 8
Language Connections 8

Mepeace.org 9
Middle East Education through Technology (MEET) 8
New Generations Technologies 8
*New Outlook Magazine* 3
*No Peace without Free Palestinian State*, Muhammad Abu Shilbaya 4
*Palestine-Israel Journal* 7
Peace Computer Centers 9
PEACEWECAN website 8
Skype during Gaza War: al-Tariq with Sulha Peace Project 10
Traubman family website of joint initiatives 8
Voice of Peace radio, Abie Nathan 4
*Windows: Magazine for All Children* 7


## Community Activism

Acco Group for Joint Living 9
Arab-Jewish Community Center of Jaffa 7
Arabic-Hebrew Studies Center in Jerusalem 7
Clore Neighborhood Center, Haifa 8
East Barta'a Free Clinic: Middle Way 9
Friendship's Way: Jaffa 5
Galilee Foundation for Value Education: Moshav Shorashim 6
Gilboa's Regional Council 9
Interns for Peace (Nitzanei Shalom/Bara'am al-Salaam) 4
Ir Amim: Jerusalem 8
Jerusalem Foundation 6
Jerusalem Inter-Cultural Center 7
Jewish Arab Community Association: Acre 6
Living in Jerusalem, Citizenship and Multiculturalism 9
Oasis of Peace Neve Shalom/ Wahat al-Salaam 4
Other Voice: Gaza and Sederot 9
Palestinian House of Friendship (Nablus) 8
Peres Center for Peace: Jaffa 7
Neighborhood Home: Jaffa 6


## Dialogue

Co-Counseling Arab-Jewish workshops 4
Committee for Israeli-Palestinian Dialogue 5
Compassionate Listening Project in Israel and Palestine 7
Covenant of the Sons of Shem 4
Greek Catholic archbishop George Hakim Haifa dialogues 3
Hanna Siniora secret Palestinian-Israeli dialogue groups 4
House of Hope, Shefaram 4

Kelman third-party approach international workshops 4
Mifgashim-Lika'at: Alternative Voice in the Galilee 8
One-to-One: Arab-Jewish Project of Hillel House 4
Prejudice reduction, communication, problem solving, sensitivity training 4
Middle East Citizen Diplomacy 7
Nonviolent Communication (NVC) 10
Palestinian Center for Rapprochement (P) 6
Wounded Crossing Borders 9

## Economy, Business

Aix Group 10
Business-to-Business Peres Center 9
Center for Jewish-Arab Economic Development (CJAED) 6
Economic Development Venture 9
Green Action 9
Israeli-Palestinian Chamber of Commerce 10
The Jasmine Project: CJAED 9
Jenin-Gilboa Tourism Projects 10
Jerusalem Community Kitchen 9
Jerusalem Women's Association with Palestinian Media and Development Institute 9
Kav Mashve: Israeli Equal Opportunity Initiative 9
Mejdi: Dual Narrative Tour Company 9
Negev Arab Businessmen's Forum 9
Negev Institute for Strategies of Peace and Development NISPED 9
Palestine Investment Fund 10
Palestine Trade Center (Paltrade) with IPCRI 9
Palestinian Agency for Food and Agriculture 9
Palestinian-Israeli Business Forum: CJAED 7
Peace Oil 9
SAHA, fair trade 9
Sharikat Haya, an Arab Women's Employment Initiative 9
Shorouq, Palestinian Society for Women 9
Sindyanna of the Galilee 9
Women's Association of Wadi Fukin 9
Young Entrepreneurs of Palestine 9
Zaytoun Collective 9

## Educational Activism and Research

Abu Ghosh High School with Pelech Religious Experimental High School for Girls 7
ALON Social Involvement Organization 7

## Political Activism

Peace Now (*Shalom Akhshav*) 4
Peace Tent and Committee of Arab Mayors 7
Police Relations Initiative: The Abraham Fund 8
Rabbis for Human Rights 6
Al-Safadi letter to President of Iran 8
Seruv 8
Shufani's trip for Arabs to Auschwitz-Birkenau
Shutafut/Mushaarakah (Partnership) 4
Soldiers against Silence 5
Twenty-First Year 6
Unified National Leadership of the Uprising 6
Wadi Ara rally for peace and against racism 6
Al-Watan Center 6
We Want Peace, Palestinian Graffiti/Sticker campaign 6
Witness the Occupation 6
Yesh Gavul 5, 6
Zochrot 8


## Political Negotiations, Parties, Policy

14 Points 6
Abu-Sharif and Mahnaimi meetings 6
Ahmad Samah al-Khalidi proposal to Zionist leaders 2
Arab Higher Committee-Magnes proposals 2
Awni Abd al-Hadi and Omar Salih al-Barghuti's and Kalvarisky's "Platform for
    Judaeo-Arab Accord" 2
Aziz Shehadeh peace plan 4
Binationalist Initiatives 1
Cairo-based Decentralization Party and anti-Ottoman Beirut Reform Society
    meeting with Zionists 1
Daud Barakat (Arab editor, *Al-Ahram*, Cairo) proposal 1
Faisal-Weizmann agreement 1
Fares Hamdan, initiatives by first Arab elected to Knesset 3
First Arab Congress: Arab and Jewish alliance 1
The Geneva Accords/Initiatives 8
Haifa Municipal Council 2
Hajj Amin al-Husayni, David Ben Gurion talks 2
Ha-Magen: Arab-Jewish alliance with Arab nationalists 1
Hashomer Hatza'ir, the Young Guard 3
Israeli Leftist parties: Matzpen, Siah, Moked, Sheli, Shasi 4
Israeli-Palestinian Negotiating Partners, Harvard 8
Israeli-Palestinian Peace Research Project 6
Joseph Abileah's Federation of Israel, Palestine, and Jordan 3
Kazim al-Husayni and Chaim Kalvarisky meetings 2
Khaled al-Hassan and Rita Hauser meetings 6
King Hassan, Morocco, call for Peace with Israel, 1958 3

Magnes-Alami binational confederation Jordan, Syria Lebanon 2
MAPAM Arab-Jewish Arab Affairs Department 3
MAPAM third congress 1958 Arab and Jewish delegates 3
MERETZ coalition 7
Musa Alami, David Ben Gurion talks 2
Naomi Chazan and Yael Dayan's talks with PLO 7
Nasif al-Khalidi and Chaim Kalvarisky plan joint conference 1
New Force party in Knesset calls for Palestinian state 3
New Paths to Peace conferences, Simcha Flapan 3
OSLO Accords Declaration of Principles, Arafat and Rabin 7
Ottoman Municipal Councils: Muslim, Jewish, Christian 1
Palestine Communist Party binational proposal 3
People's Voice 8
PLO–James Baker (US) talks 6
Progressive List for Peace: A-J 5
Rustum Bastuni elected to Knesset 3
Said Hammami peace plan for mutual recognition 4
Semitic Action's federation of Palestine, Israel, Jordan 3
Shinui: Democratic Front for Peace and Equality, Labor, Civil Rights Movement 5
Uri Avnery's Pax Semitica and *Haolam Hazeh* Arab alliance 3
Usbat al-Taharrur al-Watani (Ar. National Liberation League) and newspaper *Al-Ittihad* supports joint action 3
Zionist and Syrian nationalists leaders meeting 2

## Religious Activism

Fire for Peace: 3-day multicultural religious festival 8
Interfaith Dialogues: Hebrew University 5
Interfaith Encounter Association 8
Interfaith renovation of Anglican Church in Jerusalem 7
Interreligious Coordinating Council in Israel 6
Jerusalem Center for Jewish-Christian Relations (JCJCR) 8
Jerusalem Peacemakers 8
Middle Way: Compassionate Engagement in Society 8
Nablus Youth Federation 8
Netivot Shalom 5
Oz v'Shalom 5
Sulha Project 8
United Religions Initiative Middle East and North Africa 10

## Science, Environment, Medicine, Mental Health

Alliance of Middle Eastern Scientists and Physicians
Arab Bone Marrow Registry by Dr. Amal Bishara 9
Arava Institute for Environmental Studies 7

Association of Israeli and Palestinian Physicians for Human Rights 6
*Bridges*: Israeli and Palestinian public health magazine 8
Center for the Environment: IPCRI 7
Citizens for the Environment 6
Economic Cooperation Foundation with Palestinian Ministry of Health and Palestinian Council of Health 8
Friends of the Earth Middle East (FoEME) 7
Gaza Community Mental Health Program 6
Good Water Neighbors 8
Haganat Hateva in Sinai 4
Heart of the Matter Project 7
Humans Without Borders 8
Israeli-Palestinian Science Organization 8
Mental Health Workers for the Advancement of Peace 6
Midwives for Peace 9
NIR School of the Heart 7
Ossim Shalom: Social Workers for Peace and Welfare 6
Palestinian Galilee Society: Arab National Society for Health Research and Services 5
Palestinian-Israeli Environmental Secretariat 7
Pediatric Hemato-Oncology Unit: Peres Center for Peace 9
Save a Child's Heart 7
Sharhabil Bin Hassneh Eco Park 8
Social Working Together 8

### Sports and Physical Activism

Antarctica: Breaking the Ice 8
Arab-Jewish Walk for Fitness 8
Arab Workers' Club and Jewish Kupat Holim 2
Joggers for Peace 6
Peace Players International 9
Peace Sports School Program: Al-Quds Association for Democracy and Dialogue, Ramallah, with Peres Center 9
Seas of Peace 10
Soccer for Peace 9

### Women's Activism

Association for the Advancement of Women's Health in Israel 7
Aswat 8
Bat Shalom 7
Beyond Words 8
Bridge: feminist peace group, Haifa 4
Bridge for Peace 7

## Youth Activism

Alpert Music Center's Jewish-Arab Youth Orchestra 9
Arab-Jewish Intervention Programs 5
Arab-Jewish Young People's Clubs 2
Building Bridges for Peace 9
Budo for Peace 8
Cyprus Young Adult Workshops for Arabs and Jews 4
Djanogly Visual Arts Center: Jerusalem Foundation 9
Friendship Center in Tel Aviv 7
Friendship Village 7
Future Generation Hands Association 9
Galilee Circus 8
Harduf-Shefaram Theater Track 8
"I Am You Are" film workshop, Jerusalem Cinemateque 9
Jerusalem Circus 8
Jerusalem International YMCA peace kindergarten 9
Jewish-Arab Association for the Child and Family: Jaffa 5
Lebanese and Israeli children's orchestra: George Samaʿan 7
"Markaz" Community in Action 9
Naggar School of Photography: special needs 9
Nazareth Annual Summer Youth Labor Camps 4
Neighborhood Home: Jaffa 5
Neighbors: Makom Bagalil *8*
Nemashim, a theater commune 9
Reut/Sadaka 5
*Roadblock*, play, Arabic Qalansua High School and Hebrew Maayan-Shacher School 9
Seeds of Peace 7
Seeking Common Ground 9
Shaʿar la-Adam/Bab lil-Insan (Heb./Ar. gate to humanity) 8
Voice of Peace Choir 8
Young People Against Racism 7
Young Leaders' Summer Academy 9
Youth Leadership Development: Jaffa 7
Youth Sing a Different Song 5

# Notes

## Preface

1. Sheila H. Katz, *Women and Gender in Early Jewish and Palestinian Nationalism* (Gainesville: University Press of Florida, 2003).
2. Rashid Khalidi, *Palestinian Identity: The Construction of Modern National Consciousness* (New York: Columbia University Press, 1997), 89.
3. Mohammed Abu-Nimer, *Dialogue, Conflict Resolution, and Change: Arab-Jewish Encounters in Israel* (Albany: State University of New York Press, 1999), 44.
4. Shany Payes, *Palestinian NGOs in Israel: The Politics of Civil Society* (Taurus Academic, 2005), 191.

## Introduction

1. Elias Chacour and Mary E. Jensen, *We Belong to the Land: The Story of a Palestinian Israeli Who Lives for Peace and Reconciliation* (San Francisco: HarperSanFrancisco, 1990), 205.
2. David Grossman, "An Israel without Illusions: Stop the Grindstone of Israeli-Palestinian Violence," *New York Times*, 27 July 2014.
3. Anke Rasper, "Mending the Middle East," *Deutsche Welle*, 5 July 2012, www.dw.com/en/mending-the-middle-east/a-16072192.
4. Gene Sharp, *The Politics of Nonviolent Action* (Boston: Sargent, 1973), 64.
5. Thomas Weber and Robert J. Burrowes, "Nonviolence: An Introduction," Washington, DC: Nonviolence International, n.d. www.nonviolenceinternational.net/seasia/whatis/book.php.
6. Sari Nusseibeh with Anthony David, *Once Upon a Country: A Palestinian Life* (New York: Farrar Straus and Giroux, 2007), 305.
7. Michael N. Nagler, Tal Palter-Palman, and Matthew A. Taylor, "The Road to Nonviolent Coexistence in Palestine/Israel," website of Matthew A. Taylor, March 2007, www.matthewtaylor.net/nvcoexistpalisfinal.pdf.
8. Téa Obreht, *The Tiger's Wife: A Novel* (New York: Random House, 2011), 238.

9. Rashid Khalidi, *Palestinian Identity: The Construction of Modern National Consciousness* (New York: Columbia University Press, 1997), viii–ix.

10. Ibid., xi.

11. "The Merciful Lord of Mercy" is one of the primary descriptions of God in the Quran, and is present in the *Fatiha*, or opening.

12. Martin Luther King Jr., *Where Do We Go from Here: Chaos or Community?* (Boston: Beacon, 1967), 62–63.

## Chapter 1

1. Alan Dowty, "'A Question that Outweighs All Others': Yitzhak Epstein and the Zionist Recognition of the Arab Issue," *Israel Studies* 6, no. 1 (2001), 47.

2. Aharon Cohen, *Israel and the Arab World* (New York: Funk and Wagnalls, 1970), 97.

3. Geoffrey W. Furlonge, *Palestine Is My Country: The Story of Musa Alami* (New York: Praeger, 1969), 6.

4. Rashid Khalidi, *Palestinian Identity: The Construction of Modern National Consciousness* (New York: Columbia University Press, 1997), 6.

5. Beshara Doumani, *Rediscovering Palestine: Merchants and Peasants in Jabal Nablus, 1700–1900* (Berkeley: University of California Press, 1995), 235–236.

6. Samih K. Farsoun and Naseer Aruri, *Palestine and the Palestinians*, 2nd ed. (Boulder, CO: Westview, 2006), 23.

7. Baruch Kimmerling and Joel S. Migdal, *Palestinians: The Making of a People* (New York: Free Press, 1993), 8–9.

8. Farsoun and Aruri, *Palestine and the Palestinians*, 22.

9. Benny Morris, *Righteous Victims: A History of the Zionist-Arab Conflict, 1881–1999* (New York: Knopf, 1999), 7.

10. In Roger Owen, *The Middle East in the World Economy, 1800–1914* (London: Methuen, 1981), and Charles P. Issawi, *An Economic History of the Middle East and Northern Africa* (New York: Columbia University Press, 1982).

11. On development of Palestinian identity from 1700 to 1900, see Doumani, *Rediscovering Palestine*; from the mid-nineteenth to early twentieth century see Khalidi, *Palestinian Identity*.

12. Zachary Lockman, *Comrades and Enemies: Arab and Jewish Workers in Palestine, 1906–1948* (Berkeley: University of California Press, 1996), 43–44.

13. A reference to a book written by founder of Zionism, Theodore Herzl: *Altneuland: Old-New Land*, trans. Lotta Levensohn (Princeton, NJ: M. Wiener, 1997).

14. Morris, *Righteous Victims*, 25.

15. Neville J. Mandel, *The Arabs and Zionism before World War One.* (Berkeley: University of California Press, 1976), 47–48.

16. Najib Azuri, *Le reveil de la nation arabe* (Paris: Plon, 1905).

17. See Khalidi, *Palestinian Identity*.

18. Morris, *Righteous Victims*, 677.

19. Farsoun and Aruri, *Palestine and the Palestinians*, 51.

20. Khalidi, *Palestinian Identity*, 98–99.

21. Mandel, *Arabs and Zionism*, 30–38.

22. Ibid., 37.

23. Lockman, *Comrades and Enemies*, 51.

24. Ibid., 45.

25. Shifra Belzer in Rachel Katznelson-Shazar, *The Plough Woman: Records of the Pioneer Women of Palestine* (Westport, CT: Hyperion, 1976), 43.

26. Hannah Trager, *Pioneers in Palestine: Stories of One of the First Settlers in Petach Tikva* (Westport, CT: Hyperion, 1976), 9.

27. Ibid., 15–17.

28. Ibid., 105.

29. Morris, *Righteous Victims*, 57.

30. For further discussion, see Benjamin Beit-Hallahmi, *Original Sins: Reflections on the History of Zionism and Israel* (New York: Olive Branch, 1993).

31. Shabtai Teveth, *Ben-Gurion and the Palestinian Arabs: From Peace to War* (Oxford: Oxford University Press, 1985), 137.

32. Morris, *Righteous Victims*, 58.

33. Cohen, *Israel and the Arab World*, 97.

34. Neil Caplan, *Futile Diplomacy* (London: Frank Cass, 1983), 18–20.

35. Morris, *Righteous Victims*, 65.

36. Kimmerling and Migdal, *Palestinians*, 71.

37. Caplan, *Futile Diplomacy*, 21.

38. Ibid., 28.

39. Mark Tessler, *A History of the Israeli-Palestinian Conflict*, 2nd ed. (Bloomington: Indiana University Press, 2009), 153.

40. Morris, *Righteous Victims*, 79.

41. See the "Feisal-Weizmann Agreement," in Walter Laqueur and Barry Rubin, *The Israel-Arab Reader: A Documentary History of the Middle East Conflict*, 7th ed. (New York: Penguin, 2009), 18–20.

## Chapter 2

1. Arthur A. Goren, ed., *Dissenter in Zion: From the Writings of Judah L. Magnes* (Cambridge: Harvard University Press, 1982), 48.

2. Zachary Lockman, *Comrades and Enemies: Arab and Jewish Workers in Palestine, 1906–1948* (Berkeley: University of California Press, 1996), 118–119.

3. Rachel Yanait Ben-Zvi, *Before Golda: Manya Shochat, a Biography* (New York: Biblio, 1989), 90.

4. Issam Nassar, "Reflections on Writing the History of Palestinian Identity," *Palestine-Israel Journal* 8–9, nos. 4 and 1 (2001–2002), n.p.

5. Samih K. Farsoun and Naseer Aruri, *Palestine and the Palestinians*, 2nd ed. (Boulder, CO: Westview), 77.

6. For analysis of the situation of Palestinians under the Mandate, see Rashid Khalidi, *The Iron Cage: The Story of the Palestinian Struggle for Statehood* (Boston: Beacon, 2006).

7. Atallah Mansour, *Waiting for the Dawn: An Autobiography* (London: Secker, 1975), 9.

8. Deborah S. Bernstein, *The Struggle for Equality: Urban Women Workers in Pre-state Israeli Society* (New York: Praeger, 1987), 118.

9. Yanait Ben Zvi, *Before Golda*, 126.

10. Lockman, *Comrades and Enemies*, 69-70.

11. Simona Sharoni, *Gender and the Israeli-Palestinian Conflict: The Politics of Women's Resistance* (Syracuse, NY: Syracuse University Press, 1995), 132; Elise G. Young, *Keepers of the History: Women and the Israeli-Palestinian Conflict* (New York: Teachers College Press, 1992), 138.

12. Rachel Katznelson-Shazar, *The Plough Woman: Records of the Pioneer Women of Palestine* (Westport, CT: Hyperion, 1976), 121-123; Deborah S. Bernstein, *Constructing Boundaries: Jewish and Arab Workers in Mandatory Palestine* (Albany: State University of New York Press), 133.

13. Lockman, *Comrades and Enemies*, 119-120.

14. Ibid., 73.

15. Ibid., 124-126, 128.

16. Ibid., 135-136.

17. Ibid., 118.

18. Ibid., 85-87.

19. Shabtai Teveth, *Ben-Gurion and the Palestinian Arabs: From Peace to War* (Oxford: Oxford University Press, 1985), 119-120.

20. Lockman, *Comrades and Enemies*, 105.

21. Ibid., 88-90, 94, 98.

22. Goren, *Dissenter*, 38.

23. Paul Mendes-Flohr, ed., *A Land of Two Peoples: Martin Buber on Jews and Arabs* (New York: Oxford University Press, 1983), 3.

24. Ibid., 12, 14.

25. Martin Buber, *On Zion: the History of an Idea* (New York: Schocken, 1973), x.

26. Teveth, *Ben-Gurion*, 67-70.

27. Neil Caplan, *Futile Diplomacy* (London: Frank Cass, 1983), 65-72, 78.

28. Benny Morris, *Righteous Victims: A History of the Zionist-Arab Conflict, 1881-1999* (New York: Knopf, 1999), 105.

29. Caplan, *Futile Diplomacy*, 47-52.

30. Goren, *Dissenter*, 27.

31. Ibid., 235.

32. Ibid., 87, 97.

33. Goren, *Dissenter*, 34; Bernard Wasserstein, "The Arab-Jewish Dilemma," in *Like All the Nations?: The Life and Legacy of Judah L. Magnes*, ed. William M. Brinner and Moses Rischin (Albany: State University of New York, 1987), 188-189.

34. Goren, *Dissenter*, 35, 40.

35. Lockman, *Comrades and Enemies*, 159.

36. P. J. Vatikiotis, *Among Arabs and Jews: A Personal Experience, 1936-1990* (London: Weidenfeld and Nicolson, 1991), 20, 23.

37. Ibid., 24-28, 33-35, 56.

38. Carol J. Birkland, *Unified in Hope: Arabs and Jews Talk about Peace* (New York: Friendship, 1987), 131.

39. Elias Chacour and Mary E. Jensen, *We Belong to the Land: The Story of a*

*Palestinian Israeli Who Lives for Peace and Reconciliation* (San Francisco: HarperSan-Franscisco, 1990), 103.

40. Gideon Weigert, *My Life with the Palestinians* (Jerusalem: Jerusalem Times, 1997), 13-15, 20, 23, 26.

41. Lockman, *Comrades and Enemies*, 182-186.

42. Judah L. Magnes and Martin Buber, *Arab-Jewish Unity: Testimony before the Anglo-American Inquiry Commission for the Ihud (Union) Association* (Westport, CT: Hyperion, 1976), 12.

43. Lockman, *Comrades and Enemies*, 160-166.

44. Teveth, *Ben-Gurion*, 105.

45. David Ben-Gurion, *My Talks with Arab Leaders* (Jerusalem: Keter, 1972), vii.

46. Teveth, *Ben-Gurion*, 129-130.

47. Ben-Gurion, *My Talks*, 7-8.

48. Teveth, *Ben-Gurion*, 132.

49. Ben-Gurion, *My Talks*, 16-17.

50. Ibid., 24-27, 30-31.

51. Ibid., 32-33.

52. Caplan, *Futile Diplomacy*, 90-92, 96-100, 103.

53. Tamir Goren, "Cooperation Is the Guiding Principle?: Jews and Arabs in the Haifa Municipality during the British Mandate." *Israel Studies* 11, no. 3 (2006), 108.

54. Goren, *Dissenter*, 305.

55. Ben-Gurion, *My Talks*, 18-19, 23.

56. Teveth, *Ben-Gurion*, 149, 155-158.

57. Philip Mattar, *The Mufti in Jerusalem* (New York: Columbia University Press, 1992), 50-64.

58. Ben-Gurion, *My Talks*, 46-47.

59. Ben-Gurion, *My Talks*, 47-49, 53-54.

60. Goren, *Dissenter*, 36-37.

61. "Palestine Royal Commission Peel Report, 1937," in *The Israel-Arab Reader: A Documentary History*, 7th ed., ed. Walter Laqueur and Barry Rubin (London: Penguin, 2008), 41-42.

62. Ben-Gurion, *My Talks*, 122-124, 127, 141, 145-147, 151.

63. Ibid., 199.

64. Elie Eliachar, *Israeli Jews and Palestinian Arabs: Key to Arab-Jewish Coexistence* (Jerusalem: Council of the Sephardi Community, 1970), 9.

65. Rashid Khalidi, *Iron Cage*, 116-118.

66. Ibid., 120.

67. Birkland, *Unified in Hope*, 36.

68. For details on the League for Jewish and Arab Rapprochement, see Jos Strengholt, "A Jewish State with Cannons, Flags, and Military Decorations: Strengthening and Defeat of the Bi-nationalist Movement in Palestine 1939-1942," Binationalism blog, 28 October 2008, http://binationalism.blogspot.com.

69. Lockman, *Comrades and Enemies*, 170, 172-173, 178.

## Chapter 3

1. Martin Buber, "Genuine Dialogue and the Possibilities of Peace," in *Pointing the Way: Collected Essays* (New York: Harper, 1957), 237–238.

2. For more encounters from that period, see Carol J. Birkland, *Unified in Hope: Arabs and Jews Talk about Peace* (New York: Friendship, 1987).

3. Rashid Khalidi, *The Iron Cage: The Story of the Palestinian Struggle for Statehood* (Boston: Beacon, 2006), 107–108.

4. Zachary Lockman, *Comrades and Enemies: Arab and Jewish Workers in Palestine, 1906–1948* (Berkeley: University of California Press, 1996), 270–273.

5. Ibid., 315–317.

6. Zachary Lockman, "Railway Workers and Relational History: Arabs and Jews in British-Ruled History," in *The Israel/Palestine Question*, ed. Ilan Pappé (London: Routledge, 1999), 103.

7. Lockman, *Comrades and Enemies*, 286–287.

8. Ibid., 323–325.

9. Ibid., 292, 299, 303–304.

10. Joel Beinin, *Was the Red Flag Flying There? Marxist Politics and the Arab-Israeli Conflict in Egypt and Israel, 1948–1965* (London: I. B. Tauris, 1990), 40.

11. Lockman, *Comrades and Enemies*, 327–328, 332–334.

12. Ibid., 337, 341–342.

13. Judah L. Magnes and Martin Buber, *Arab-Jewish Unity: Testimony before the Anglo-American Inquiry Commission for the Ihud (Union) Association* (Westport, CT: Hyperion, 1976), 9–10.

14. Arthur A. Goren, ed., *Dissenter in Zion: From the Writings of Judah L. Magnes* (Cambridge, MA: Harvard University Press, 1982), 38, 40, 46, 49.

15. Khalidi, *Iron Cage*, 105–139.

16. *The Future of Palestine*, prepared by the Arab Office, London, 1947 (Westport, CT: Hyperion, 1976), 81, 83.

17. Lockman, *Comrades and Enemies*, 341, 351, 355.

18. Goren, *Dissenter*, 55–56, 461.

19. Mohammed Abu-Nimer, *Dialogue, Conflict Resolution, and Change: Arab-Jewish Encounters in Israel* (Albany: State University of New York Press, 1999), 29.

20. Homi K. Bhabha, *The Location of Culture* (London: Routledge, 1994), 139.

21. Uri Avnery, *My Friend, the Enemy* (Westport, CT: Hill, 1986), 190.

22. Birkland, *Unified in Hope*, 101.

23. Raja Shehadeh, *Strangers in the House: Coming of Age in Occupied Palestine* (South Royalton, VT: Steerforth, 2002), 3–7, 9, 27–28.

24. P. J. Vatikiotis, *Among Arabs and Jews: A Personal Experience, 1936–1990* (London: Weidenfeld and Nicolson, 1991), 83.

25. Ibid., 85.

26. Birkland, *Unified in Hope*, 136.

27. Anthony G. Bing, *Israeli Pacifist: The Life of Joseph Abileah* (Syracuse, NY: Syracuse University Press, 1990), 214.

28. Amos Oz, *A Tale of Love and Darkness* (Orlando: Harcourt, 2004), 314–319.

29. Rashid Khalidi, *Palestinian Identity: The Construction of Modern National Consciousness* (New York: Columbia University Press, 1997), 178, 180–190.

30. Shany Payes, *Palestinian NGOs in Israel: The Politics of Civil Society* (London: Tauris Academic Studies, 2005), 6.

31. Hanan Ashrawi, *This Side of Peace: A Personal Account* (New York: Simon and Schuster, 1995).

32. Simona Sharoni, *Gender and the Israeli-Palestinian Conflict: The Politics of Women's Resistance* (Syracuse, NY: Syracuse University Press, 1995), 133.

33. Beinin, *Was the Red Flag*, 213.

34. Lockman, *Comrades and Enemies*, 359.

35. Avnery, *My Friend*, 194.

36. Amos Elon and Sana Hassan, *Between Enemies: A Compassionate Dialogue between an Israeli and an Arab* (New York: Random House, 1974) 97, 106-108.

37. Avnery, *My Friend*, 28-29.

38. Uri Avnery, "A Federation—Why Not?" *Gush Shalom*, 10 August 2013, http://zope.gush-shalom.org/home/en/channels/avnery/1376051927.

39. Avnery, *My Friend*, 32.

40. Gideon Weigert, *My Life with the Palestinians* (Jerusalem: Jerusalem Times, 1997), 74-75.

41. Mordechai Bar-On, *In Pursuit of Peace: A History of the Israeli Peace Movement* (Washington, DC: United States Institute of Peace, 1996), 2-3.

42. *New Outlook*, July 1957.

43. *New Outlook*, January/February 1993, 3.

44. *New Outlook*, July 1957, 14, 21, 42.

45. Birkland, *Unified in Hope*, 137.

46. Ibid., 125-126.

47. Abu-Nimer, *Dialogue*, 59.

48. Website of Givat Haviva, accessed 2 May 2014, www.givathaviva.org.

49. Maxine Kaufman-Nunn, *Creative Resistance: Anecdotes of Nonviolent Action by Israeli-Based Groups* (Jerusalem: Alternative Information Center, 1993), 26-28.

50. Bar-On, *In Pursuit of Peace*, 201-202.

51. Eliahu Elath, *Jewish-Arab Relations in Israel* (New York: American Histadrut Cultural Exchange Institute, 1967), 5, 6, 10-14.

52. Ari Shavit, *My Promised Land: The Triumph and Tragedy of Israel* (New York: Spiegel, 2013), 148-150.

53. Khalidi, *Iron Cage*, 136-147.

## Chapter 4

1. Carol J. Birkland, *Unified in Hope: Arabs and Jews Talk about Peace* (New York: Friendship, 1987), 32.

2. Simha Flapan, *Zionism and the Palestinians* (London: Croom Helm, 1979), 13-14.

3. Samih K. Farsoun and Naseer Aruri, *Palestine and the Palestinians*, 2nd ed. (Boulder, CO: Westview, 2006), 5.

4. Mark Tessler, *A History of the Israeli-Palestinian Conflict*, 2nd ed. (Bloomington: Indiana University Press, 2009), 425.

5. Raja Shehadeh, *Strangers in the House: Coming of Age in Occupied Palestine* (South Royalton, VT: Steerforth, 2002), 57, 63–64.

6. Ibid., 48, 76.

7. Ibid., 49–51, 68–74.

8. Hanan Ashrawi, *This Side of Peace: A Personal Account* (New York: Simon and Schuster, 1995), 22–23.

9. Ibid., 31.

10. Ibid., 32, 51.

11. Sandy Tolan, *The Lemon Tree: An Arab, a Jew, and the Heart of the Middle East* (New York: Bloomsbury, 2006).

12. Birkland, *Unified in Hope*, 32.

13. Gideon Weigert, *My Life with the Palestinians* (Jerusalem: Jerusalem Times, 1997), 58, 67.

14. Ibid., 54, 57.

15. American Friends Service Committee, *Search for Peace in the Middle East* (Philadelphia: American Friends Service Committee, 1970), v–vii, 52.

16. Farsoun and Aruri, *Palestine and the Palestinians*, 143–161.

17. Anita Weiner, Arnon Bar-On, and Eugene Weiner, *The Abraham Fund Directory of Institutions and Organizations Fostering Coexistence between Jews and Arabs in Israel*, 1st ed. (New York: Abraham Fund, 1991), 123.

18. Ibid., 146, 542, 554.

19. *Ibid.*, 475–476.

20. Weigert, *My Life*, 70.

21. Tessler, *History*, 475–477.

22. Ibid., 481–485, 489.

23. Mohammed Abu-Nimer, *Dialogue, Conflict Resolution, and Change: Arab-Jewish Encounters in Israel* (Albany: State University of New York Press, 1999), 44–45.

24. Ibid., 19–26.

25. Weiner, Bar-On, and Weiner, *Abraham Fund Directory*, 121.

26. Ibid., 93.

27. Birkland, *Unified in Hope*, 112–113.

28. Ricky Sherover-Marcuse, "Liberation Theory: Axioms and Working Assumptions about the Perpetuation of Social Oppression," nypolisci.org, accessed 30 June 2014, http://nypolisci.org/files/poli15/Readings/Liberation%20Theory.pdf.

29. Ron Scolnik, "In Memory of Rabbi Bruce Cohen, Interns for Peace," Partners for a Progressive Israel website, 13 August 2010, http://progressiveisrael.org/in-memory-of-rabbi-bruce-cohen-interns-for-peace.

30. Ari Shavit, *My Promised Land: The Triumph and Tragedy of Israel* (New York: Spiegel, 2013), 255.

31. Uri, Avnery, *My Friend, the Enemy* (Westport, CT: Hill) 1986, 190.

32. Mordechai Bar-On, *In Pursuit of Peace: A History of the Israeli Peace Movement* (Washington, DC: United States Institute of Peace, 1996), 102–107.

33. Reuven Kaminer, *The Politics of Protest: The Israeli Peace Movement and the Palestinian Intifada* (Brighton, UK: Sussex Academic, 1996), 23–24.

34. Janet Aviad and Yitzhak Galnoor, *Peace Is Greater than Greater Israel* (pamphlet; Jerusalem: Peace Now, 1979).

35. Middle East Project website, www.middleeastproject.org, accessed 14 June 2012.

36. Weiner, Bar On, and Weiner, *Abraham Fund Directory*, 133.

37. Ibid., 603, 633.

38. Ibid., 284.

39. Kaminer, *Politics of Protest*, 25, 29, 32–33; Bar-On, *In Pursuit of Peace*, 205.

40. Riah Abu el-Assal, *Caught In Between: The Extraordinary Story of an Arab Palestinian Christian Israeli* (London: SPCK, 1999), 87.

41. Peter Demant, "Unofficial Contacts and Peacemaking: Israeli-Palestinian Dialogue, 1967–1993," in *Israel in the Nineties: Development and Conflict*, ed. Frederick Lazin and Gregory Mahler (Gainesville: University Press of Florida, 1996), 78–79.

42. Avnery, *My Friend*, 68, 111–112, 114.

43. Ibid., 122, 129, 140–146.

44. Avnery, "The Ghetto Within," *Counter Punch*, 23 March 2012, www.counter punch.org/2012/03/23/the-ghetto-within.

45. Demant, "Unofficial Contacts," 77, 80; Kaminer, *Politics of Protest*, 21.

## Chapter 5

1. Uri Avnery, *My Friend, the Enemy* (Westport, CT: Hill, 1986), 196.

2. Ibid., 333.

3. Grace Feuerverger, *Oasis of Dreams: Teaching and Learning Peace in a Jewish-Palestinian Village in Israel* (New York: Routledge, 2001), xv, 124.

4. Mordechai Bar-On, *In Pursuit of Peace: A History of the Israeli Peace Movement* (Washington, DC: United States Institute of Peace, 1996), 123, 124.

5. Avnery, *My Friend, the Enemy*, 196, 198–200.

6. Shany Payes, *Palestinian NGOs in Israel: The Politics of Civil Society* (London: Tauris Academic, 2005), 1.

7. Bar-On, *In Pursuit of Peace*, 127–133.

8. Ibid., 155.

9. Reuven Kaminer, *The Politics of Protest: The Israeli Peace Movement and the Palestinian Intifada* (Brighton, UK: Sussex Academic, 1996), 35.

10. Bar-On, *In Pursuit of Peace*, 151.

11. Ibid., 146.

12. Kaminer, *Politics of Protest*, 35.

13. Carol J. Birkland, *Unified in Hope: Arabs and Jews Talk about Peace* (New York: Friendship, 1987, 44, 48–49.

14. Raja Shehadeh, *Occupier's Law: Israel and the West Bank* (Washington, DC: Institute for Palestine Studies), 1988.

15. "A Brief History of Al-Haq," Al-Haq website, accessed 21 May 2015, www .alhaq.org/about-al-haq/brief-history.

16. Amitabh Pal, *"Islam" Means Peace: Understanding the Muslim Principle of Nonviolence Today* (Westport, CT: Praeger, 2011), 184.

17. Birkland, *Unified in Hope*, 94.

18. "Philosophy," Library on Wheels for Nonviolence and Peace Association

website, accessed 14 July 2012, www.lownp.com/portal/index.php?option=com
_content&view=article&id=75:philosophy&catid=57:home-page&Itemid=53.

19. Nafez Assaily and Andrew Rigand, "The Intifada," in *Nonviolent Struggle and Social Defence*, ed. Shelley Anderson and Janet Larmore (London: War Resisters' International, 1991), https://www.wri-irg.org/books/nvsd.htm#Heading10.

20. "An Interview with Ibrahim Issa," Hope Flowers School website, accessed 16 June 2014, www.hopeflowersschool.org/ibrahim-issa.html.

21. Avnery, *My Friend*, 246.

22. Ibid., 255, 256, 273.

23. Ibid., 301, 303, 304.

24. Birkland, *Unified in Hope*, 128.

25. Bar-On, *In Pursuit of Peace*, 190, 191.

26. Kaminer, *Politics of Protest*, 38, 45.

27. Riah Abu el-Assal, *Caught in Between: The Extraordinary Story of an Arab Palestinian Christian Israeli* (London: SPCK, 1999), 87.

28. Avnery, *My Friend*, 326.

29. Kaminer, *Politics of Protest*, 106.

30. Peter Demant, "Unofficial Contacts and Peacemaking: Israeli-Palestinian Dialogue, 1967–1993," in *Israel in the Nineties: Development and Conflict*, ed. Frederick Lazin and Gregory Mahler (Gainesville: University Press of Florida, 1996), 82–84.

31. Kaminer, *Politics of Protest*, 106, 119.

32. Bar-On, *In Pursuit of Peace*, 210, 215, 217, 218.

33. Amal Kawar, "Palestinian Women's Activism," in *Palestinian Women of Gaza and the West Bank*, ed. Suha Sabbagh (Bloomington: Indiana University Press, 1998), 235.

34. Penny Rosenwasser, *Voices from a "Promised Land:" Palestinian and Israeli Peace Activists Speak Their Hearts, Conversations with Penny Rosenwasser* (Willimantic, CT: Curbstone, 1992), 49–50.

35. Sahar Khalifeh, "Comments by Five Women Activists: Siham Abdullah, Amal Kharisha Barghouthi, Rita Giacaman, May Mistakmel Nassar, Amal Wahdan," in *Palestinian Women of Gaza and the West Bank*, ed. Suha Sabbagh (Bloomington: Indiana University Press, 1998), 210.

36. Ayala Emmett, *Our Sisters' Promised Land: Women, Politics, and Israeli-Palestinian Coexistence* (Ann Arbor, MI: University of Michigan Press, 1996), 95.

37. Meredith Alexander, "Palestinian Women Encounter Roadblocks on the Path to Political Participation, Professor Says" *Stanford Report*, 27 April 2001, http://news.stanford.edu/news/2001/may2/beinin-52.html.

38. Peace Women across the Globe is an organization of activists in Switzerland. In 2005 it chose 1,000 women for the Nobel Peace Prize. Scalo Publishers, *1000 Peacewomen across the Globe* (Zurich, Switzerland: Scalo Publishers, 2006), www.1000peacewomen.org/en/who-we-are/history-30.html.

39. Sara Helman, "Peace Movements in Israel," in Jewish Women's Archive's online encyclopedia of Jewish women, accessed 16 June 2014, http://jwa.org/encyclopedia/article/peace-movements-in-israel.

40. Simona Sharoni, *Gender and the Israeli-Palestinian Conflict: The Politics of Women's Resistance* (Syracuse, NY: Syracuse University Press, 1995), 134.

41. Website of *Isha L'Isha Haifa Feminist Center*, accessed 26 June 2012, www .isha.org.il.

42. Bar-On, *In Pursuit of Peace*, 166–170.

43. Demant, "Unofficial Contacts," 82–84.

44. Bar-On, *In Pursuit of Peace*, 185.

45. Oded Haklai, *Palestinian Ethnonationalism in Israel* (Philadelphia: University of Pennsylvania Press, 2011), 168.

46. Website of the Galilee Society: The Arab National Society for Health Research and Services, accessed 16 August 2014.

47. Mohammed Abu-Nimer, *Dialogue, Conflict Resolution, and Change: Arab-Jewish Encounters in Israel* (Albany: State University of New York Press, 1999), 38–39.

48. Ibid., 30–33, 36.

49. David Hall-Cathala. *The Peace Movement in Israel, 1967–1987* (New York: St. Martin's, 1990).

50. Abu-Nimer, *Dialogue*, 59.

51. Website of Sadaka-Reut: Arab-Jewish Youth Partnership, accessed 29 July 2013, www.reutsadaka.org.

52. Margherita Drago, "Dangerous Liaisons: Perceptions on Arab/Jewish Intermarriage in Israel," Culture Matters blog, 9 August 2011, https://culture matters.wordpress.com/2011/08/09/dangerous-liaisons-perceptions-on-arab jewish-intermarriage-in-israel/.

53. Birkland, *Unified in Hope*, 15.

54. Demant, "Unofficial Contacts," 81.

## Chapter 6

1. Ayala Emmett, *Our Sisters' Promised Land: Women, Politics, and Israeli-Palestinian Coexistence* (Ann Arbor, MI: University of Michigan Press, 1996), 39, 40.

2. Hanan Ashrawi, *This Side of Peace: A Personal Account* (New York: Simon and Schuster, 1995), 63.

3. Sandy Tolan, *The Lemon Tree: An Arab, a Jew, and the Heart of the Middle East* (New York: Bloomsbury, 2006).

4. For details of Palestinian nonviolence see Mary E. King, *A Quiet Revolution: The First Palestinian Intifada and Nonviolent Resistance* (New York: Nation, 2007).

5. "The Early Years," on website of the Al-Watan Center, accessed 17 June 2012, http://www.alwatan.org/part2/early.html.

6. Website of the Arab Association for Human Rights, accessed 10 June 2012, https://arabhra.wordpress.com.

7. "Panorama Centre," WebGaza.net, May 2006, accessed 1 August 2012.

8. Website of *Muwatin*: The Palestinian Institute for the Study of Democracy, accessed 24 May 2014, http://web.muwatin.org.

9. Website of the Palestinian Center for Peace and Democracy, accessed 15 August 2013, http://pcpd.org/en/node/1.

10. Abdel Hamid Afana, "A Model for Community Care in Gaza," *Palestine-Israel Journal* 10, no. 4 (2003).

11. Michael N. Nagler, Tal Palter-Palman, and Matthew Taylor, "The Road to Nonviolent Coexistence in Palestine/Israel," available on the website of Matthew A. Taylor, n.d., www.matthewtaylor.net/nvcoexistpalisfinal.pdf.

12. Linda Gradstein, "Palestinians Claim Tax Is Unjust, Many Don't Pay," (Fort Lauderdale, Fla.) *Sun-Sentinel*, 8 October 1989.

13. Maxine Kaufman-Nunn, *Creative Resistance: Anecdotes of Nonviolent Action by Israeli-Based Groups* (Jerusalem: Alternative Information Center, 1993), 65.

14. Penny Rosenwasser, *Voices from a "Promised Land": Palestinian and Israeli Peace Activists Speak Their Hearts, Conversations with Penny Rosenwasser* (Willimantic, CT: Curbstone, 1992), 29.

15. Reuven Kaminer, *The Politics of Protest: The Israeli Peace Movement and the Palestinian Intifada* (Brighton, UK: Sussex Academic, 1996), xii, 50–52, 122.

16. Mordechai Bar-On, *In Pursuit of Peace: A History of the Israeli Peace Movement* (Washington, DC: United States Institute of Peace, 1996), 222–225; Kaminer, *Politics of Protest*, 60.

17. Bar-On, *In Pursuit of Peace*, 225–232.

18. Kaminer, *Politics of Protest*, 67, 79.

19. Bar-On, *In Pursuit of Peace*, 237, 244.

20. Kaminer, *Politics of Protest*, 174–178.

21. Kaufman-Nunn, *Creative Resistance*, 79, 80.

22. Kaminer, *Politics of Protest*, 184.

23. Bar-On, *In Pursuit of Peace*, 234–235.

24. Peter Demant, "Unofficial Contacts and Peacemaking: Israeli-Palestinian Dialogue, 1967–1993," in *Israel in the Nineties: Development and Conflict*, ed. Frederick Lazin and Gregory Mahler (Gainesville: University Press of Florida, 1996), 91.

25. Website of Al-Qasemi College, accessed 21 June 2012, http://www.qsm.ac.il/pr.

26. Bar-On, *In Pursuit of Peace*, 255.

27. Kaminer, *Politics of Protest*, 137.

28. Bar-On, *In Pursuit of Peace*, 258.

29. Kate Rix, "Music Groups Transcend Politics in the Middle East," Berkeley Research, University of California at Berkeley, 12 February 2010, http://vcresearch.berkeley.edu/news/music-groups-transcend-politics-middle-east.

30. Kaminer, *Politics of Protest*, 148.

31. Kaminer, *Politics of Protest*, 139, 143.

32. Hubert Campfens, ed., *Community Development around the World: Practice, Theory, Research, Training* (Toronto: University of Toronto Press, 1997), 223.

33. Kaminer, *Politics of Protest*, 149–150.

34. Kaufman-Nunn, *Creative Resistance*, 49.

35. Website of the Interreligious Coordinating Council of Israel, accessed 2 August 2014, http://rhr.org.il/eng/icci.

36. Sarah Kaminker, "Palestinian-Israeli Economic Cooperation: A View from the Field," *Palestine-Israel Journal* 6, no. 3 (1999); and "Center for Jewish-

Arab Economic Development" on the website of the Inter-Agency Task Force on Israeli Arab Issues, accessed 6 November 2013, www.iataskforce.org/entities /view/105.

37. Kaminer, *Politics of Protest*, 151.

38. Kaufman-Nunn, *Creative Resistance*, 67.

39. Bassam Abu-Sharif and Uzi Mahnaimi, *Best of Enemies: The Memoirs of Bassam Abu-Sharif and Uzi Mahnaimi* (Boston: Little, Brown, 1995) 226, 229, 233, 255, 256.

40. Ibid., 257–258, 260.

41. Bar-On, *In Pursuit of Peace*, 245, 246, 260.

42. Kaminer, *Politics of Protest*, 110.

43. Ibid., 99, 105–108.

44. Bar-On, *In Pursuit of Peace*, 262.

45. Kaminer, *Politics of Protest*, 118.

46. Kaufman-Nunn, *Creative Resistance*, 15.

47. Kaminer, *Politics of Protest*, 122, 128.

48. Kaufman-Nunn, *Creative Resistance*, 51, 78.

49. See Anita Weiner, Arnon Bar-On, and Eugene Weiner, *The Abraham Fund Directory of Institutions and Organizations Fostering Coexistence between Jews and Arabs in Israel*, 1st ed. (New York: Abraham Fund, 1991).

50. Website of Sikkuy: The Association for the Advancement of Civic Equality, accessed 1 May 2012, http://www.sikkuy.org.il/?lang=en.

51. Website of Citizens for the Environment in the Galilee, accessed 30 July 2012, http://cfenvironment.org.il/index.php/english.

52. Website of Center for Creativity in Education and Cultural Heritage, accessed 21 August 2013, https://sites.google.com/site/ccechfund/home.

53. Seth Freedman, "Child's Play," *Guardian*, 9 March 2007.

54. Website of Ein Yael, accessed 20 July 2013, www.einyael.co.il; and the website of the Jerusalem Foundation, www.jerusalemfoundation.org/culture /museums-and-cultural-centers/ein-yael-living-museum.aspx.

55. Mohammed Abu-Nimer, *Dialogue, Conflict Resolution, and Change: Arab-Jewish Encounters in Israel* (Albany: State University of New York Press, 1999), 59.

56. Mitchell G. Bard, *Building Bridges: Lessons for America from Novel Israeli Approaches to Promote Coexistence* (Chevy Chase, MD: American-Israeli Cooperative Enterprises, 1997).

57. Shany Payes, *Palestinian NGOs in Israel: The Politics of Civil Society* (London: Tauris Academic, 2005), 216.

58. Abu Nimer, *Dialogue*, 58.

59. Hanan Ashrawi, *This Side of Peace: A Personal Account* (New York: Simon and Schuster, 1995), 59.

60. Ibid., 63–64.

61. Nahla Abdo-Zubi, "Women of the Intifada: Gender, Class, and National Liberation," *Race and Class*, 32, no. 4 (1991), 25.

62. Simona Sharoni, *Gender and the Israeli-Palestinian Conflict: The Politics of Women's Resistance* (Syracuse, NY: Syracuse University Press, 1995), 135.

63. Ayala Emmett, *Our Sisters' Promised Land: Women, Politics, and Israeli-*

*Palestinian Coexistence* (Ann Arbor, MI: University of Michigan Press, 1996), 39, 40.

64. Ashrawi, *This Side of Peace*, 37–38.

65. Emmett, *Our Sisters' Promised Land*, 20.

66. Kaminer, *Politics of Protest*, 83–89.

67. Barbara Swirski and Marilyn P. Safir, *Calling the Equality Bluff: Women in Israel* (New York: Pergamon, 1991).

68. Emmett, *Our Sisters' Promised Land*, 15.

69. Kaminer, *Politics of Protest*, 92, 93.

70. Rosenwasser, *Voices from a Promised Land*, 105.

71. Kaminer, *Politics of Protest*, 94, 96.

72. Emmett, *Our Sisters' Promised Land*, 15–16.

73. Ashrawi, *This Side of Peace*, 60–61.

74. Bar-On, *In Pursuit of Peace*, 242.

75. Rosenwasser, *Voices from a Promised Land*, 64–68, 74–78.

76. Bar-On, *In Pursuit of Peace*, 243.

77. Ashrawi, *This Side of Peace*, 63.

78. Kaminer, *Politics of Protest*, 157, 172.

79. Emmett, *Our Sisters' Promised Land*, 97–99.

80. Rosenwasser, *Voices from a Promised Land*, 23, 97–98, 101.

81. Emmett, *Our Sisters' Promised Land*, 64–68.

82. Ibid., 133–134, 148.

83. Thanks to Stephen Zunes for comments on Palestinian-Saddam relations.

84. Kaminer, *Politics of Protest*, 186–188, 193–195.

85. Ibid., 206–207.

86. Rosenwasser, *Voices from a Promised Land*, 207.

87. Kaminer, *Politics of Protest*, 196.

88. Kaufman-Nunn, *Creative Resistance*, 73.

89. Demant, "Unofficial Contacts," 89–91.

90. Kaminer, *Politics of Protest*, 214.

91. Raja Shehadeh, *Strangers in the House: Coming of Age in Occupied Palestine* (South Royalton, VT: Steerforth, 2002), 232.

92. Bar-On, *In Pursuit of Peace*, 292, 295, 296.

93. Ibid., 291.

94. Ashrawi, *This Side of Peace*, 175.

95. Demant, "Unofficial Contacts," 91.

96. Hillel Schenker, "Chronicles of Peace Activism," *Palestine-Israel Journal* 5, no. 1 (1998).

## Chapter 7

1. "Israel-Palestine Liberation Organization Agreement: 1993," http://avalon.law.yale.edu/20th_century/isrplo.asp.

2. Mary Ann French and Roxanne Roberts, "Peace in Their Time: A Bit Dazed, A Bit Dazzled, the Peacemakers Celebrate," *Washington Post*, 14 September 1993.

3. Mordechai Bar-On, *In Pursuit of Peace: A History of the Israeli Peace Movement* (Washington, DC: United States Institute of Peace, 1996), 297.

4. Ayala Emmett, *Our Sisters' Promised Land: Women, Politics, and Israeli-Palestinian Coexistence* (Ann Arbor, MI: University of Michigan Press, 1996), 1–2, 174–176.

5. Peter Demant, "Unofficial Contacts and Peacemaking: Israeli-Palestinian Dialogue, 1967–1993," in *Israel in the Nineties: Development and Conflict*, ed. Frederick Lazin and Gregory Mahler (Gainesville: University Press of Florida, 1996), 92.

6. Reuven Kaminer, *The Politics of Protest: The Israeli Peace Movement and the Palestinian Intifada* (Brighton, UK: Sussex Academic, 1996), 215.

7. Bar On, *In Pursuit of Peace*, 301–304.

8. Maxine Kaufman-Nunn, *Creative Resistance: Anecdotes of Nonviolent Action by Israeli-Based Groups* (Jerusalem: Alternative Information Center, 1993), 19.

9. Riah Abu al-Assal, *Caught In Between: The Extraordinary Story of an Arab Palestinian Christian Israeli* (London: SPCK, 1999), 133.

10. Emmett, *Our Sisters' Promised Land*, 180, 193–194.

11. Edy Kaufman, Shukri B. Abed, and Robert L. Rothstein, *Democracy, Peace, and the Israeli-Palestinian Conflict* (Boulder, CO: Lynne Rienner, 1993), 319.

12. Ibid., 8, 10, 41, 56, 61.

13. Website of the Arab-Jewish Community Center, accessed 29 September 2012, http://ajccjaffa.wix.com/ajcc.

14. John Wallach and Michael Wallach, *The Enemy Has a Face: The Seeds of Peace Experience* (Washington, DC: United States Institute of Peace, 2000), 33, 42, 46, 49, 50, 53.

15. Ibid., 44, 55–61, 63, 66, 67, 69, 87–97, 111.

16. Demant, "Unofficial Contacts," 93.

17. For the full text see "Israel-Palestine Liberation Organization Agreement: 1993," http://avalon.law.yale.edu/20th_century/isrplo.asp. UN Resolution 242 calls for Israeli withdrawal from lands captured in the 1967 war.

18. Shimon Peres and David Landau, *Battling for Peace: A Memoir* (New York: Random House, 1995), 301–302.

19. Emmett, *Our Sisters' Promised Land*, 194–195.

20. Thomas L. Are, *Israeli Peace/Palestinian Justice: Liberation Theology and the Peace Process* (Atlanta: Clarity, 1994), i.

21. Bassam Abu-Sharif and Uzi Mahnaimi, *Best of Enemies: The Memoirs of Bassam Abu-Sharif and Uzi Mahnaimi* (Boston: Little, Brown, 1995), vii, 7, 9, 54. Mahnaimi was a soldier and military intelligence operator. Abu-Sharif was a PLO leader, a mastermind of terrorist acts and hijackings, and a survivor of the Mossad's attempt to assassinate him with a bomb disguised as a book about Che Guevara.

22. "About Us," on the website of the *Palestine-Israel Journal*, accessed 18 June 2013, http://www.pij.org/about.php.

23. Website of Friends of the Earth Middle East, accessed 20 August 2014, www.foeme.org.

24. "Israel Palestine Center for Environment," on the website of the Israel Palestine Center for Research and Information, accessed 20 August 2014, http://ipcri.org/httpdocs/IPCRI/E-Projects.html.

25. Benjamin E. Brinner, *Playing across a Divide: Israeli-Palestinian Musical Encounters* (Oxford: Oxford University Press, 2009), 9.

26. Ibid., 123.

27. Ibid., 128–130.

28. Ibid., 150–153.

29. Ibid., 152.

30. "Our History," on the website of Windows: Channels for Communication, accessed on 18 June 2015, http://www.win-peace.org.

31. Musa Isa Barhoun and Ben Mollo, "Building Religious/Cultural Bridges between Israeli and Palestinian University Students," *Eubios Journal of Asian and International Bioethics* 9 (1999), 55.

32. "The Project For Arab-Jewish Dialogue At Bar-Ilan University," on the website for the Pluralism Project at Harvard University, accessed 22 June 2013, http://pluralism.org/profiles/view/74256.

33. "What We Do: Projects and Programs," on the website of the Civic Forum Institute, accessed 18 June 2015, http://www.cfip.org.

34. "History," on the website of the Jerusalem Center for Women, accessed 1 September 2013, www.j-c-w.org/index.php?option=com_content&task=view&id=22&Itemid=9.

35. "Bat Shalom," on the website Insight on Conflict, accessed 23 June 2014, www.insightonconflict.org/conflicts/israel-palestinian-territories/peacebuilding-organisations/bat-shalom/.

36. Daphna Golan, "'Separation,' 'Normalization' and Occupation: The Dilemmas of a Joint Venture by Palestinian and Israeli Women," *Palestine-Israel Journal* 2 no. 2 (1995).

37. "*Tali Raz—Nisan Young Women Leaders*," an interview on YouTube, uploaded 3 September 2007 and accessed 24 July 2014, www.youtube.com/watch?v=9M5NPAag1kI.

38. "Nisan Young Women Leaders," on the website of the Global Fund for Women, accessed 9 May 2013, www.globalfundforwomen.org.

39. "Association for the Advancement of Women's Health in Israel," on the website of La-Briut, accessed 11 November 2013, www.la-briut.org.il/english/info/.

40. Emmett, *Our Sisters' Promised Land*, 1.

41. Avi Shlaim, "The Rise and Fall of the Oslo Peace Process," in *International Relations of the Middle East*, ed. Louise L'Estrange Fawcett (Oxford: Oxford University Press, 2005), 241–261.

42. "The Question of Palestine," UN General Assembly Security Council, 1 July 1996, accessed 18 July 2012, https://unispal.un.org/DPA/DPR/unispal.nsf/5ba47a5c6cef541b802563e000493b8c/b3e70bb64c50472c8525636900474283?OpenDocument; for more details, see Richard Roth, "Arab Leaders Call Summit a Success," CNN, 23 June 1996, www.cnn.com/WORLD/9606/23/summit.wrap/.

43. Shlaim, "Rise and Fall of the Oslo Peace Process."

44. David Grossman and Haim Watzman, *Death as a Way of Life: From Oslo to the Geneva Accords* (New York: Picador, 2004), 4–5.

45. "Roundtable: The Future of People-to-People." *Palestine-Israel Journal* 12–13, nos. 4, 1 (2005–2006).

46. Website of Adalah: The Legal Center for Arab Minority Rights in Israel, accessed 14 October 2012, www.adalah.org/en.

47. Website of the Palestinian Center for Democracy and Conflict Resolution, accessed 18 June 2012, www.pcdcr.org/eng/.

48. Website of the Palestinian Center for Human Rights, accessed 2 July 2014, www.pchrgaza.org/portal/en/.

49. Website of the Peace and Democracy Forum, accessed 16 June 2012, www.pdf-palestine.org.

50. Website of Middle East Nonviolence and Democracy, accessed 18 June 2013, www.mendonline.org.

51. Ibid.

52. Issam Sartawi Center for the Advancement of Peace and Democracy description on the website of Al-Quds Open University, accessed 14 June 2014, www.alquds.edu/en/151-centers-and-institutes/issam-sartawi-center-for-peace-and-democrac.html.

53. Website of Wi'am: Palestinian Conflict Resolution and Transformation Center, accessed 7 July 2012, www.alaslah.org.

54. "Beit Arabiya," on the website of the Israeli Committee against House Demolitions, accessed 17 July 2014, http://icahd.org/tours/beit-arabiya/.

55. Website of Bimkom: Planners for Planning Rights, accessed 5 October 2013, http://bimkom.org/eng/.

56. Website of the Jerusalem Intercultural Center, accessed 5 October 2013, http://jicc.org.il.

57. Arabic-Hebrew Studies Center, on the website of the Jerusalem Intercultural Center, accessed 5 October 2013, http://jicc.org.il/the-arabic-hebrew-studies-center-in-jerusalem-2008-9/.

58. Ahseea Ahmed, "Contesting Discourse: Can Deliberative Democracy Mitigate Protracted Ethnic Conflict in Israel?" Master's thesis, Simon Fraser University, 2005, 63, accessed 5 October 2013, http://summit.sfu.ca/item/10163.

59. Website of the Compassionate Listening Project, accessed 11 May 2014, www.compassionatelistening.org.

60. Gene Knudsen Hoffman, "An Enemy Is One Whose Story We Have Not Heard," in *Essays by Gene Knudsen Hoffman: Quaker Peace Activist and Mystic*, ed. Anthony Manousos (Torrance, CA: Friends Bulletin, 2003), 302.

61. Frida Kerner Furman, "Compassionate Listening as a Path to Conflict Resolution," *Journal for the Study of Peace and Conflict* (2009-2010), 24-38.

62. Gene Knudsen Hoffman, Cynthia Monroe, and Leah Green, *Compassionate Listening: An Exploratory Sourcebook about Conflict Transformation*, ed. Dennis Rivers, n.p.: New Conversations, 2008.

63. Webpage of the Palestine Center for Conflict Resolution and Reconciliation, accessed 3 November 2013, www.mideastweb.org/ccrr/.

64. Website of the Parents Circle Families Forum, accessed 14 July 2014, www.theparentscircle.com/Content.aspx?ID=2#.Vln4CIR10cI.

65. Website of the Peres Center for Peace, accessed 1 July 2013, www.peres-center.org.

66. "History and Mission," on the website of the Arava Institute, accessed 24 June 2014.

67. Michael J. Zwirn, "Promise and Failure: Environmental NGOs and Palestinian-Israeli Cooperation," *Middle East Review of International Affairs* 5, no. 4 (2001), 9–10.

68. "SACH in the News," on the website of Save a Child's Heart, accessed 18 June 2015, www.saveachildsheart.com.

69. "About Us," on the website of the Nir School of the Heart, accessed 22 November 2012, http://nirschool.org/html/fs_about_mission.html.

70. "Pieces for Peace," MidEastWeb, July 2000, accessed 15 May 2013, www.mideastweb.org/pieces4peace.htm.

71. "About Us," on the website of the Negev Coexistence Forum for Civil Equality, accessed 5 August 2012, www.dukium.org.

72. Am Johal, "Interview with Devorah Brous," *Dissident Voice* newsletter, 11 January 2008, http://dissidentvoice.org/2008/01/interview-with-devorah-brous/.

73. Website of the Galilee Multicultural Theater, accessed 21 October 2013, www.thegalilee.org/index.php?lang=us.

74. Website of the Umm el-Fahem Art Gallery, accessed 14 June 2013.

75. Website of the Kayan-Feminist Organization, accessed 23 July 2013, www.kayan.org.il/en/.

76. Website of the Haifa Women's Crisis Shelter, accessed 1 August 2012, www.hwcs.org.il/HWCS/index.asp?DBID=1&LNGID=1.

77. "History," on the website of Mahapach-Taghir, accessed 21 July 2013, http://mahapach-taghir.org/about/history.

78. Website of Hand in Hand: Center for Jewish-Arab Education in Israel, accessed 25 August 2012, www.handinhandk12.org.

79. A New Way, accessed 24 May 2014, www.anewway.org.il/english.html.

80. ALON Social Involvement Organization, accessed 2 May 2012, www.amutat-alon.org.il.

81. Website of Friendship Village: International Center for Education for Peace and Human Rights in a Multicultural Society, accessed 12 November 2012, http://friendshipvillage.homestead.com/Home.html.

82. Website of Merchavim, accessed 18 November 2012, www.machon-merchavim.org.il/?lang=en.

83. Avi Shlaim, "Rise and Fall of the Oslo Peace Process."

## Chapter 8

1. Amelia Thomas, "The Jerusalem Circus Symbolizes Hope," *Middle East Times*, 11 March 2005.

2. "Our Peoples Can Live Together in Peace and Friendship," *The Guardian*, 19 January 2004.

3. Barry Davis, "Walking the Tightrope," *Jerusalem Post*, 15 March 2007.

4. "About Us," on the website of the Galilee Foundation for Value Education, accessed 6 June 2013, http://eng.makom-bagalil.org.il/about_us/.

5. Julie M. Norman, *The Second Palestinian Intifada: Civil Resistance* (London: Routledge, 2010); Julie Norman with Maia Carter Hallward, eds. *Nonviolent Resis-*

*tance in the Second Intifada: Activism and Advocacy* (New York: Palgrave Macmillan, 2011).

6. Website of Taʿayush: Arab-Jewish Partnership, accessed 29 June 2014.

7. "Who We Are," on the website of Tawasul, accessed 29 June 2014, http://tawasul.ps/?page_id=33.

8. Website of the Palestinian Center for Policy and Survey Research, accessed 1 May 2014.

9. Description of the Palestinian Center for Research and Cultural Dialogue on the Partners in Palestine website, www.fnst-jerusalem.org/our-work/partners-in-israel/.

10. "Dialogue Program," on the website of the Palestinian Academic Society for the Study of International Affairs, accessed 16 July 2012, www.passia.org.

11. Website of Ir-Amim: For an Equitable and Stable Jerusalem with an Agreed Political Future, accessed 20 August 2013, www.ir-amim.org.il/en.

12. "About," on the website of the Coalition of Women for Peace, accessed 30 June 2013, http://www.coalitionofwomen.org/about-1/about/?lang=en.

13. Website of Aswat: Palestinian Lesbian Women, accessed 29 June 2013, www.aswatgroup.org/en.

14. Website of Anarchists against the Wall, accessed 14 May 2012, www.awalls.org.

15. "Mission Statement," on the website of the Geneva Initiative, accessed 21 July 2012, http://www.geneva-accord.org/mainmenu/mission-statement.

16. "Who We Are," on the website of Peace Now, accessed 2 August 2012, http://peacenow.org.il/eng/content/who-we-are.

17. Website of the One Voice Movement, accessed 30 July 2012, www.onevoicemovement.org.

18. "The Israeli Palestinian Negotiating Partners," on Harvard Law School's Program on Negotiation website, accessed 12 June 2012, www.pon.harvard.edu/category/research_projects/meni/ipnp/.

19. "Neighbors for Joint Development in the Galilee," on the website of the Inter-Agency Task Force, accessed 3 May 2012, www.iataskforce.org/entities/view/154.

20. "An Alternative Voice in the Galilee: Encounters Inter-Cultural Community Center," on the website of the Inter-Agency Task Force, accessed 25 July 2012, www.iataskforce.org/entities/view/299.

21. "Policing in a Divided Society," on the website of the Abraham Fund Initiatives, accessed 1 July 2012, www.abrahamfund.org/5863.

22. Website of the Arab-Jewish Center for Equality, Empowerment, and Cooperation–Negev Institute for Strategies of Peace and Development, accessed 7 July 2012, http://en.ajeec-nisped.org.il.

23. Website of the Citizens' Accord Forum between Jews and Arabs in Israel, accessed 18 June 2015, www.caf.org.il.

24. See the "Tools for Change" tab on the website of Just Vision, accessed 20 June 2015, www.justvision.org/resources.

25. "Jewish Palestinian Success," on the website of the Traubman Family, accessed 15 July 2012, http://traubman.igc.org/peace.htm.

26. Encounter-EMEM@yahoogroups.com.

27. "Key Milestones," on the website of Language Connections, accessed 21 June 2015, www.languageconnections.org/?page_id=13.

28. "Dugrinet," on the website of the Galilee Foundation for Value Education, accessed 17 June 2012, http://eng.makom-bagalil.org.il/dugrinet/.

29. "About" page at Bitterlemons.net, accessed 10 October 2013.

30. See the Traubman family website for information: http://traubman.igc.org /call-now.htm.

31. Jeremy Grange, "Line of Hope Links Palestinians and Israelis," *BBC News*, 17 August 2007, http://news.bbc.co.uk/2/hi/middle_east/6948034.stm.

32. "Peace We Can" website of the Arik Institute for Reconciliation, Tolerance, and Peace, accessed 12 August 2012, www.arikpeace.org.

33. "Community Histories by Youth in the Middle East," on the website of the International Center for Ethics, Justice, and Public Life at Brandeis University, accessed 3 August 2012, https://brandeis.edu/ethics/about/projects/past/chyme /index.html.

34. Website of Middle East Education through Technology, accessed 20 October 2012, http://meet.mit.edu.

35. "About," on the website of *All For Peace Radio*, accessed 26 October 2012, http://www.allforpeace.org/en/pages/אודות.

36. Carol Daniel Kasbari, "Examination of Peace Journalism in Israel and the Occupied Palestinian Territories: Challenges and Opportunities," *Global Media Journal*, 1 December 2006.

37. Website of the Jerusalem Peacemakers, accessed 20 November 2012.

38. "What is Sulha?" on the website of the Sulha Peace Project, accessed 20 November 2012, http://sulha.com.

39. "Middle Way: Compassionate Engagement in Society," on the website of Insight on Conflict, accessed 29 September 2012, www.insightonconflict.org. http://www.middleway.org.il/English/

40. "Dialogue between Israelis and Palestinians," *Wajibu: Journal of Social and Religious Concern*, 25 January 2003, http://africa.peacelink.org/wajibu/articles/art _2124.html.

41. "Projects," on the website of the Interfaith Encounter Association, accessed 31 August 2012, https://interfaithencounter.wordpress.com/groupseventsprojects /projects/.

42. Daniel Rossing, "New Local Jewish-Christian Relationship," on the website of the Jerusalem Center for Jewish-Christian Relations, April 2004, www .jcjcr.org/category/new-local.

43. "Petition Online," on the now-defunct website of the Alliance of Middle Eastern Scientists and Physicians, accessed 30 August 2012.

44. Now-defunct website of the Israeli-Palestinian Science Organization, accessed 30 August 2012.

45. A. Manenti, "*Bridges*, the Israeli-Palestinian Public Health Magazine," *The European Journal of Public Health* 15, no. 4 (2005), 437.

46. Etgar Lefkovits, "Using Technology to Develop Arab-Jewish Ties," *New York Times*, 6 June 2003.

47. Website of Ecopeace, formerly Friends of the Earth Middle East, accessed 25 August 2012, http://www.foeme.org/www/?module=home.

48. Website of Budo for Peace, accessed 20 August 2012, www.budoforpeace .org.

49. "The Jewish-Arab Youth Orchestra," website of Youth Music Israel, accessed 20 August 2012, www.youth-music.org.il/index.php/en/the-arab-jewish -orchestra.

50. "Voice of Peace Choir," website of the Arab-Jewish Community Center of Jaffa, accessed 21 August 2012, http://ajccjaffa.wix.com/ajcc#!choral-programs /c230q.

51. Website of the School for Peace, accessed 21 August 2012, http://sfpeace .org.

52. Website of the Walter Lebach Institute for Jewish-Arab Coexistence through Education, accessed 21 August 2012, www.dayan.tau.ac.il/education /coexistence/symposia.htm.

53. "Language as a Cultural Bridge," website of the Abraham Fund Initiatives, accessed 18 August 2012, www.abrahamfund.org/5865.

54. Or Kashti, "Spoken Arabic Studies Counter Anti-Arab Prejudice among Israeli Students," *Haaretz*, 20 December 2013.

55. "At a Glance: Bridge over the Wadi," on the website of Hand in Hand: Center for Jewish Arab Education in Israel, accessed 15 August 2012, www.hand inhandk12.org/inform/schools/wadi-ara.

56. "House of Devotion," on the website of *Sha'ar La'Adam*, accessed 15 June 2015, http://adam-insan.org.il/?page_id=193.

57. "Neighbors," on the website of the Galilee Foundation for Value Education, accessed 23 July 2014, http://eng.makom-bagalil.org.il/newneighbors/.

58. "About the Museum Ein Dor Archaeological Museum," on the website of the Ein-Dor Museum of Archeology, accessed 30 July 2014, www.eindormuseum .co.il/content.php?actions=browse&id=4733.

59. "Artists without Walls," Open Society Archives, accessed 24 November 2014, http://w3.osaarchivum.org/galeria/the_divide/chapter19.html.

60. Ibid.

61. "The Film," on the website of the Promises Project, accessed 1 May 2012, www.promisesproject.org/film.html.

62. "Crossing the Lines," on the website of the Compassionate Listening Project, accessed 14 July 2012, www.compassionatelistening.org/store/dvds -videos/220/crossing-the-lines.

63. "Clore Neighborhood Center: Arab-Jewish Coexistence," on the website of the Leo Baeck Community Center, accessed 22 July 2012, www.leobaeck.org .il/page2.asp?category=2099.

64. Website of the All Nations Café, accessed 25 July 2012, http://allnations cafe.org.

65. Website of Chefs for Peace, accessed 12 July 2012, http://chefs4peace .weebly.com.

66. Website of Together Beyond Words: Empowering Women and Promoting Peace, accessed 23 June 2012, www.en.beyondwords.org.il.

67. "Circlework in the Middle East," on the website of the Institute for Circlework, accessed 22 June 2012, http://instituteforcirclework.org/discover-circlework/international-work/#sthash.uosYpi0L.dpbs.

68. Website of Creativity for Peace, accessed 21 July 2012, www.creativityforpeace.com.

69. "Social Workers—Working Together," on the Jerusalem Foundation website, accessed 21 June 2012, http://jerusalemfoundation.co4.codeoasis.com/project_overview.aspx?TAB=0&MID=551&CID=561&PID=678.

70. "A Brief History," on the Machsom Watch website, accessed 21 June 2013, www.machsomwatch.org/en/HistoryHeb.

71. Website of Seruv, accessed 13 July 2012, www.seruv.org.il/english/default.asp.

72. "Combatants Letter," on the website of Seruv, accessed 13 July 2012, www.seruv.org.il/english/combatants_letter.asp.

73. Ben White, "A Hidden History in the Holy Land," *Sojourners*, August 2010, and Norma Musih, "Learning the Nakba as a Condition for Peace and Reconciliation," on the website of Zochrot, July 2005, www.zochrot.org/en/article/52320.

74. "Interview with Gamila, 2005" on the website of Just Vision, accessed 12 June 2012, www.justvision.org/portrait/863/highlights.

75. "Humans without Borders: One Women's Quest to Overcome the Divides of Occupation," on the website of Insight on Conflict, accessed 10 June 2012, http://www.insightonconflict.org/2010/01/humans-without-borders-one-womans-quest-to-overcome-the-divides-of-occupation/.

76. Tim McGirk, "Teaching Auschwitz to the Palestinians," *Time*, 8 July 2008.

77. "Shoah and Tell: An Arab's Holocaust Museum," Israelity Bites blog, 28 January 2010, http://israelitybites.blogspot.com/2010/01/shoah-and-tell-arabs-holocaust-museum.html.

78. Charles A. Radin, "Muslim Opens Holocaust Museum in Israel," *Boston Globe*, 6 May 2005.

79. Mahmoud Al-Sadafi, "Other Victims of Denial," *Monthly Review*, 14 December 2006, http://mrzine.monthlyreview.org/2006/alsafadi141206.html.

80. Aviv Lavie, "Partners in Pain," *Haaretz*, 5 February 2003.

81. Ibid.

82. Alan Cowell, "End to Boycott of Israeli Universities Is Urged," *New York Times*, 20 May 2005.

83. Associated Press, "Palestinian Academic Opposes Israel Boycott," 18 June 2006, www.ynetnews.com/articles/0,7340,L-3264160,00.html.

84. "George Sa'adeh," on the website of Just Vision, accessed 21 June 2012, www.justvision.org/portrait/820/highlights.

85. Benny Barbash, "Dispatches from Israel," *Peacework* magazine, 1 March 2002.

86. "The Summit: The Mountain of Israeli-Palestinian Friendship, Antarctica," Common Ground News Service, 17 January 2004.

## Chapter 9

1. Marina Cantacuzino, *The Forgiveness Project: Stories for a Vengeful Age* (Philadelphia, PA: Jessica Kingsley, 2015), 60–61.

2. "Zohar Shapira," on the website of The Forgiveness Project, 26 May 2010, http://theforgivenessproject.com/stories/zohar-shapira-israel/.

3. Cantacuzino, *The Forgiveness Project*, 62.

4. Stephen Zunes, "U.S. Role in Lebanon Debacle," *Foreign Policy in Focus*, 18 May 2007.

5. Zara Zhang, "Israeli, Palestinian Group's Performance Promotes Political Unity through Music," *The Crimson*, 23 February 2014.

6. Website of Yesh Din, accessed 31 July 2013, www.yesh-din.org.

7. Website of Gisha: Legal Center for Freedom of Movement, accessed 30 May 2014, http://gisha.org.

8. Website of Al-Tariq, accessed 25 July 2012, https://altariq.wordpress.com.

9. Website of the Peres Center, accessed 1 June 2012, www.peres-center.org.

10. Cale Salih, "Bone Marrow Registry in Jerusalem Offers Hope to Arab Cancer Patients," *Al-Monitor*, 27 December 2012.

11. "Midwives for Peace," on the website of Madre, accessed 20 June 2013, www.madre.org/page/palestine-midwives-for-peace—palestinian-medical-relief-society—zakher-association-58.html.

12. Ibid.

13. Nabila Espanioly, on the website of Shatil, http://english.shatil.org.il/activist-profiles/. http://www.shatil.org.il/

14. Anne Usher, "The Great Divide," *Esquire*, September 2011, 100–103.

15. Carol Daniel Kasbari, "Israel-Palestine: Going Beyond the Dialogue of Words," *TEDxJaffa*, 2 November 2011, YouTube, www.youtube.com/watch?v=LWiZMXEK_E8.

16. Katie Knorovsky, "Lessons from the Holy Land," on National Geographic's Intelligent Travel blog, 23 September 2013, http://intelligenttravel.nationalgeographic.com/2013/09/23/lessons-from-the-holy-land/.

17. Mohammed Daraghmeh, "Agriculture: A Story of Palestinian-Israeli Cooperation in Times of Conflict," Common Ground News Service, 1 July 2005, www.commongroundnews.org/article.php?id=834.

18. For more examples of Paltrade–Peres Center ventures, see Daniel Gavron, *Holy Land Mosaic: Stories of Cooperation and Coexistence between Israelis and Palestinians* (New York: Rowman and Littlefield, 2007), 190–192.

19. "Green Action Events: The SAHA Project Takes Off," on the Green Prophet website, 10 December 2008.

20. "SAHA, an Israeli Fair Trade Revolution," on the Peace Oil blog, 17 February 2010, http://peacoil.blogspot.com/2010/02/saha-israeli-fair-trade-revolution.html.

21. "Overview," on the Sindyanna of the Galilee website, accessed 2 August 2014, www.sindyanna.com/about-us/overview/.

22. Peace Oil website, accessed 23 July 2013, www.peaceoil.org.

23. Nicky Blackburn, "Altering the Future of Israeli Arab Women," on

the website Israel 21c: Uncovering Israel, 4 March 2007, www.israel21c.org /altering-the-future-of-israeli-arab-women-one-at-a-time/.

24. Website of AJEEC-NISPED, accessed 14 July 2012, http://en.ajeec-nisped .org.il.

25. "The Abraham Fund Initiatives," on the website of International Women's Day, accessed 4 May 2015, www.internationalwomensday.com/abrahamfund# .Vi_nV0s5TnY.

26. "Employment and Economic Development," on the website of the Abraham Fund Initiatives, accessed 30 June 2013, www.abrahamfund.org/5864.

27. Website of Kav Mashve, accessed 21 July 2013, www.kavmashve.org.il /english/.

28. Kenneth Bob, "Antidote to Cynicism: The Gilboa-Jenin Connection," on the Ameinu blog, 3 September 2009, www.ameinu.net/blog/letters-from-leadership /antidote-to-cynicism-the-gilboa-jenin-connection/.

29. Moshe Gilad, "Between the Gilboa and Jenin," *Haaretz*, 7 December 2010.

30. "Middle Way: Compassionate Engagement in Society," on the Insight on Conflict website, accessed 17 November 2013, www.insightonconflict.org /conflicts/israel-palestinian-territories/peacebuilding-organisations/middleway/.

31. "Acre Group for Joint Living," Shatil Profiles, accessed 3 May 2013, http:// english.shatil.org.il/activist-profiles/.

32. Website of Other Voice, accessed 26 July 2014, www.othervoice.org /welcome-eng.htm.

33. "The Museum," on the website of Museum on the Seam, accessed 25 July 2013, www.mots.org.il/eng/TheMuseum/TheMuseum.asp.

34. "Frames of Reality," on the website of the Peres Center for Peace, accessed 20 August 2013, www.peres-center.org/Frames_of_Reality.

35. Patricia Smith Melton, "Sixty Years, Sixty Voices: Israeli-Palestinian Women" (Washington, DC: Peace X Peace, 2008).

36. "Jewish Arab Orchestra Performs Maqam Dulab Hijaz Peace Music," with Eliana Gilad conducting, http://www.mp3tunes.tk/download?v=SmwRTekuxSs.

37. *Neighbours*, The Galilee Multicultural Theater, 29 May 2012, YouTube, www.youtube.com/watch?v=v7Mfq7RykHI.

38. "Activist Profiles," on the website of Shatil, accessed 30 August 2013, http:// english.shatil.org.il/activist-profiles/.

39. Donald Macintyre, "Israelis Stage Daring Saga of Abandoned Palestinian Raised as a Jew," *The Independent*, 14 April 2008.

40. Lisa Alcalay Klug, "In Israel, Where Art Imitates Messy Life," *New York Times*, 31 December 2005.

41. "Israeli-Palestinian Comedy Tour," 4 February 2008, YouTube, www.you tube.com/watch?v=sz_AUEf6pJY.

42. Hany Abu-Assad and Tirzah Agazzi, "Conversation: *Paradise Now* Director," *Tikkun Magazine*, 27 March 2008.

43. "About the Film," on the *Refusing to Be Enemies* website, accessed 22 July 2012, http://refusingtobeenemies.org/film.html.

44. A. O. Scott, "Inside a Veteran's Nightmare," *New York Times*, 25 December 2008.

45. Website of Neve Shalom/Wahat al-Salam, accessed 2 November 2013, http://wasns.org.

46. Website of Seeds of Peace, accessed 6 July 2013, www.seedsofpeace.org.

47. Website of Sadaka-Reut, accessed 6 July 2013, www.reutsadaka.org.

48. Website of Hand In Hand, accessed 10 June 2013, www.handinhandk12.org.

49. "The Erna D. Leir Peace Kindergarten of the Jerusalem International YMCA," on the website of its funder the Jerusalem Foundation, accessed 6 July 2013, www.jerusalemfoundation.org.

50. Website of Peace Child, accessed 12 June 2014, http://peacechild.org.

51. Miriam Asnes, "No Rest on This Sabbath: A Weekend Retreat with Nemashim," *Middle East Web*, 6–7 January 2006, www.mideastweb.org/nemashim /january2006.htm.

52. Seth Freedman, "Child's Play," *Guardian*, 9 March 2007.

53. Erin Elizabeth Breeze and Melodye Feldman, *Building Bridges for Peace, an Intervention for Israeli, Palestinian, and American Teens: A Report on Theory, Best Practices, and Evaluation after Fifteen Years* (Denver, CO: Seeking Common Ground, 2008), www.buildingbridgesshift.org/wp-content/uploads/2013/05/Best -Practices-Report.pdf.

54. Website of Windows: Channels for Communication, accessed 1 November 2013, www.win-peace.org.

55. "Adam Institute for Democracy and Peace," on the website of the Jerusalem Foundation, accessed 1 November 2013, www.jerusalemfoundation.org /coexistence/education/the-adam-institute-for-democracy-and-peace.aspx.

56. Website of the Jerusalem Foundation, accessed 1 November 2013, www .jerusalemfoundation.org.

57. "Middle East," on the website of Peace Players International, accessed 20 July 2012, www.peaceplayersintl.org/our-programs/middle-east.

58. "International Conference on Education for Peace and Democracy," *Asia Research News*, 26 November 2006.

59. "UNESCO Chair for Multiculturalism in Teacher Training," on the website of Beit Berl, accessed 26 November 2012, www.beitberl.ac.il/english/research /unesco/pages/default.aspx.

60. Tamara Traubman, "Sociology Professor Becomes First Arab Dean of Israeli University," *Haaretz*, 10 October 2005.

61. David Rudge, "Israeli Arab Appointed Dean of University for First Time," *Jerusalem Post*, 10 November 2005.

62. Website of the Jewish-Arab Center, University of Haifa, accessed 2 June 2013, http://jac2.haifa.ac.il/index.php/en/home.html.

63. Website of the Future Generation Hands Association, accessed 22 June 2013, www.fgha2005.org/en/.

64. "Goldberg IIE Prize Awarded to Fresh Start Israeli and Palestinian Young Professionals," on the website of the Institute of International Education, 23 June 2009, www.iie.org/en/Who-We-Are/News-and-Events/Press-Center /Press-Releases/2009/2009-06-23-Goldberg-IIE-Prize-Awarded-To-Fresh-Start.

65. Website of Hagar Association: Jewish-Arab Education For Equality, accessed 20 June 2012.

66. Website of Ein Bustan: Sowing Seeds of Hope and Peace, accessed 2 June 2013, www.ein-bustan.org.

67. "Salaam Shalom: Teaching Children in the Middle East Pathways to Peace," *Waldorf Today*, accessed 21 June 2014, www.waldorftoday.com.

68. Website of Soccer for Peace, accessed 14 July 2013, www.soccerforpeace .com.

69. Osseily Hanna, "Heartbeat: Palestinian and Israeli Youth Musicians on Debut Tour in US," *Huffington Post*, 19 February 2013.

70. Website of Heartbeat, accessed 12 July 2014, http://heartbeat.fm/about/.

71. Description of Heartbeat Jerusalem on the website of the Alliance for Middle East Peace, accessed 10 November 2014, www.allmep.org/index .php?option=com_content&view=article&id=5&Itemid=4.

72. Website of Masks Off, accessed 11 July 2013, www.masksoff.org.

73. Beresheet Lashalom Foundation, accessed 24 July 2014, www.beresheetla shalom.org.

74. Website of Peace NGO Forum, accessed 15 August 2014, www.peacengo .org/en/ListOfOrganizations.

75. "A Holistic Approach to Peace: Connecting NGOs and Spreading Aware-ness," Choosing to See blog, 17 September 2011, https://choosingtosee.wordpress .com/2011/09/17/building-bridges-between-peace-ngos/.

76. Mepeace.org, accessed 20 July 2014.

77. Heidi Basch, "Online Peace Ongoing," *Palestine-Israel Journal*, October 2006.

78. "Peace Computer Centers," on the website of Peres Center for Peace, ac-cessed 24 August 2013, www.peres-center.org/Peace_Computer_centers.

79. Website of Alliance for Middle East Peace, accessed 22 May 2013, www .allmep.org.

## Chapter 10

1. Ronit Avni, "Just Vision: In search of Israeli and Palestinian Morning-After Leadership," in *Bullets and Bombs: Grassroots Peacebuilding between Israelis and Pales-tinians*, ed. Judith Kuriansky (Westport, CT: Praeger, 2007), 167.

2. Mohammed Abu-Nimer and Ned Lazarus, "The Peacebuilder's Paradox and the Dynamics of Dialogue: A Psychosocial Portrait of Israeli-Palestinian En-counters," in *Bullets and Bombs: Grassroots Peacebuilding between Israelis and Pales-tinians*, ed. Judith Kuriansky (Westport, CT: Praeger, 2007), 19.

3. Lourdes Garcia-Navarro, "Influence of Israel's Leftist Peace Movement Wanes," National Public Radio, 22 October 2010.

4. Jodi Rudoren and Jeremy Ashkenas, "Netanyahu and the Settlements," *New York Times*, 12 March 2015.

5. Shany Payes, *Palestinian NGOs in Israel: The Politics of Civil Society* (London: Tauris Academic, 2005), 190.

6. Michelle I. Gawerc, *Prefiguring Peace: Israeli-Palestinian Peacebuilding Partnerships* (Lanham, MD: Lexington, 2012), 227–228.

7. Ibid., 228–230.

8. Ari Shavit, "War Clouds over My Sons' Future," *The Sunday Times*, 13 July 2014, www.thesundaytimes.co.uk/sto/news/focus/article1433645.ece.

9. See his tribute to his daughters on the Daughters for Life Foundation website, http://daughtersforlife.com.

10. "Our Story," on the website of the Daughters for Life Foundation, accessed 2 June 2014, http://daughtersforlife.com/about/our-story/.

11. "A Story of Diverse Citizens," available at traubman.igc.org, http://traub man.igc.org/gazahelp.pdf.

12. United Religions Initiative Middle East and North Africa, accessed 20 May 2012, www.uri.org/?e=app.blog.listByRegion&region_id=7.

13. "Israeli-Palestinian Partnership Launches Start-Up," Ynetnews, 15 July 2009, www.ynetnews.com/articles/0,7340,L-3746717,00.html.

14. Website of the Israeli-Palestinian Chamber of Commerce, accessed 4 June 2014, www.ipcc.org.il.

15. Moshe Gilad, "Between the Gilboa and Jenin." *Haaretz*, 7 December 2010.

16. The album, *Tomorrow Is Coming*, is available through AllMusic: www.all music.com/album/tomorrow-is-coming-mw0002119020.

17. Miriam Kresh, "Seeds of Bliss Chews Your Way to Peace in the Middle East," Green Prophet website, 15 October 2012.

18. Website of Seas of Peace, accessed 26 June 2015, http://seasofpeace.org.

19. Catherine Rottenberg, "Hagar: Jewish-Arab Education for Equality, Creating a Common Future in Israel," on the website of the Institute for Advanced Study, Summer 2013, www.ias.edu/about/publications/ias-letter/articles /2013-summer/rottenberg-hagar.

20. Project Harmony's Tumblr page, "The Human Side: Stories of Israel-Palestine," accessed 22 June 2015, http://projectharmonyisrael.tumblr.com.

21. Website of Shutafut/Sharakah, accessed 12 June 2014, www.shutafut -sharakah.org.il/en/category/toward-and-equal-and-shared-society/.

22. "NVC for People of Israel and Palestine 9 Day Training," on the website of Nonviolent Communication, accessed 7 July 2014, https://www.cnvc.org /about-Israel-Palestine-9-day-training.

23. "Interfaith Women Inaugurate Garden of the Mothers," on the website of United Religions Initiative, accessed 4 August 2014, www.uri.org.

24. On the website of Sha'ar la-Adam/Bab lil-Insan, accessed 7 July 2014, www .adam-insan.org.il/?page_id=500#!home/c19ig.

25. *My So-Called Enemy*, directed by Lisa Gossels, Good Egg Productions, 2010.

26. Ethan Bronner, "Where Politics Are Complex, Simple Joys at the Beach," *New York Times*, 27 July 2011.

27. Ibid.

28. Payes, *Palestinian NGOs in Israel*.

29. Ibid., 189.

30. "A Discussion with Mohammed Abu-Nimer, Professor, School of International Service, American University," on the website of the Berkley Center for Religion, Peace, and World Affairs, Georgetown University, 13 June 2010, http:// berkleycenter.georgetown.edu/interviews/a-discussion-with-mohammed-abu -nimer-professor-school-of-international-service-american-university.

31. Mohammed Abu-Nimer, *Dialogue, Conflict Resolution, and Change: Arab-Jewish Encounters in Israel* (Albany: State University of New York Press, 1999), 150, 155–156.

32. Nadia Nasser-Najjab, "Post-Oslo Dialogue: An Evaluation." *Palestine-Israel Journal* 12–13, nos. 4 and 1 (2005–2006).

33. Gottleib, Lynn, "Boycotts, Nonviolence, and Palestinian-Israeli Conflict Transformation," *Fellowship of Reconciliation Magazine* (Summer 2010).

34. Nasser-Najjab, "Post-Oslo Dialogue."

35. Hind Khoury, "Civil Society: From Advocacy to Social Change," *Palestine-Israel Journal* 18, no. 2–3 (2012).

36. Salim Tamari, "Kissing Cousins," *Palestine-Israel Journal* 12–13, nos. 4 and 1 (2005–2006).

37. Daniel Bar-Tal, "Farewell after Four Challenging Years," *Palestine-Israel Journal* 12, no. 2–3 (2005).

38. "Discussion with Mohammed Abu-Nimer."

39. Abu-Nimer, *Dialogue*, 151.

40. Abu-Nimer and Lazarus, "Peacebuilder's Paradox," 19.

41. Frida Kerner Furman, "Religion and Peacebuilding: Grassroots Efforts by Israelis and Palestinians," *Journal of Religion, Conflict, and Peace* 4, no. 2 (2012), 119.

42. Ibid., 119.

43. Nadia Nasser-Najjab and Lee Pearlman, "The Future of People-to-People," *Palestine-Israel Journal* 12–13, nos. 4 and 1 (2005–2006).

44. Julia Chaitin, *Peace-building in Israel and Palestine: Social Psychology and Grassroots Initiatives* (New York: Palgrave Macmillan, 2011), 155.

45. "Still Campaigning for Coexistence," *The Economist*, 30 August 2007.

46. Furman, "Religion and Peacebuilding," 24–38.

47. Ziad AbuZayyad, "Making Peace between Peoples," *Palestine-Israel Journal* 12–13, nos. 4 and 1 (2005–2006).

48. Payes, *Palestinian NGOs in Israel*, 226, 228.

49. Michael N. Nagler, *The Search for a Nonviolent Future: A Promise of Peace for Ourselves, Our Families, and Our World* (Maui, HI: Inner Ocean, 2004).

50. Edward Said, "The One-State Solution," *New York Times*, 10 January 1999.

51. Payes, *Palestinian NGOs in Israel*, 5.

52. Rashid Khalidi, *The Iron Cage: The Story of the Palestinian Struggle for Statehood* (Boston: Beacon, 2006), xxxiv.

53. Gershon Baskin and Zakaria Al-Qaq, "Years of Experience of Strategies for Peace Making," *International Journal of Politics, Culture, and Society* 17, no. 3 (2004), 544.

54. Ali Abu Awwad in the film *Encounter Point*, dir. Ronit Avni, Julia Bacha.

55. Interview with Ali Abu Awwad, on website of Just Vision, 2005, accessed 16 November 2014, www.justvision.org/portrait/799/interview; Ilene Prusher, "Where Palestinians and Settlers Meet as Equals," *Haaretz*, 13 March 2015.

56. Thanks to Gordon Fellman for suggesting this language.

57. Emmanuel Levinas and Jill Robbins, *Is It Righteous to Be? Interviews with Emmanual Levinas* (Stanford University Press, 2002), 176.

58. Interview with Sami Adwan, on website of Just Vision, 2005, accessed 23 July 2012, http://www.justvision.org/portrait/846/interview.

59. Ron Pundak, "More Relevant Than Ever: People-to-People Peacebuilding Efforts in Israel and Palestine," *Palestine-Israel Journal* 18, nos. 2-3 (2012).

60. Ibid.

61. August 1969 letter to the former Czech Communist Party chair Alexander Dubček, translated in Vaclav Havel, *Disturbing the Peace: A Conversation with Karel Huizdala* (New York: Vintage, 1991), 115.

62. Howard Zinn, *A Power Governments Cannot Suppress* (San Francisco: City Lights, 2006), 270.

# Bibliography

## Books and Articles

Abdo-Zubi, Nahla. "Women of the Intifada: Gender, Class, and National Liberation." *Race and Class* 32, no. 4 (1991): 19–34.

Abu-Assad, Hany, and Tirzah Agazzi. "Conversation: *Paradise Now* Director." *Tikkun Magazine*, 27 March 2008.

Abu el-Assal, Riah. *Caught In Between: The Extraordinary Story of an Arab Palestinian Christian Israeli*. London: SPCK, 1999.

Abu-Nimer, Mohammed. *Dialogue, Conflict Resolution, and Change: Arab-Jewish Encounters in Israel*. Albany: State University of New York Press, 1999.

Abu-Nimer, Mohammed, and Ned Lazarus. "The Peacebuilder's Paradox and the Dynamics of Dialogue: A Psychosocial Portrait of Israeli-Palestinian Encounters." In *Bullets and Bombs: Grassroots Peacebuilding between Israelis and Palestinians*, ed. Judith Kuriansky. Westport, CT: Praeger, 2007.

Abu-Sharif, Bassam, and Uzi Mahnaimi. *Best of Enemies: The Memoirs of Bassam Abu-Sharif and Uzi Mahnaimi*. Boston: Little, Brown, 1995.

AbuZayyad, Ziad. "Making Peace between Peoples." *Palestine-Israel Journal* 12–13, nos. 4 and 1 (2005–2006).

Afana, Abdel Hamid. "A Model for Community Care in Gaza." *Palestine-Israel Journal* 10, no. 4 (2003).

Alexander, Meredith. "Palestinian Women Encounter Roadblocks on the Path to Political Participation, Professor Says." *Stanford Report*, 27 April 2001. http://news.stanford.edu/news/2001/may2/beinin-52.html.

American Friends Service Committee. *Search for Peace in the Middle East*. Philadelphia: American Friends Service Committee, 1970.

Are, Thomas L. *Israeli Peace/Palestinian Justice: Liberation Theology and the Peace Process*. Atlanta: Clarity, 1994.

Ashrawi, Hanan. *This Side of Peace: A Personal Account*. New York: Simon and Schuster, 1995.

Asnes, Miriam. "No Rest on This Sabbath: A Weekend Retreat with Nemashim," *Middle East Web*, 6–7 January 2006, www.mideastweb.org/nemashim/january 2006.htm.

Assaily, Nafez, and Andrew Rigand. "The Intifada." In *Nonviolent Struggle and Social Defence*, ed. Shelley Anderson and Janet Larmore. London: War Resisters' International, 1991. https://www.wri-irg.org/books/nvsd.htm#Heading10.

Aviad, Janet, and Yitzhak Galnoor. *Peace Is Greater than Greater Israel* (pamphlet). Jerusalem: Peace Now, 1979.

Avnery, Uri. "A Federation—Why Not?" *Gush Shalom*, 10 August 2013. http://zope.gush-shalom.org/home/en/channels/avnery/1376051927.

———. "The Ghetto Within." *Counter Punch*, 23 March 2012. www.counterpunch.org/2012/03/23/the-ghetto-within.

———. *My Friend, the Enemy*. Westport, CT: Hill, 1986.

Avni, Ronit. "Just Vision: In Search of Israeli and Palestinian Morning-After Leadership," pp. 167–170 in *Beyond Bullets and Bombs: Grassroots Peacebuilding between Israelis and Palestinians*, ed. Judith Kuriansky. Westport, CT: Praeger, 2007.

Azuri, Najib. *Le reveil de la nation arabe*. Paris: Plon, 1905.

Barbash, Benny. "Dispatches from Israel." *Peacework* magazine, 1 March 2002.

Bard, Mitchell G. *Building Bridges: Lessons for America from Novel Israeli Approaches to Promote Coexistence*. Chevy Chase, MD: American-Israeli Cooperative Enterprise, 1997.

Barhoun, Musa Isa, and Ben Mollo. "Building Religious/Cultural Bridges between Israeli and Palestinian University Students." *Eubios Journal of Asian and International Bioethics* 9 (1999): 55.

Bar-On, Mordechai. *In Pursuit of Peace: A History of the Israeli Peace Movement*. Washington, DC: United States Institute of Peace, 1996.

Bar-Tal, Daniel. "Farewell after Four Challenging Years." *Palestine-Israel Journal* 12, no. 2–3 (2005).

Basch, Heidi. "Online Peace Ongoing." *Palestine-Israel Journal*, October 2006.

Baskin, Gershon, and Zakaria Al-Qaq. "Years of Experience of Strategies for Peace Making." *International Journal of Politics, Culture, and Society* 17, no. 3 (2004).

Beinin, Joel. *Was the Red Flag Flying There? Marxist Politics and the Arab-Israeli conflict in Egypt and Israel, 1948–1965*. London: I. B. Tauris, 1990.

Beit-Hallahmi, Benjamin. *Original Sins: Reflections on the History of Zionism and Israel*. New York: Olive Branch, 1993.

Ben-Gurion, David. *My Talks with Arab Leaders*. Jerusalem: Keter, 1972.

Berkley Center for Religion, Peace, and World Affairs. "A Discussion with Mohammed Abu-Nimer, Professor, School of International Service, American University." On the website of the Berkley Center for Religion, Peace, and World Affairs, Georgetown University, 13 June 2010. http://berkleycenter.georgetown.edu/interviews/a-discussion-with-mohammed-abu-nimer-professor-school-of-international-service-american-university.

Bernstein, Deborah S. *Constructing Boundaries: Jewish and Arab Workers in Mandatory Palestine*. Albany: State University of New York Press, 2000.

———. *The Struggle for Equality: Urban Women Workers in Pre-state Israeli Society*. New York: Praeger, 1987.

Bhabha, Homi K. *The Location of Culture*. London: Routledge, 1994.

Bing, Anthony G. *Israeli Pacifist: The Life of Joseph Abileah*. Syracuse, NY: Syracuse University Press, 1990.

Birkland, Carol J. *Unified in Hope: Arabs and Jews Talk about Peace*. New York: Friendship, 1987.

Bob, Kenneth. "Antidote to Cynicism: The Gilboa-Jenin Connection," on the Ameinu blog, 3 September 2009, www.ameinu.net/blog/letters-from-leadership /antidote-to-cynicism-the-gilboa-jenin-connection/.

Breeze, Erin Elizabeth, and Melodye Feldman. *Building Bridges for Peace, an Intervention for Israeli, Palestinian, and American Teens: A Report on Theory, Best Practices, and Evaluation after Fifteen Years*. Denver, CO: Seeking Common Ground, 2008. www.buildingbridgesshift.org/wp-content/uploads/2013/05 /Best-Practices-Report.pdf.

Brinner, Benjamin E. *Playing across a Divide: Israeli-Palestinian Musical Encounters*. Oxford: Oxford University Press, 2009.

Brinner, William M., and Moses Rischin. *Like All the Nations?: The Life and Legacy of Judah L. Magnes*. Albany: State University of New York, 1987.

Bronner, Ethan. "Where Politics are Complex, Simple Joys at the Beach." *New York Times*, 27 July 2011.

Buber, Martin. "Genuine Dialogue and the Possibilities of Peace." In *Pointing the Way: Collected Essays*. New York: Harper, 1957.

———. *I and Thou*, 2nd ed., trans. R. Gregor Smith. Edinburgh: T. & T. Clark, 1958.

———. *On Zion: the History of an Idea*. New York: Schocken, 1973.

———. *Pointing the Way: Collected Essays*. New York: Harper, 1957.

Campfens, Hubert, ed. *Community Development around the World: Practice, Theory, Research, Training*. Toronto: University of Toronto Press, 1997.

Cantacuzino, Marina. *The Forgiveness Project: Stories for a Vengeful Age*. Philadelphia, PA: Jessica Kingsley, 2015.

Caplan, Neil. *Futile Diplomacy*. London: Frank Cass, 1983.

Chacour, Elias, and Mary E. Jensen. *We Belong to the Land: The Story of a Palestinian Israeli Who Lives for Peace and Reconciliation*. San Francisco: HarperSanFrancisco, 1990.

Chaitin, Julia. *Peace-building in Israel and Palestine: Social Psychology and Grassroots Initiatives*. New York: Palgrave Macmillan, 2011.

Cohen, Aharon. *Israel and the Arab World*. New York: Funk and Wagnalls, 1970.

Cowell, Alan. "End to Boycott of Israeli Universities Is Urged." *New York Times*, 20 May 2005.

Daraghmeh, Mohammed. "Agriculture: A Story of Palestinian-Israeli Cooperation in Times of Conflict." Common Ground News Service, 1 July 2005. www .commongroundnews.org/article.php?id=834.

Davis, Barry. "Walking the Tightrope." *Jerusalem Post*, 15 March 2007.

Demant, Peter. "Unofficial Contacts and Peacemaking: Israeli-Palestinian Dialogue, 1967-1993." Pp. 73-104 in *Israel in the Nineties: Development and Conflict*, ed. Frederick Lazin and Gregory Mahler. Gainesville: University Press of Florida, 1996.

"Dialogue between Israelis and Palestinians." *Wajibu: Journal of Social and Religious*

*Concern*, 25 January 2003. http://africa.peacelink.org/wajibu/articles/art_2124 .html.

Doumani, Beshara. *Rediscovering Palestine: Merchants and Peasants in Jabal Nablus, 1700–1900.* Berkeley: University of California Press, 1995.

Dowty, Alan. "'A Question that Outweighs All Others': Yitzhak Epstein and the Zionist Recognition of the Arab Issue." *Israel Studies* 6, no. 1 (2001): 47.

Drago, Margherita. "Dangerous Liaisons: Perceptions on Arab/Jewish Intermarriage in Israel." Culture Matters blog, 9 August 2011. https://culturematters .wordpress.com/2011/08/09/dangerous-liaisons-perceptions-on-arabjewish -intermarriage-in-israel/.

Elath, Eliahu. *Jewish-Arab Relations in Israel.* New York: American Histadrut Cultural Exchange Institute, 1967.

Eliachar, Elie. *Israeli Jews and Palestinian Arabs: Key to Arab-Jewish Coexistence.* Jerusalem: Council of the Sephardi Community, 1970.

Elon, Amos, and Sana Hassan. *Between Enemies: A Compassionate Dialogue between an Israeli and an Arab.* New York: Random House, 1974.

Emmett, Ayala. *Our Sisters' Promised Land: Women, Politics, and Israeli-Palestinian Coexistence.* Ann Arbor, MI: University of Michigan Press, 1996.

Farsoun, Samih K., and Naseer Aruri. *Palestine and the Palestinians*, 2nd ed. Boulder, CO: Westview, 2006.

Feuerverger, Grace. *Oasis of Dreams: Teaching and Learning Peace in a Jewish-Palestinian Village in Israel.* New York: Routledge, 2001.

Flapan, Simha. *Zionism and the Palestinians.* London: Croom Helm, 1979.

Freedman, Seth. "Child's Play." *Guardian*, 9 March 2007.

French, Mary Ann, and Roxanne Roberts. "Peace in Their Time: A Bit Dazed, A Bit Dazzled, the Peacemakers Celebrate." *Washington Post*, 14 September 1993.

Furlonge, Geoffrey W. *Palestine Is My Country: The Story of Musa Alami.* New York: Praeger, 1969.

Furman, Frida Kerner. "Compassionate Listening as a Path to Conflict Resolution." *Journal for the Study of Peace and Conflict* (2009–2010): 24–38.

———. "Religion and Peacebuilding: Grassroots Efforts by Israelis and Palestinians." *Journal of Religion, Conflict, and Peace* 4, no. 2 (2012): 119.

*The Future of Palestine*, prepared by the Arab Office, London, 1947. Westport, CT: Hyperion, 1976.

Garcia-Navarro, Lourdes. "Influence of Israel's Leftist Peace Movement Wanes." National Public Radio, 22 October 2010.

Gavron, Daniel. *Holy Land Mosaic: Stories of Cooperation and Coexistence between Israelis and Palestinians.* New York: Rowman and Littlefield, 2007.

Gawerc, Michelle I. *Prefiguring Peace: Israeli-Palestinian Peacebuilding Partnerships.* Lanham, MD: Lexington, 2012.

Gilad, Moshe. "Between the Gilboa and Jenin." *Haaretz*, 7 December 2010.

Golan, Daphna. "'Separation,' 'Normalization,' and Occupation: The Dilemmas of a Joint Venture by Palestinian and Israeli Women." *Palestine-Israel Journal* 2, no. 2 (1995).

Goren, Arthur A., ed. *Dissenter in Zion: From the Writings of Judah L. Magnes.* Cambridge, MA: Harvard University Press, 1982.

Goren, Tamir. "Cooperation Is the Guiding Principle?: Jews and Arabs in the

Haifa Municipality during the British Mandate." *Israel Studies* 11, no. 3 (2006): 108–141.

Gottleib, Lynn. "Boycotts, Nonviolence, and Palestinian-Israeli Conflict Transformation." *Fellowship of Reconciliation Magazine*, Summer 2010.

"Green Action Events: The SAHA Project Takes Off." On the Green Prophet website, 10 December 2008.

Grossman, David. "An Israel without Illusions: Stop the Grindstone of Israeli-Palestinian Violence." *New York Times*, 27 July 2014.

Grossman, David, and Haim Watzman. *Death as a Way of Life: From Oslo to the Geneva Accords*. New York: Picador, 2004.

Haklai, Oded. *Palestinian Ethnonationalism in Israel*. Philadelphia: University of Pennsylvania Press, 2011.

Hall-Cathala, David. *The Peace Movement in Israel, 1967–1987*. New York: St. Martin's, 1990.

Hanna, Osseily. "Heartbeat: Palestinian and Israeli Youth Musicians on Debut tour in US." *Huffington Post*, 19 February 2013.

Havel, Vaclav. *Disturbing the Peace: A Conversation with Karel Huizdala*. New York: Vintage, 1991.

Helman, Sara. "Peace Movements in Israel." In Jewish Women's Archive's online encyclopedia of Jewish women. Accessed 16 June 2014. http://jwa.org /encyclopedia/article/peace-movements-in-israel.

Herzl, Theodor. *Altneuland: Old New Land*, trans. Lotta Levensohn. Princeton, NJ: M. Wiener, 1997.

Hoffman, Gene Knudsen. "An Enemy Is One Whose Story We Have Not Heard." In *Essays by Gene Knudsen Hoffman: Quaker Peace Activist and Mystic*, ed. Anthony Manousos. Torrance, CA: Friends Bulletin, 2003.

Hoffman, Gene Knudson, Cynthia Monroe, and Leah Green. *Compassionate Listening: An Exploratory Sourcebook about Conflict Transformation*, ed. Dennis Rivers. N.p.: New Conversations, 2008.

"Israel-Palestine Liberation Organization Agreement: 1993." http://avalon.law .yale.edu/20th_century/isrplo.asp.

Issawi, Charles P. *An Economic History of the Middle East and Northern Africa*. New York: Columbia University Press, 1982.

Kaminer, Reuven. *The Politics of Protest: The Israeli Peace Movement and the Palestinian Intifada*. Brighton, UK: Sussex Academic, 1996.

Kaminker, Sarah. "Palestinian-Israeli Economic Cooperation: A View from the Field." *Palestine-Israel Journal* 6, no. 3 (1999).

Kasbari, Carol Daniel. "Examination of Peace Journalism in Israel and the Occupied Palestinian Territories: Challenges and Opportunities," *Global Media Journal*, 1 December 2006.

———. "Israel-Palestine: Going Beyond the Dialogue of Words." TEDxJaffa, 2 November 2011. www.youtube.com/watch?v=LWiZMXEK_E8.

Kashti, Or. "Spoken Arabic Studies Counter Anti-Arab Prejudice among Israeli Students." *Haaretz*, 20 December 2013.

Katz, Sheila H. *Women and Gender in Early Jewish and Palestinian Nationalism*. Gainesville: University Press of Florida, 2003.

Katznelson-Shazar, Rachel. *The Plough Woman: Records of the Pioneer Women of Palestine*. Westport, CT: Hyperion, 1976.

Kaufman, Edy, Shukri B. Abed, and Robert L. Rothstein. *Democracy, Peace, and the Israeli-Palestinian Conflict*. Boulder, CO: Lynne Rienner, 1993.

Kaufman-Nunn, Maxine. *Creative Resistance: Anecdotes of Nonviolent Action by Israeli-Based Groups*. Jerusalem: Alternative Information Center, 1993.

Kawar, Amal. *Daughters of Palestine: Leading Women of the Palestinian National Movement*. Albany: State University of New York Press, 1996.

―――. "Palestinian Women's Activism." Pp. 233–244 in *Palestinian Women of Gaza and the West Bank*, ed. Suha Sabbagh. Bloomington: Indiana University Press, 1998.

Khalidi, Rashid. *The Iron Cage: The Story of the Palestinian Struggle for Statehood*. Boston: Beacon, 2006.

―――. *Palestinian Identity: The Construction of Modern National Consciousness*. New York: Columbia University Press, 1997.

Khalifeh, Sahar. "Comments by Five Women Activists: Siham Abdullah, Amal Kharisha Barghouthi, Rita Giacaman, May Mistakmel Nassar, Amal Wahdan." Pp. 192–215 in *Palestinian Women of Gaza and the West Bank*, ed. Suha Sabbagh. Bloomington: Indiana University Press, 1998.

Khoury, Hind. "Civil Society: From Advocacy to Social Change." *Palestine-Israel Journal* 18, nos. 2–3 (2012).

Kimmerling, Baruch, and Joel S. Migdal. *Palestinians: The Making of a People*. New York: Free Press, 1993.

King, Martin Luther, Jr. *Where Do We Go from Here: Chaos or Community?* Boston: Beacon, 1967.

Klug, Lisa Alcalay. "In Israel, Where Art Imitates Messy Life." *New York Times*, 31 December 2005.

Knorovsky, Katie. "Lessons from the Holy Land." National Geographic's Intelligent Travel blog, 23 September 2013. http://intelligenttravel.national geographic.com/2013/09/23/lessons-from-the-holy-land/.

Kuriansky, Judith, ed. *Beyond Bullets and Bombs: Grassroots Peacebuilding between Israelis and Palestinians*. Westport, CT: Praeger, 2007.

Laqueur, Walter, and Barry Rubin. *The Israel-Arab Reader: A Documentary History of the Middle East Conflict*, 7th ed. New York: Penguin, 2009.

Lavie, Aviv. "Partners in Pain." *Haaretz*, 5 February 2003.

Lefkovits, Etgar. "Using Technology to Develop Arab-Jewish Ties." *New York Times*, 6 June 2003.

Lockman, Zachary. *Comrades and Enemies: Arab and Jewish Workers in Palestine, 1906–1948*. Berkeley: University of California Press, 1996.

―――. "Railway Workers and Relational History: Arabs and Jews in British-Ruled History." Pp. 99–128 in *The Israel/Palestine Question*, ed. Ilan Pappé. London: Routledge, 1999.

Macintyre, Donald. "Israelis Stage Daring Saga of Abandoned Palestinian Raised as a Jew." *The Independent*, 14 April 2008.

Magnes, Judah L., and Martin Buber. *Arab-Jewish Unity: Testimony before the Anglo-American Inquiry Commission for the Ihud (Union) Association*. Westport, CT: Hyperion, 1976.

Mandel, Neville J. *The Arabs and Zionism before World War One*. Berkeley: University of California Press, 1976.

Manenti, A. *"Bridges*, the Israeli-Palestinian Public Health Magazine." *The European Journal of Public Health* 15, no. 4 (2005): 437.

Manousos, Anthony, ed. *Essays by Gene Knudsen-Hoffman: Quaker Peace Activist and Mystic*. Torrance, CA: Friends Bulletin, 2003.

Mansour, Atallah. *Waiting for the Dawn: An Autobiography*. London: Secker, 1975.

Mattar, Philip. *The Mufti in Jerusalem*. New York: Columbia University Press, 1992.

McGirk, Tim. "Teaching Auschwitz to the Palestinians." *Time*, 8 July 2008.

Melton, Patricia Smith. *Sixty Years, Sixty Voices: Israeli and Palestinian Women*. Washington, DC: Peace X Peace, 2008.

Mendes-Flohr, Paul R., ed. *A Land of Two Peoples: Martin Buber on Jews and Arabs*. New York: Oxford University Press, 1983.

Morris, Benny. *Righteous Victims: A History of the Zionist-Arab Conflict, 1881–1999*. New York: Knopf, 1999.

Musih, Norma. "Learning the Nakba as a Condition for Peace and Reconciliation." On the website of Zochrot, July 2005. http://www.zochrot.org/en/article/52320.

Nagler, Michael N. *The Search for a Nonviolent Future: A Promise of Peace for Ourselves, Our Families, and Our World*. Maui, HI: Inner Ocean, 2004.

Nagler, Michael N., Tal Palter-Palman, and Matthew A. Taylor. "The Road to Nonviolent Coexistence in Palestine/Israel." Available on the website of Matthew A. Taylor, n.d. www.matthewtaylor.net/nvcoexistpalisfinal.pdf.

Nassar, Issam. "Reflections on Writing the History of Palestinian Identity." *Palestine-Israel Journal* 8–9, nos. 4 and 1 (2001–2002).

Nasser-Najjab, Nadia. "Post-Oslo Dialogue: An Evaluation." *Palestine-Israel Journal* 12–13, nos. 4 and 1 (2005–2006).

Nasser-Najjab, Nadia, and Lee Pearlman. "The Future of People-to-People." *Palestine-Israel Journal* 12–13, nos. 4 and 1 (2005–2006).

Norman, Julie M. *The Second Palestinian Intifada: Civil Resistance*. London: Routledge, 2010.

Norman, Julie M., and Maia Carter Hallward, eds. *Nonviolent Resistance in the Second Intifada: Activism and Advocacy*. New York: Palgrave Macmillan, 2011.

Nusseibeh, Sari, with Anthony David. *Once Upon a Country: A Palestinian Life*. New York: Farrar, Straus and Giroux, 2007.

Obreht, Téa. *The Tiger's Wife: A Novel*. New York: Random House, 2011.

Owen, Roger. *The Middle East in the World Economy, 1800–1914*. London: Methuen, 1981.

Oz, Amos. *A Tale of Love and Darkness*. Orlando: Harcourt, 2004.

Pal, Amitabh. *"Islam" Means Peace: Understanding the Muslim Principle of Nonviolence Today*. Westport, CT: Praeger, 2011.

"Palestine Royal Commission Peel Report, 1937," pp. 41–42 in *The Israel-Arab Reader: A Documentary History*, 7th ed., ed. Walter Laqueur and Barry Rubin. London: Penguin, 2008.

Pappé, Ilan. *The Israel/Palestine Question*. London: Routledge, 1999.

Payes, Shany. *Palestinian NGOs in Israel: The Politics of Civil Society.* London: Tauris Academic, 2005.

Peres, Shimon, and David Landau. *Battling for Peace: A Memoir.* New York: Random House, 1995.

Prusher, Irene. "Where Palestinians and Settlers Meet as Equals." *Haaretz,* 13 March 2015.

Pundak, Ron. "More Relevant Than Ever: People-to-People Peacebuilding Efforts in Israel and Palestine." *Palestine-Israel Journal* 18, nos. 2–3 (2012).

Radin, Charles A. "Muslim Opens Holocaust Museum in Israel." *Boston Globe,* 6 May 2005.

Rasper, Anke. "Mending the Middle East." *Deutsche Welle,* 5 July 2012. www .dw.com/en/mending-the-middle-east/a-16072192.

Rix, Kate. "Music Groups Transcend Politics in the Middle East." Berkeley Research, University of California at Berkeley, 12 February 2010. http:// vcresearch.berkeley.edu/news/music-groups-transcend-politics-middle-east.

Rosenwasser, Penny. *Voices from a "Promised Land": Palestinian and Israeli Peace Activists Speak Their Hearts, Conversations with Penny Rosenwasser.* Willimantic, CT: Curbstone, 1992.

Rossing, Daniel. "New Local Jewish-Christian Relationship." On the website of the Jerusalem Center for Jewish-Christian Relations, April 2004. www.jcjcr .org/category/new-local.

Rottenberg, Catherine. "Hagar: Jewish-Arab Education for Equality, Creating a Common Future in Israel." On the website of the Institute for Advanced Study, Summer 2013. www.ias.edu/about/publications/ias-letter /articles/2013-summer/rottenberg-hagar.

"Roundtable: The Future of People-to-People." *Palestine-Israel Journal* 12–13, nos. 4, 1 (2005–2006).

Rudge, David. "Israeli Arab Appointed Dean of University for First Time." *Jerusalem Post,* 10 November 2005.

Rudoren, Jodi, and Jeremy Ashkenas. "Netanyahu and the Settlements." *New York Times,* 12 March 2015.

Sabbagh, Suha, ed. *Palestinian Women of Gaza and the West Bank.* Bloomington: Indiana University Press, 1998.

Al-Sadafi, Mahmoud. "Other Victims of Denial." *Monthly Review,* 14 December 2006. http://mrzine.monthlyreview.org/2006/alsafadi141206.html.

Said, Edward W. "The One-State Solution." *New York Times,* 10 January 1999.

Salih, Cale. "Bone Marrow Registry in Jerusalem Offers Hope to Arab Cancer Patients." *Al-Monitor,* 27 December 2012.

Scalo Publishers. *1000 Peacewomen Across the Globe.* Zurich, Switzerland: Scalo Publishers, 2006.

Schenker, Hillel. "Chronicles of Peace Activism." *Palestine-Israel Journal* 5, no. 1 (1998).

Scolnik, Ron. "In Memory of Rabbi Bruce Cohen, Interns for Peace." Partners for a Progressive Israel website, 13 August 2010. http://progressiveisrael.org/in -memory-of-rabbi-bruce-cohen-interns-for-peace.

Scott, A. O. "Inside a Veteran's Nightmare." *New York Times,* 25 December 2008.

Sharoni, Simona. *Gender and the Israeli-Palestinian Conflict: The Politics of Women's Resistance.* Syracuse, NY: Syracuse University Press, 1995.

Sharp, Gene. *The Politics of Nonviolent Action.* Boston: Sargent, 1973.

Shavit, Ari. *My Promised Land: The Triumph and Tragedy of Israel.* New York: Spiegel, 2013.

———. "War Clouds over My Sons' Future." *The Sunday Times*, 13 July 2014. http://www.thesundaytimes.co.uk/sto/news/focus/article1433645.ece.

Shehadeh, Raja. *Occupier's Law: Israel and the West Bank.* Washington, DC: Institute for Palestine Studies, 1988.

———. *Strangers in the House: Coming of Age in Occupied Palestine.* South Royalton, VT: Steerforth, 2002.

Sherover-Marcuse, Ricky. "Liberation Theory: Axioms and Working Assumptions about the Perpetuation of Social Oppression." nypolisci.org, accessed 30 June 2014, http://nypolisci.org/files/poli15/Readings/Liberation%20Theory .pdf.

Shlaim, Avi. "The Rise and Fall of the Oslo Peace Process," pp. 241–261 in *International Relations of the Middle East*, ed. Louise L'Estrange Fawcett. Oxford: Oxford University Press, 2005.

"Shoah and Tell: An Arab's Holocaust Museum." Israelity Bites blog, 28 January 2010. http://israelitybites.blogspot.com/2010/01/shoah-and-tell-arabs -holocaust-museum.html.

"Still Campaigning for Coexistence." *The Economist*, 30 August 2007.

Strengholt, Jos. "A Jewish State with Cannons, Flags, and Military Decorations: Strengthening and Defeat of the Bi-nationalist Movement in Palestine 1939–1942." Binationalism blog, 28 October 2008. http://binationalism.blogspot .com.

"The Summit: The Mountain of Israeli-Palestinian Friendship, Antarctica." Common Ground News Service, 17 January 2004.

Swirski, Barbara, and Marilyn P. Safir. *Calling the Equality Bluff: Women in Israel.* New York: Pergamon, 1991.

Tamari, Salim. "Kissing Cousins." *Palestine-Israel Journal* 12–13, nos. 4 and 1 (2005–2006).

Tessler, Mark. *A History of the Israeli-Palestinian Conflict*, 2nd ed. Bloomington: Indiana University Press, 2009.

Teveth, Shabtai. *Ben-Gurion and the Palestinian Arabs: From Peace to War.* Oxford: Oxford University Press, 1985.

Thomas, Amelia. "The Jerusalem Circus Symbolizes Hope." *Middle East Times*, 11 March 2005.

Tolan, Sandy. *The Lemon Tree: An Arab, a Jew, and the Heart of the Middle East.* New York: Bloomsbury, 2006.

Trager, Hannah. *Pioneers in Palestine: Stories of One of the First Settlers in Petach Tikva.* Westport, CT: Hyperion, 1976.

Traubman, Tamara. "Sociology Professor Becomes First Arab Dean of Israeli University." *Haaretz*, 10 October 2005.

Usher, Anne. "The Great Divide." *Esquire*, September 2011, 100–103.

Vatikiotis, P. J. *Among Arabs and Jews: A Personal Experience, 1936–1990.* London: Weidenfeld and Nicolson, 1991.

Wallach, John, and Michael Wallach. *The Enemy Has a Face: The Seeds of Peace Experience*. Washington, DC: United States Institute of Peace, 2000.

Wasserstein, Bernard. "The Arab-Jewish Dilemma." In *Like All the Nations?: The Life and Legacy of Judah L. Magnes*, ed. William M. Brinner and Moses Rischin. Albany: State University of New York, 1987.

Weber, Thomas, and Robert J. Burrowes. "Nonviolence: An Introduction." Washington DC: Nonviolence International, n.d. www.nonviolenceinternational .net/seasia/whatis/book.php.

Weigert, Gideon. *My Life with the Palestinians*. Jerusalem: Jerusalem Times, 1997.

Weiner, Anita, Arnon Bar-On, and Eugene Weiner. *The Abraham Fund Directory of Institutions and Organizations Fostering Coexistence between Jews and Arabs in Israel*, 1st ed. New York: Abraham Fund, 1991.

White, Benjamin. "A 'Hidden History' in the Holy Land." *Sojourners*, August 2010.

Yanait Ben-Zvi, Rachel. *Before Golda: Manya Shochat, a Biography*. New York: Biblio, 1989.

Yeshurun, Halit. "'Exile Is So Strong Within Me, I May Bring It to the Land': A Landmark 1996 Interview with Mahmoud Darwish." *Journal of Palestine Studies* 42, no. 1 (2012): 46–70.

Young, Elise G. *Keepers of the History: Women and the Israeli-Palestinian Conflict*. New York: Teachers College Press, 1992.

Zhang, Zara. "Israeli, Palestinian Group's Performance Promotes Political Unity through Music." *The Crimson*, 23 February 2014.

Zinn, Howard. *A Power Governments Cannot Suppress*. San Francisco: City Lights, 2006.

Zunes, Stephen. "U.S. Role in Lebanon Debacle." *Foreign Policy in Focus*, 18 May 2007.

Zwirn, Michael J. "Promise and Failure: Environmental NGOs and Palestinian-Israeli Cooperation." *Middle East Review of International Affairs* 5, no. 4 (2001): 9–10.

# Resources

## Bands

Alei Hazayit
Bustan Abraham
White Bird

## Music

"Born Here," DAM (song)
"Bukra fi Mishmish," Heartbeat (song)
*Stop Using Drugs*, Tamer Nafer (album)
*Tomorrow Is Coming*, Seeds of Peace (album)
"Zaman al-Salam," by Yair Dalal, performed by the Norwegian Philharmonic at the Nobel Peace Prize Ceremony, Oslo, 1994

## Plays

*Masks Off*, by E. Angelica and Yehuda Calo Livne, Teatro Arcobaleno Rainbow Theater
*Neighbors*, Galilee Multicultural Theater
*Roadblock*, written and performed by teens from Qalansua High School and Ma'ayan-Shacher School
*Return to Haifa*, adapted from eponymous novella by Ghassan Kanafani, Cameri Theater of Tel Aviv
*Six Actors in Search of a Plot*, by Mohammad el-Thaher with Arab and Jewish teens from Peace Child Israel; performed by Peace Child Israel

## Films

*Budrus*, Just Vision; dir. Julia Bacha, 2009
*Crossing the Lines: Palestinians and Israelis Speak with the Compassionate Listening Project*; Hwosch Productions, 2002
*Encounter Point*, Just Vision; dir. Ronit Avni and Julia Bacha, 2006
*The Haifa War Diary—Eli and Nasser*, prod. Eli Levi and Nasser Nasser; dir. Gili Shapira and Avishai Kfir, 2006
*Knowledge Is the Beginning*, EuroArts Music International; dir. Paul Smaczny, 2005
*Lemon Tree*, Eran Riklis Productions; dir. Eran Riklis, 2008
*My So-Called Enemy*, Good Egg Productions; dir. Lisa Gossels, 2010
*Paradise Now*, Warner Independent Pictures; dir. Hany Abu-Assad, 2005
*Promises*, Promises Film Project; dir. Justine Shapiro, B. Z. Goldberg, and Carlos Bolado, 2002
*Refusing to Be Enemies: The Zeituna Story*, Minerva Project; dir. Laurie White, 2007
*Waltz with Bashir*, Razor Film Produktion; dir. Ari Folman, 2008
*West Bank Story*, prod. Pascal Vaguelsy, Amy Kim, Ashley Jordan, Ravi Malhotra, and Bill Boland; dir. Ari Sandel, 2005

# Index